WITH LOVE

Born in London of Irish parents, Theodora FitzGibbon is currently living near Dublin with her husband George Morrison, the film-maker and photographic archivist. Cookery editor of *Image* magazine and the *Irish Times*, she has contributed to many other periodicals including *Homes and Gardens* and *Harper's Bazaar*. Her novel, *Flight of the Kingfisher*, was made into a successful BBC TV play. Theodora FitzGibbon has written over twenty-five books, three of which were awarded bronze medals at the Frankfurt International Food Fair and one of which won a special Glenfiddich award.

WITH LOVE

THEODORA FITZGIBBON

Pan Books
London and Sydney

With Love to Caitlin
and
In memoriam
Peter and Dylan

First published 1982 by Century Publishing Co. Ltd
This edition published 1983 by Pan Books Ltd,
Cavaye Place, London SW10 9PG

ISBN 0 330 26943 7
Photoset by Parker Typesetting Service, Leicester
Printed and bound in Great Britain by
Collins, Glasgow

CONTENTS

PLATES

PART ONE
PETER'S BOOK
(1938 to 1943)

Prologue

The first time I saw him was in the Café Flore, Paris, in 1938. Usually I went to the Deux Magots next door, or when I wanted to indulge my taste for red plush, gold, and painted mirrors, the Brasserie Lipp opposite.

His appearance and manner attracted me as much as his looks. He was a large man with a beautifully shaped head: his hair, which was dark brown, inclined to chestnut at the sides, started high on his forehead, and was worn long enough to curl gently in the nape of his neck. Immaculately so. A prominent nose, under which was a well-trimmed long, silky moustache, a well-shaped full mouth, and the most extraordinary eyes. They were deep reddish brown, very large, but set slightly slanting in his face. Their expression was one of sleepy amusement. The eyebrows followed the shape of the eyes, and did not come down at the corners, so that they gave him a curiously Mephistophelean look. He was beautifully dressed in a dark striped suit, cream silk shirt, a buttonhole, and I think a monocle hung around his neck. He looked magnificent. I had never seen anyone even remotely like him.

I never did again, until I saw Josef Kheifit's haunting film *The Lady with the Little Dog* in 1961. The leading actor, Alexander Batalov, looked remarkably like he did then, and not only looked, but has a similar walk, and manner.

He had a very elegantly bound book open in front of him, and from time to time he would look up, and mark his place with the tip of his finger at the bottom of the book. His hands were very large, but he used them delicately. He glanced at me, then looked away. I then opened my book, Stanislavsky's *My Life in Art*, which was my bible, and made a pretence of reading. After a while he was joined by a very striking looking woman, beautifully dressed, over whom he fussed, and attended. They drank champagne, which made me feel thirsty, and quite took the gold from the autumn morning. From time to time friends would pass their table, stop and talk for a few minutes, then go on their way. The friends looked interesting too, and it all seemed marvellously urbane. So much so that the young man who was taking me to Fontainebleau that afternoon got very short shrift through no fault of his own.

At that time I had only a few acquaintances in Paris, mostly friends of my father's or relatives of people I knew in Ireland. They didn't interest me greatly, nor I them. But I loved Paris. I used all the money I got for my birthday or Christmas to get over there on various pretexts. Old school-friends; study; anything that came into my head and would satisfy my family. I was used to, and liked, being alone, and wandering about a strange and fascinating city thrilled me. Until this day I had had one consuming desire: to be a very good actress; and it was to this end that I was in Paris now. It was the time of Louis Jouvet, Jean Gabin, Madeleine Ozeray, Françoise Rosay, Marie Bell, Danielle Darrieux, and many great names of the French theatre. Jean Cocteau was a magician who could write plays, novels, poems or films with equal facility. I spent all available time and money at the theatre or cinema, sometimes going straight from one to the other. The rest of the time I went to the Louvre, sat in cafés, or just wandered about.

My theatrical career wasn't going the way I wanted it to at all. Owing to my being quite tall and blonde, I was always cast as the 'other woman', a figure prominent in the plays of those years. In fact, I can't think of a successful contemporary play without her. After doing this in good repertory companies like Coventry or Birmingham, it reached the nadir when I was again cast as the 'other woman' in a film with Elisabeth Bergner. I was then eighteen and playing a woman of forty, whilst Miss Bergner seemed about forty, and was playing a girl of eighteen. It seemed to me that I was too young to be playing character parts, but no others came my way. To my knowledge I had never met an 'other woman', at least not the way they were portrayed in my scripts. Nowadays the 'other woman' is often the central character, and a much more human person.

The pattern of my day was changed: I went to the Flore and studied someone who was more fascinating to me than

Louis Jouvet. Sometimes there would be a large party at his table. All the women were beautiful and the men, if not all handsome, were worth looking at. There was always conversation and a certain amount of laughter, presumably when pearls of wit fell from one of the lips. It was tantalizing, but full of interest, rather like watching a silent film. There was no opportunity to get into this magic circle: the membership was obviously limited. I started going there earlier and earlier in the hope that he would be alone again but, when he was, I could think of no way to introduce myself. The wildest schemes flitted into my mind, and flitted out again equally quickly. One day he did drop an envelope on the floor and I went to pick it up, but alas, he retrieved it first. I was rewarded with a nod. On the day when he wasn't there in the morning, I went back again in the evening and asked Pascal the waiter what his name was, but he couldn't make out which *monsieur* I was talking about. I couldn't even make out his nationality, as I was never quite near enough to hear his accent. He spoke both French and English to his companions, and he could have been either, or even Russian.

One day I sat deliberately quite far away, so that I could point him out to Pascal and get his name. Pascal was good at that, but he came back with a very unsatisfactory answer: it sounded like 'Poulum', and meant nothing to me, nor did it give any clue as to his nationality. Nevertheless, the day came when Pascal summoned me, bent low over me, and said he had found out that 'Poulum' took photographs, good photographs too, so he'd heard. It was all a bit disappointing, and for a day I let the Flore get on without me. Pascal took quite an interest in me on account of this, and never missed a chance to try to bring about a meeting, but either he was too intimidating for Pascal, or there were too many of those beauties about. The beauties came in all sizes and colours. Their clothes were outstanding, and in some cases *outré,* but looked right on them. The accepted dress for young women in the morning in those days, was the tailor-made suit, or *le tailleur*, as the French called it. Almost my entire wardrobe consisted of *les tailleurs* in various materials which, after seeing Garbo and Marlene Dietrich at the cinema, I enlivened alternately with a large floppy hat or a small black beret according to the mood I was in. My black tailor-made I had inherited from a rather chic friend of my mother's. It had a wrap-over skirt, which when one crossed one's legs showed a large amount of calf. This was thought very dashing, and it was my favourite. However, even that must have looked tame compared to some of those beauties' outfits.

If I am giving the impression that I was a lonely young girl tossing on my bed at night, I must correct it. I was twenty years old, quite considerably travelled, had had a certain amount of success, and was in the middle of a nice cosy uncomplicated love affair in London. This all took place during my two weeks away, for reassessment of myself and other people – a habit started very early on in life, and still kept to. Anyway this watching and waiting was not my style, and I was getting a bit impatient. The effect that this man seen across a café had on me was not one of immediate love or desire: it was fascination. A curious feeling, and one that has never happened to me again.

For the next few days I had little time to indulge in my new pastime as some Irish friends arrived in Paris, and we did all the things that young and gay people like to do at any time. I got home too late to get up in time to get to the Flore before lunch, and the whole episode took on an air of unreality, almost of having happened in another century.

On the way home from a party the night before I left Paris, we stopped at the Flore for a nightcap and something to eat. It all looked very different at three in the morning: the change was quite startling. As we were leaving about an hour later, he came in with a crowd of people. They were in elaborate fancy dress: one woman looked exquisite as a black cat, and a magnificently tall, tawny-haired woman shimmered in gold. There was a man in an elegant Domino costume. He was dressed in tails, with a red-lined black cloak. Under his arm he carried a large eagle's head made out of *papier mâché*. It was this bizarre memory that I carried back with me during the long London winter.

Chapter One

In fact the winter wasn't long at all. The spectre of the 'other woman' was well and truly laid, mainly due to my being cast in the first play written by Anatole de Grunwald, later to become extremely well known in film circles as a producer. He was a gentle, slim, dark-haired man in his twenties; shy in manner, he nevertheless was able to make a point firmly when he wished. When he became successful during the war, he was kind and helpful, and got me several small parts in films. A charming companion, and one I would have liked to have seen more of, but the partner in my cosy love affair had taken a very jealous turn, and hated to let me out of his sight. This I found very tiring, so I wriggled out of that situation as gracefully as I could.

When I wasn't working in the theatre, I worked as a mannequin, as modelling was called then. The top mannequins were always almost six feet tall but, owing to having very slender legs and arms and a small head, I looked at least three inches taller than I was. I found being a mannequin very unsatisfactory after acting as I hadn't got a clothes-horse mentality. That is, until I found Ronald Traquair, a young Scotsman with a *salon* in Grosvenor Street.

A *salon* is just about all he had: the other rooms in which he lived were almost bare of furniture, and often there wasn't enough money to go round. This made the whole procedure much more interesting, and I really felt I had to sell the clothes for him. They were made of rich velvets, brocades and silks; they were beautiful and romantic, and I looked good in them. I only worked part-time for him, usually when he had an important client or when he had the money. Sometimes he would show his clothes at night, and I would rush from rehearsals to Grosvenor Street. John Gielgud and John Perry often brought clients to see the clothes. Afterwards, if the killing had been good, we would go out and buy a bottle of whisky for twelve shillings and sixpence, and come back and queen it in the downy-cushioned chairs of the *salon*, with the log fire burning discreetly; we were sometimes joined by the chief cutter, a dear little woman who was crippled, and who adored Traquair. He was very good looking, but wasn't a ladies man. Nevertheless we were very fond of each other.

On Grand National day 1939 I put ten shillings on Marmaduke Jinks which came home at fifty to one. I took Traquair out to dinner, and found I had plenty left to get to Paris for Easter. The fare was about three pounds, and one could live comfortably in Paris on five pounds a week. I never saw Traquair again, as he was killed in a car accident shortly afterwards.

The strong sweet-sour smell of Paris; the aroma of garlic and olive oil; the taste of Pernod; the gritty feeling of French cigarettes between one's lips; the vitality and realism of the people: the city where to excrete was human, and to urinate, if not divine, at least a natural function. All this contrasted vividly with the lavender and dust smell of London. The weather was cold and clear, with a watery spring sun which bathed the buildings in a pale gold light. It was crowded with visitors, and it was often hard to find a table on one's own in the cafés. Pascal was delighted to see me again, and would look round for a suitable table for me to sit at. His choice was not always mine, but I didn't like to hurt his feelings.

On the third day I was there Pascal was standing near the door of the Flore, and looked quite excited when he saw me. He fussed over me so much that I didn't notice where I was going. He sat me down at a small table alongside the glass partition at the side, dusted the table vigorously and inquired my order. I looked up and saw who was at the next table, not an arm's length from me. But could it be? Yes, it was 'Poulum', but 'Poulum' wearing a different coat.

My eyes started their examination at marble table-top level. A large drawing pad took up most of the table, and as he drew I saw that he was left-handed, but those large, surgeon's hands went swiftly across the paper. The cuff above the hand was frayed and dirty: the suit was shiny and covered in what looked like a grey powder; the monocle and buttonhole were gone, the hair still curled, but not immaculately, the moustache needed trimming, but it was undoubtedly 'Poulum'. He looked up and smiled. I smiled back; he was much more approachable in these clothes. He settled himself in the chair, and took a swallow of the red wine he was drinking.

'I wonder,' he said: 'I wonder if you would mind sitting at my table as you distract me sitting where you are?'

I moved at his request. He went on sketching, and try as I might I couldn't see what he was drawing. We sat in silence for some time and I was beginning to feel uncomfortable, when he closed the drawing pad and turned towards me. I looked up and met his gaze, trying desperately not to blink. He put his head on one side and the enormous eyes roamed all over my face. They had an amusing, quizzical expression. It seemed to go on for a very long time. Then in a soft, pleasantly drawling voice, he said:

'You're a very pretty girl, but you won't do.'

My heart contracted. 'Won't do for what?'

'For some very boring photographs I have to take.'

'But I thought . . .' I had been about to say that I thought he was a photographer, then stopped suddenly, as this would assume too much knowledge.

'But you thought what, my dear?' he said in an amused voice.

I stuttered, and said I thought he was an artist, a painter, anything that came into my head.

He seemed rather pleased by this, and seemed not to have noticed my awkwardness. His head went right down on one side, almost to his shoulder.

'Well, I suppose I am, but there are still those boring photographs. Let's talk about something else. You, for instance.'

He was surprisingly easy to talk to, and appeared to be interested in what I was saying. Once he laughed quite loudly at some observation I made, although I didn't think it was all that funny. Drinks came and went; perhaps we were a little bit tipsy. I had that odd feeling that I had known him for years and that we had just picked up a conversation where it had left off some time ago, the way you can with very old friends. It got very late, and suddenly my young belly gave a loud rumble.

'Heavens, you *must* be hungry; come back and have luncheon at my place.'

Pascal was summoned, and smiled benignly over us. It was quite embarrassing, and I was frightened he would say something about last year. There were endless saucers to be counted, and I offered to pay my share, but was airily waved aside.

We left the Flore, turned right, and he strode rapidly on – so quickly that I was sure I would lose him amongst the crowds; but he was very tall and easy to pick out. We turned right again, he still walked quickly with his head down slightly, as if he had forgotten that I was with him. Then he stopped dead, turned round and faced me square on. My head came about level with his chin. He bent down and said:

'I don't think I have very much to eat at home.' He said this apologetically, and his eyes held mine.

'Well, we'll buy something on the way there.'

'An excellent idea, except that I haven't any money left.'

It was agreed that I would buy the food from a *charcuterie*, as he had bought the drinks earlier. We picked out some good-looking terrine, pâté de marcassin, and cornichons, then we stopped several times again and bought bread, butter, cheese, and chicorée frisée. The episode had an air of unreality: I couldn't believe that I was with 'Poulum', even though it wasn't the 'Poulum' of last year. Neither of us had thought to inquire the other's name, so he was still 'Poulum' to me. Once we had done the shopping he walked at a normal pace, and there was an air of intimacy, almost of secrecy, between us. On passing a wine shop I said:

'Let's buy a bottle of champagne.'

'Champagne?' He said it as if I had said, 'Let's go up in a balloon.'

It was on the tip of my tongue to say, 'But you love

champagne.' I desisted, but we bought it, and carried all our parcels like children at Christmas.

I don't know what sort of 'place' I had thought of 'Poulum' living in; there hadn't been any time to think. We were beside an old hotel and it was there we stopped. A small beady-eyed man who looked as if he never went out gave us a key. We walked up endless flights of stairs, and when it seemed there couldn't be any more, we were there.

The room was an attic of large proportions, with a skylight on one side. It was cold, the patterned wallpaper was peeling and almost the entire floor space was covered with pieces of screwed-up paper. They looked like surrealist children's boats. The bed hadn't been made for some time, was rumpled, crumpled and littered with tubes of paint, more pieces of paper and a beautiful silk dressing gown rolled into a ball. There were the ashes of a fire in the grate, empty wine bottles, stained glasses, dirty plates, and more tubes of paint on the shelf above the fireplace. An easel stood in the centre of the room, and on it was a half-finished painting of a large room, empty except for a trestle table. The walls and floor of the room were painted in very delicate rainbow colours, each hue merging into the next. The contrast between the painted room and the actual one was startling. There was a sagging armchair by the fireplace and a hard chair with a cane bottom by the easel. Stacks of disordered newspapers were in one corner and a small pile of logs. The other furniture was sparse and battered.

Halfway across the room he turned, and with a grand sweep of the arm pointed to the armchair.

'Do sit down, I'll have a fire going in a minute.'

He went about the room, picking up the pieces of paper, which he arranged pyramid fashion on top of some books on a chest of drawers. I attempted to help him, but was waved aside.

'Don't you do it: I know where they go.'

It seemed impossible that anyone would know where they went, but nevertheless the careful arrangement went on. I shivered slightly, involuntarily.

'I'll light the fire then . . .'

But I was not allowed to touch anything. He behaved as if it was a very grand apartment, which only needed a switch to transform it. I eyed the food on the bed, and my belly made another ominous rumble.

'Goodness, I'm forgetting you've probably a healthy young appetite. We'll just wash up a few plates. I don't like the servants poking about, they disturb all my things.'

It was difficult to know what to answer, so I said nothing but busied myself in preparing the meal. The table was covered with paints and a palette, so I spread it out on the floor in front of the now crackling fire. He sat in the armchair and I sat on the floor, and we ate and ate and ate – so quickly, that we forgot the champagne, and had finished a bottle of red wine that was open.

'Oh, the champagne . . . well, we can have it with our dessert.'

The dessert was one wizened apple which we ate, bite and bite about, between us. The after-glow of the food and the warmth of the fire turned the room into the one on the easel. I felt sleepy and must have looked it, for he said:

'Do lie down on the bed, I'll make a space for you. I want to do some more to this painting before the light goes.'

When I woke up it was quite dark, and he was sitting in front of the fire with his chin resting on one hand. It was a characteristic pose. Cigarette smoke curled in the dim red glow. As I stirred, he moved over to the bed and switched on a lamp. He sat on the side, and took the lobe of my ear between his finger and thumb.

'It was pleasant having a sleeping muse in my room,' he said.

His hand moved about my face, and took hold of my chin, which he raised up to face the light. My hair, which I wore in a coil in the nape of my neck, had come undone and fell about my shoulders. A hairpin dug in my neck at the back. He wound my hair round his fingers, put it back behind my ears and turned my face in profile. It was as though he was examining a piece of sculpture.

'Surely your hair can't really be that gold colour.'

It was, and he drew his lips together.

'You have very pretty ears . . . and blue veins behind your eyes like my mother had. I've never seen anyone with those blue veins except her.' He sighed, and I luxuriated under the flattery.

'You look almost transparent in this light. Pity, I like dirty, black-haired women.'

I sat up, and said I must be going.

'Going – but where on earth do you think you're going to? I thought you were going to be my muse.'

'But . . . I don't even know your name, and I'm going back to London the day after tomorrow.'

'We can soon change all that; what on earth does a pretty girl like you want to live in London for?'

They were all very difficult questions to answer, so I suggested that we went out to have a drink. I had the feeling that I was playing a part in a play, and hadn't learnt the lines.

'I haven't any money until next week,' he said sadly.

I turned out my handbag on the bed, and we counted what I had left.

'Heavens, you *are* a rich little creature. This will last us for weeks if we go carefully.'

It was all said so gently, and with such obvious child-like pleasure, that I laughed aloud. I wondered briefly how he was going to survive until the money came next week, and what had happened to all those beauties, but I said nothing, got up and started to coil up my hair.

'Don't screw it all up like that. Leave it hanging down, it looks beautiful.'

'But, I can't just go round with it hanging all down my back like a child.'

'It makes you look pre-Raphaelite.'

I went out with it all hanging down my back like a child, and felt acutely uncomfortable to begin with. Nobody at that time had long hair falling all over the place. Either tight curls or short hair was the fashion, and I didn't know quite what a pre-Raphaelite was, except it sounded quite nice.

We went to a nearby café and sat there for hours, talking entirely about ourselves. He seemed to regard me as some sort of freak, and kept picking out a word from my conversation and rolling it about his lips, like a wine taster exploring.

'Actress . . . Irish . . . Tipperary . . . twenty-one . . . Russian . . . H'm, m'm . . .'

Then he looked at me and said:

'I don't believe a word of it.'

'Why would I make up a story to tell you? It's not a very exciting one at that.'

'Oh, don't ask me to explain what goes on in the mind of an imaginative little creature like you.'

He treated me as if I was a strange little animal that he should be wary of. When he said something nice, it was retracted in the next sentence, as if he thought I might take some advantage, or even bite. His whole manner would change from one of concern to one of making me concerned. You had to be quick, and you had to be right. One moment he was a mature man of forty, and the next like a schoolboy. It was like seeing different facets of a room in a piece of cut crystal.

The next day we went to the Flore, and Pascal beamed over me, asked how I was and at the same time cast a knowing eye.

'You seem to be very well known here, why haven't I seen you before?' he asked. He said this in a very proprietory way.

'I haven't been to Paris since last year.'

I hope that this would provoke some explanation for his apparent change of fortune.

'Oh, last year,' he sighed, 'that seems like ten years ago to me.'

The days lengthened into weeks: I wrote to my maternal grandmother in London, and made some feasible suggestions as to why I should stay in Paris. Grandma, who had brought me up, was nobody's fool, and answered rather shrewdly, saying no doubt my French would be useful to me 'later on', but to be certain not to get trapped as she wouldn't trust those Germans an inch, especially that Hitler. She did, however, enclose a pure white, crinkly five-pound note. I bought a much needed pair of silk stockings, and the rest went on food and drink.

The atmosphere in Paris was tense in certain quarters. Hitler had occupied Prague; rumours were circulating that Poland would be next, which were reinforced when Chamberlain said that 'in that event, the British and French governments would lend all support in their power'. When one dared to think about the prospect, it was exceptionally gloomy. Poison gas, bombs, the huge casualty lists of the 1914-18 war ran in front of one's eyes like a piece of film. At my age, it was pleasanter to hope and to do all the things that might be denied me later on. The horrors were put at the back of one's mind, and it was only when more and more men appeared in army uniform on the streets that the horrors pushed themselves forward. There was after all the feeling of safety induced by the impregnable Maginot Line.

The day-to-day excitement of my life overshadowed everything. I helped to take the 'boring photographs', which weren't in the least so, and I showed such aptitude that he wanted to teach me more about it. But, if anything, I wanted to be on the other side of the camera, although I liked helping to fix lights and process the film. The photographs 'Poulum' took were not in the least boring, they were quite remarkable: not only for their imaginative qualities, but also for the technical surprises and innovations he employed. I had never seen anything like them, and they look as good today as they did then. Most of the portrait photographs of the thirties were set pieces, with the sitters looking as they thought they looked: heavy retouching and stiff poses. His photographs were startling because they captured their subjects spontaneously in their environments, a thing at that time hardly to be found in the work of any British photographer, though characteristic of the work of Cartier-Bresson. Not that his photographs resembled those of Cartier-Bresson in style, for 'Poulum' had a quite individual way of using a single light, and sometimes a surrealist quality of allowing large areas to fall into complete shadow from which salient features would emerge strikingly illuminated, with remarkable dramatic interest.

He was a passionate surrealist, as were most of his friends and the painters he admired. He taught me to understand the gaiety and perspicacity of surrealism, for which I have always been grateful. The big surrealist exhibition of 1936 was still talked about; Mariette Oppenheim with her fur tea-cups and saucers was a good friend of his, and a very attractive girl. I got to know many of the 'beauties' and they weren't frightening: particularly Eleonor, or Leonor Fini, the cat-woman of the previous year, a brilliant and original painter, and Lady Iya Abdy the beautiful tawny-haired Russian, photographs of whom were in all the glossy magazines.

The smell of paint and linseed oil; the studios of the painters, each one as individual as the individual artist . . .

Eugene Berman, the Russian painter, was always in a dressing gown with daubs of paint over it (I never saw him out of doors). When one's visit had lasted long enough he would say:

'Well, I must draw the curtains now and get back to my painting!'

I loved his dark, desolate landscapes and ruins.

Max Ernst, then in his forties, with an impish sense of fun . . . We once spent several hours going across Paris without treading on a line in the paving stones. His studio was a rectangular room with heavy dark furniture, relieved by a few comfortable Second Empire chairs. It contrasted strongly with the rococo style prevalent in the apartment of Salvador Dali – huge gilt looking-glasses, ornate but beautiful plaster work, and Gesso decoration on the large doors. A surrealist touch was a full-size stuffed polar bear which stood in one corner of a dark panelled room, where several vivid and unforgettable Dali pictures hung.

The young, saturnine-looking Balthus, whose name was Balthasar Klossowsky, and his beautiful Swiss wife Nuche, lived in the sixteenth-century palace of the Archbishops of Rouen, in Paris. He was a young man, a pupil of André Derain's and highly thought of. He painted his wife and also did a number of drawings to illustrate *Wuthering Heights.* Curiously he had been partly educated in Yorkshire and was an enthusiastic Anglophile. He couldn't understand my being critical of the English, so I had to give him a brief rundown of Irish history, at which 'Poulum' sniffed and told him not to believe a word of it.

When brought to the sixteenth-century house on the Quai de Saint Augustin to meet Picasso, the huge barn-like studio with the tiered stove at one end and the vast canvases propped here, there and everywhere overawed me, so I said very little and was hardly noticed, I thought. Then Picasso came over to me and examined me with eyes burning like the hot Spanish sun, and in a staccato voice said:

'Vos bras sont très beaux.'

From then on, if I wasn't there, he would ask where was the girl with the beautiful arms.

Giacometti, the sculptor, André Derain, Tristan Zara, Christian (Bébé) Bérard, – all of them were living and working in the Paris of those prewar days. (If many of these names are now household words, it was not the case then. At a collected exhibition of their work, at Mayer's Gallery in London, just before this time, half the pictures were unsold, and those purchased went for very little.)

There were not only painters, but men of letters, such as André Breton, Louis Aragon, Henri de Montherlant, Jean Cocteau, André Mesens, and Antoine de Saint-Exupèry, who was a man of action and charm, and a superb writer. *Vol de Nuit* is a perfect example of his lucid and beautiful prose; and his tiny dark-haired wife, Consuelo, was a particular friend.

Such then was the intellectual atmosphere, as I saw it, in Paris in 1939. It is not being overdramatic to say that it changed my life, for from then on I have associated myself entirely with creative people.

Chapter Two

Although it was stimulating and exciting, it was not all honey. There was often no money at all, and we existed on dry bread rubbed with garlic. The garlic taste remained long after the bread had been digested, and gave one the feeling of having eaten more recently. As a change, we had bread smeared with mustard, when there was any mustard. I couldn't go past the local *charcuterie* because it made my mouth water so, and always had to take a much more circuitous route. It seemed not to affect 'Poulum' at all, or if it did he never mentioned it. There was to be no compromise; one painted and nothing else mattered. From time to time small sums of money appeared, I never knew from where or how much they were. The bills were paid, or something given on account; we had perhaps one good meal, a bottle of wine; canvas and paints were bought, and then back to the bread and garlic. One was always hungrier the day after the meal, which bears out Rabelais's words: 'Appetite comes with eating!'

He liked me to be in the room when he painted, so I tidied it up as much as I was allowed. I did the bed one day when he was out. It yielded a rich hoard of old tubes of paint, several empty matchboxes, two forks, a saucer and what looked like the skin of a kipper or dried herring. It looked very nice when I had finished, for I had found a faded cover in the wardrobe and put it on. I sat back in the armchair to admire my handiwork. But not for long! When he came home and saw it, instead of praising me, he was furious. His face went quite red with temper and he stripped the covers down.

'I hate made beds,' he shouted, 'there's something so squalid about them.'

I was too astonished to speak, but rushed over and wrestled with the bed clothes the other side. I treated that old bed like a treasured possession that had to be guarded.

'Squalid!' I yelled. '*You* are ostentatious in your squalidness.'

He stopped and turned quickly. 'What did you say?'

'I said you were ostentatious in your squalidness.'

'That's a very good line,' he said. 'I must remember it.'

I didn't tell him then that it came from W. B. Yeats's *A Vision* because I was too angry.

It was our first quarrel, and I went for my coat.

'But you can't go just because I don't like tidy beds.' He took me by the shoulders, and shook me very gently. 'You can't . . .'

It was finally agreed that the bed could be made, but must be ruffled, or preferably laid on straight away, so that it didn't look like the bed of a *petit-bourgeois* family.

I would lie on it and read his books. The elegantly leather-bound one that I remembered from last year was Benjamin Constant's *Adolphe*.

With the exception of *Le Sofa* by Crébillon, in which the sofa tells the story of all the love affairs it has witnessed, his library read like a list of French classics: Daudet, the Goncourt Brothers, Diderot, Flaubert, Stendhal, Turgenev, and Prosper Merimée. The latter's short stories of werewolves were new to me and I revelled in them. There was also a marvellous book called *Maldoror*, written, I think, by the Frenchman Count Lautréamont. It was weird and exciting, and highly thought of by the Surrealists. The only English book was *New Writing* edited by John Lehmann, and a current copy of *Horizon* magazine edited by Cyril Connolly and financed to a certain extent by Peter Watson, both of whom 'Poulum' knew. Once he came back with a volume of Racine's plays which was pushed into my hand with the words:

'If you're going to be an actress, you'd better start learning some of this.'

I found the alexandrines a bit heavy going.

Being a very fast reader I was often accused of 'not having read them properly', and would be tested on certain passages. My French wasn't all that good to start with, and I got seriously caught out over *la diligence* in one of Daudet's books: how could I have guessed it meant stage-coach? From then on the lessons got more intense, and when it was too dark to paint we often sat for hours over my instruction. I certainly learned more than I had done at various convents all over the place; but then convents are like Hilton Hotels, they vary little from country to country.

It was the hunger that made me think about ways of getting food. Always thin, I was becoming quite emaciated. I found that I couldn't read a passage about a meal without almost drooling. When the next sum of money turned up, I commandeered a small part of it and suggested that we should cook over the fire. This was thought marvellously practical, and he even made some sort of little trivet out of strong wire to hold a saucepan. I bought all the materials for a real curry, the most flavoursome meal I could think of.

'A curry? Like all those dreadful Anglo-Indians in Hove?'

'No, not like the Anglo-Indians in Hove, but like the Indian Indians in India. It won't be hot and peppery.'

'Well . . .' his nose twisted round disapprovingly. 'Well, perhaps just this once.'

I got all the spices and ground them up by hand: the smell from the cardamoms, coriander, cumin, mace, cloves, cinnamon, ginger, turmeric and peppers was like a magnificent *hors d'oeuvre.* A great pot of *dal*, Indian lentil soup, bubbled and spat over the glowing wood.

We ate until our bellies swelled up like poisoned pups. He had to admit it was good, although he did rather take the gilt off it by saying that next time I must try my hand with a *boeuf à la mode.* I wasn't too sure how to do that, so I kept quiet.

But from then on we had at least one hot meal a day: Irish stew, creamy and delicious, not swimming in liquid; bortsch, vegetable soups, and little chunks of meat grilled over the fire on skewers in true Cossack fashion. Actually, he didn't really approve of food that wasn't French, but it was difficult to perform *haute cuisine* dishes over that cramped little fire. The extra food gave me back my customary energy: my mind became more alert, and lying on the bed reading French classics most of the day began to pall. Being a muse was a rather sedentary occupation.

I pressed the black *tailleur*, bought a gay scarf, slapped on the black beret à la Dietrich, and went off to look for a job. The fact that I hadn't got a *carte de travail* didn't deter me. That would come, no doubt. I chose Molyneux first of all, because he was the acknowledged master of *le tailleur*. It took a bit of getting past the scented *vendeuse*, but I burbled on about Traquair and several other people I had worked for in London, and eventually I was promised an appointment.

As it turned out he was a charming Irish gentleman, whose name was pronounced *Molynoox*, and it was the French-Scottish name of the Auld Alliance, Traquair, that had stimulated his interest. He was, in fact, looking for the 'English Rose' type. Thank God my family in Tipperary never knew!

The job was on a temporary basis until the season was over in June. It wasn't demanding, and the money was nice. I could still be a muse on Sundays and Mondays, which was enough for anyone. I was delighted to be able to write some concrete news to my grandmother, who was getting restive. 'Poulum' didn't like my being away for most of the day, but we had very sybaritic weekends which made up for it.

Our relationship was in many ways an odd one, as one might expect from living with so curious a person. He could on occasions be very off-putting, almost intimidating and, at other times, warm, tender and full of spontaneous gaiety. Always outspoken, there were however many things I could not ask him: he would tell you so much, and then shut down suddenly, inexplicably, as though he was frightened to reveal too much of himself to another person. He was more afraid than I realized, but then I was not without some apprehension myself, and at that age one is still finding out a lot about oneself. He was particularly reticent when discussing his relationships with women, although he did tell me of eating baked jacket potatoes and caviare with one of his girls. The usual clichés of love or sex could not be applied to him. Generally undemonstrative, he would then astound one by being almost sentimental. Sometimes I would think he loved me, and at other times he seemed quite indifferent. But if I suggested returning to England he would get fussed, his shoulders would hunch up so that his neck almost disappeared, his eyes would become even larger and fill with a melancholy expression. I did not know his age, nor did I inquire, but I assumed it was about forty. These are small details, but ones not usually withheld in an intimate relationship.

His mind worked quite slowly, but logically. If I asked a question of an intellectual nature he would consider it for some minutes, even hours, and several times he said he would think about it and let me know in a few days' time. Then surely, in two or three days when I had almost forgotten asking it, he would come up with a long, detailed and comprehensive answer. He liked to instruct, and what he taught me I have never forgotten.

I did however find out what the crumpled pieces of paper were for. He was at that time experimenting with *trompe l'œil* painting. Whole canvases were painted of them, and were so realistic that once I went to pick them up.

Young people when they relax usually adopt untidy attitudes. Sitting up straight in a chair smacks of childhood training, and is a sign of inhibition in the young, or approaching middle age in older people. While I was curled up on the bed and listening to him talk, he would often stroke my hair, my shoulder or behind my ear. Then I would stretch out and luxuriate. I behaved like a cat, he said, and therefore he would call me Puss. Always after that, I was known as Puss or Pussy, although I don't think I was catlike in other ways.

Very early on I found I could make him laugh. Not the laughter associated with polite conversation, but so that the tears would come out of his eyes. He had a delighted, delightful laugh that made one feel good. It was always the comic situation that provoked it. Anecdotes about my family in Ireland were certain successes, although he always said he didn't believe a word of them. To him Ireland was as remote as Siberia. Certainly he never realized how close to the truth are the stories of Somerville and Ross. He must have thought I was much more imaginative than in fact I am, as I come from a rum, very individual family. My great-great-uncle coined his own money in Cloughjordan, King's County, in the 1870s and always used it. As children we would play with some of the coins. Now, alas, only pennies are left, but we all still have a total disregard for the coin of the realm!

He in turn would regale me by talking about his friends so vividly that I would think I had met them. Only once he spoke of his family. He said his mother had been wildly impractical with money and, when remonstrated with by his father for spending too much on housekeeping, had fed them both on nothing but rice pudding for three days.

Some days when I was working he would drink with his friends in the Flore. I was seldom brought out, but when I suggested a meeting, he would say that he would like to be alone with me, as he hadn't seen me all day. In many ways it was like living in the nineteenth century, when a person's public and private activities were markedly separate.

At the back of my mind I knew that I would have to return to England sometime, even if only for a visit. I had come away initially for a long weekend, and now it was months. I could not go on making excuses indefinitely. The news in Europe was disquieting: there were prolonged and unsatisfactory negotiations with Russia, and Hitler was a real and very near menace.

A letter arrived from my agent saying that a play I had toured in was being brought to London. I must come back for rehearsals. I did not envisage the reaction the letter would have when I showed it. First, utter sadness, the shoulders hunched, and tears: then impatience and temper. Finally he walked out of the little room I had come to love. I walked about it all night, touching the objects I knew were a part of him: stoking the fire, doing anything that would make the night shorter. He was not back by the time I had to leave in the morning. I came back again in the evening; the empty room mocked me. Had the actions been reversed, I would of course have stayed. It was a difficult decision, one that I would not like to have to make again. I left a long letter saying that I would come over for a few days when I knew what was happening, and that I was taking the copy of Prosper Merimée with me as a hostage.

My letter was unanswered.

Chapter Three

Peter Rose Pulham, for that was his name, was born in England in 1910. His mother was Scottish, and his father's family came from Pulham in Norfolk. He was very proud that his family was mentioned in Fuller's 'Worthies', the finest work of the seventeenth-century English historian Thomas Fuller, called *The History of the Worthies of England*.

His mother died when he was twelve years old, and it undoubtedly had an adverse effect on him. His memories of her were affectionate and romantic, but cautious.

Of his early life and schooling I know nothing. He disliked school so much that he could never bear to talk about it. At the age of nineteen he went to Worcester College, Oxford, and read, I think, English literature. He loved Oxford, and when talking of his days there it was always summer: sparkling and magical. Many of the friends he made there, such as Desmond Ryan and Graham Eyres Monsell, were his friends for life. His descriptions of Oxford were almost Proustian, and told with the same meticulous affection.

He came down from Oxford in his early twenties, without getting a degree, having decided he wanted to take photographs. He seldom talked of unpleasant periods of his life, for he had no self-pity, but I gathered that this decision displeased his banker father, who gave him a comparatively small sum of money (about a hundred pounds) to go ahead, but told him not to expect any more.

Painstakingly he taught himself to take photographs, and his original, individual style was almost immediately recognized and acclaimed. It became the fashionable thing to be photographed by Rose Pulham, and many a well-known English beauty sat for him. He worked for some years with *Harper's Bazaar* in both London and Paris. The long Regency windows of his Berkeley Square apartment opened on to a balcony above the green trees of the gardens below: the air was soft and quiet in the evenings when the traffic ceased. Weekends were spent in the houses of the rich. For several years he was content. He had success and the feeling of well-being it brings. He was still experimenting with techniques in his work, and enjoyed the company of the women he desired and the friends he wanted. A lot of money was made, and equally quickly spent. Tchelitchew drew his portrait: he was a handsome man in his twenties, charming and witty. Life was fair.

Success is a tyrant. It can be like climbing a beanstalk which waves perilously when you are at the top. The world of advertising reaches out to an original creative talent, then proceeds to superimpose its own imprint over it, thus restricting the mind of the creator. The bridle is slipped on, and whilst that is hardly noticed, the girths are tightened on the saddle, feet are put into the stirrups, and the faceless rider has acquired spurs or a whip. In those circumstances there are two courses ahead: to trot gently around the ring like a fat-backed circus pony, or to dig in your toes, refuse and unseat the rider.

The latter course was taken by Peter. He was asked to take more and more photographs which were not to his liking, so quite firmly, and suddenly, he dug in his toes.

He said he had taken all the photographs he ever wanted to take, and henceforth the visual side of his imagination would be applied to painting. He would finish only those photographs he was contracted for. Carefully, laboriously, he taught himself to paint, as he had previously taught himself to take photographs. He prepared himself for years of arduous lonely work. He would ask no one to undergo this with him; if they were prepared to share his hardships that was another matter, but they must not expect a comfortable bourgeois life. There would be no compromise.

Painting was to become the enduring preoccupation of his life. Everything else was secondary.

This was the man, at the age of twenty-eight, that I met in 1939.

Chapter Four

Back in London *Goodbye Mr Chips* was playing to packed houses in the cinema, whilst H. G. Wells's *The Shape of Things to Come* enjoyed a more restricted audience. Will Hay, Moore Marriott and Graham Moffat cavorted in *Ask a Policeman*. Professor Joad argued endlessly on the wireless, Dodie Smith's play was still running, Margaret Lockwood was the reigning British film star, and the hit song was 'Deep Purple'.

The summer air was hot and heavy, trembling with the unease that means thunder. The streets were crowded, guttural voices of German refugees mingling with the familiar cockney or other English accents. It was much more tense than Paris had been: middle-aged people with vivid memories of the First World War showed their worry on their faces, and young men were uncertain as to whether to enlist in the army or take up their careers. Leaflets on how to detect poison gas or handle incendiary bombs were distributed; gas-masks, for those who had not got them at the time of the Munich crisis, were issued; air-raid shelters were being erected, trenches dug, and Anderson shelters like corrugated kennels were put up in suburban gardens. There were advertisements for air-raid wardens on a voluntary basis, also fire-watchers, and Red Cross personnel.

My mother had a German-Jewish refugee girl staying with her in London, who told us horrifying stories of life in Germany. It cast a gloom over the usually cheerful house as she sat in the evenings sorting out the innumerable railway tickets she had bought in Germany, to spend the money she could not bring, and deciding which one to sell next.

It was hard to concentrate on anything. The lines of the play seemed more banal than I remembered them, and I frequently thought of giving it up. But money had to be earned, and this was the best way for me to do it. I felt trapped.

I worried about Peter, and wrote saying that I would do the play for three months and then come back. He replied with a curt little note:

> Dear Pussy,
>
> Please do not worry about me for I am quite all right, and painting well. I miss you very much, but don't hurry back as I will probably have changed my mind by the time you get here . . .

We rehearsed in the empty Aldwych Theatre. Romney Brent, the American actor, was the producer, and I lived in the enclosed world of the theatre which seemed more real than the strange outside one. The play opened at the Richmond Theatre on August Bank holiday Monday, as a try-out to London. The notices were, on the whole, good but there were complications about the London theatre. We were to be 'on call', and 'they' would let us know. A restless lethargy settled on me: the fear of rejection if I went to Paris; uncertainty, unhappiness and possibly no success in London.

I took the crowded mail-boat to Ireland with its smell of stout, and frying bacon and eggs: the soft voices of my countrymen, even the songs they sang in the saloon, soothed me.

Desolate dignified Dublin in the early hours of the morning. Kingsbridge station, Portarlington first stop, Limerick Junction, strangely enough in Tipperary, then Limerick. The battered old AC motor: the avenue of chestnut trees at Annesgrove, the tiger-skin rugs, the old rocking horse, sweet, lined, welcoming faces. The smell of a sweating horse, wet leather, the old jennet, turf fires burning, hams boiling, bread baking, all as evocative as the smell of paint and linseed oil.

Dash, Beauty, Trixie, Finn, bounded towards me with frenzied greetings. Old Dolly's muzzle under my arm; Slieve Kimalta, the Hill of the Sorrows, mist-enshrouded, from the bedroom window. The vividness of the far-stretching acres at Ballymackey which my ancestors had trod for over three hundred years. Raking the ashes at four in the morning, hot whisky, and talk talk, talk.

'Would you not stay?'

Would that I could.

In London the strange wailing noise of the air-raid siren sounded, monotonously disturbing the stillness, and alarming the blackbirds. Rita Mayer, the German girl, straight away clapped on her gas-mask. The flaps of rubber around her cheeks made loud farting noises as she breathed.

'For heaven's sake, tell her to take it off. There's no gas, and it looks so depressing.'

'I don't know how to say it in German.'

'You were taught by German nuns . . . a year in Vienna. . .'

'But we didn't learn the German for gas and gas-masks.'

'Keinen gas. Nehmen Sie es ab.'

But as long as she stayed with us the gas-mask was put on when the siren went.

My mother and I said that if we were going to be bombed we would like to see what hit us, so we took a whisky and soda into the garden and sat under the beech tree. From time to time Rita's gas-masked head would appear at the window. She looked very sinister. The quiet was menacing, as though the whole of London held its breath. Even the birds were silent.

Was it the same in Paris?

'Let's have another. . .'

The voice made me start, and moving to replenish the glasses, the cheerful noise of the all-clear blew.

All day long the numbness continued. Stories circulated that half London had been destroyed, we were lucky. In fact a civilian plane had arrived from France, unannounced, but owing to censorship we were not to know that for many years. Orders and instructions were relayed at intervals on the wireless, as the radio was then called. Check the black-out curtains; no torches or even smoking in the streets;

theatres and cinemas closed; identity cards; rationing details to be given later. Register; volunteer; evacuation of women and children; tighten our belts.

Oh darling, will I never see you again?

Waiting, always waiting. Waiting for news, for buses, for trains, the stations teeming with evacuees going out and coming back. Waiting for bombs that never fell; gas. Waiting for casualties in dreary improvised rooms. Worst of all, waiting in queues: for food, for forms to be filled in, for things that would never happen. The misery of doing nothing, waiting to be told what to do. Maybe.

It became known as the Great Bore War.

As all wars are going to be over by Christmas, everyone tried to live as normal a life as was allowed. With all theatres still closed in London, I went back to being a mannequin in the daytime, with a voluntary war job some evenings. The approaching winter, early darkness and frost, made travelling on the infrequent buses – all services had been cut to conserve petrol – much more exhausting than a full day's work. All young men and women were compelled to register for the forces. New ministries were suddenly opened, to deal with National Service, shipping, blockade, food and propaganda. Old ministries were moved, overnight it seemed, to the West Country or Wales. Many rich people went to their country houses to find them commandeered for the forces or evacuees. Some went to Canada or the United States, for money could still be moved out of England. The Civil Service, never popular with the masses, was having a field day. Uninspiring and sometimes incomprehensible posters, such as 'YOUR resolution will bring US victory', appeared on walls. Social order must be maintained, and we were told to carry with us our gas-masks, read official instructions, and proceed *quietly* with our affairs! The Civil Service's idea of affairs was not mine.

Lord Gort was Commander-in-Chief of the British Expeditionary Force in France; the French garrisoned the Maginot Line. There was no fighting, for the blockade would win the war. All we had to do was wait, presumably as quietly as possible. In December the German pocket battleship *Graf Spee*, which had been raiding cargo ships in the south Atlantic, was fired on and damaged by British ships, then forced into Montevideo harbour where she was scuttled on Hitler's orders. Britannia ruled the waves all right, and Montevideo was a long way away.

About this time in the phoney war I met Yvonne Chudleigh. She was working at the same place as I was, and at first sight we smilingly pussy-footed around each other like cats. In fact, even when I knew her better, she was so unlike me that it is remarkable we got on so well.

For she was a prototype John Betjeman girl: blonde, tall, attractive to look at and devoted to playing tennis. Far from being an intellectual, her close friends called her 'Bonehead'. She deliberately made remarks designed to provoke astonishment and laughter. That was her great charm: warmth, and being basically so sure that she didn't mind making a fool of herself. It made everyone else feel better, not superior, but better and gayer. For of course she was not foolish at all. Although a few years younger than me, she knew exactly what she wanted, and in the nicest possible way went ahead and got it. If she couldn't discuss metaphysical problems with the next man, she could cook a good simple dinner, make excellent and original clothes, and amuse. Yvonne also had that most under-rated of qualities, common sense. She had two brothers, both in their twenties: Neil, who at nineteen married a French women ten years his senior, survived the war in the Royal Air Force, had children, and lived happily ever after; and Derek, who had made a disastrous marriage which had just ended in divorce. When I met him he was working as a journalist, wanted to write a book, but was unable to settle down to it, as he was awaiting his call-up papers.

They all came from Chudleigh in Devonshire, and their ancestor was the famous, or infamous, and beautiful maid-of-honour Elizabeth Chudleigh, who in 1744 had secretly married Augustus John Hervey, afterwards Third Earl of Bristol. When he succeeded to the title, Hervey sought to divorce her. She appears to have been heartily sick of him by then, and to avoid scandal Elizabeth declared herself unmarried and was thus pronounced a spinster by the court. Within a month she had married the Second Duke of Kingston, with whom she had been living, and shocked licentious London society in a number of ways, but particularly by appearing at a ball in a transparent dress with little or nothing on underneath. Kingston died four years later. His nephew, who wished to inherit the money, declared her a bigamist, and Elizabeth hurried back from Rome where she was being received with honour by Pope Clement XIV and was tried in the House of Lords in 1776. She was found guilty but retained the fortune. Thereafter she lived briefly in Calais, then St Petersburg, on an estate which she called 'Chudleigh'. She died in Paris in 1788. There was a little of Elizabeth Chudleigh in all of them.

Yvonne and Derek had a penthouse flat in Chelsea, and were looking for someone to share it with them. Yvonne and I worked together; I was deadly sick of the long bus journeys, and the ticket sorting at home. It was the obvious answer, so for nearly six months we three lived a pleasant and uninhibited life together.

Chapter Five

In 1939 the small London borough of Chelsea still retained some of the pastoral quality of earlier days. Although the famous eighteenth- and nineteenth-century pleasure gardens of Ranelagh and the Cremorne were no more, old men still talked vividly of them, as though they had closed the year before. Charles II's old hunting lodge was transformed into the Pheasantry drinking club, and that of Henry VIII was a children's kindergarten, but it did not require great imagination to visualize the marshy land running down to the river being inhabited by mallard, snipe and woodcock.

The King's Road on the northern side was named after Charles II, and a dilapidated terrace of houses between Manresa Road and Carlyle Square were said to have been built to house the court mistresses. They stood back from the road, with pretty trees in front, leaning with a drunken air, slightly disreputably to one side.

Chelsea is bounded on the southern side by the Thames, and Sir Joseph Bazalgette's beautiful embankment, interspersed with Battersea, Albert, and Chelsea bridges, and it is along this stretch that the Royal Hospital was instituted by Charles II at Nell Gwynne's behest, for invalid and old soldiers. The scarlet and blue uniforms are still worn by the pensioners.

In Saxon times it was called Cealchythe, and a synod was held there in 785; in the sixteenth century it is Chelcith, which became Chelsea. For many hundreds of years it attracted writers, painters and craftsmen, and it was perhaps unique in that rich and poor lived side by side.

The tomb of Sir Thomas More, the author of *Utopia*, lies in the close of Chelsea Old Church. In the seventeenth century Chelsea housed the painter Sir John Lawrence, and the poet laureate Thomas Shadwell. The eighteenth century brought the opening of the china porcelain factory, and the famous Chelsea china. Other celebrated inhabitants included the Irish physician and collector Sir Hans Sloane, Francis Atterbury, and Dean Jonathan Swift; Steele and Smollett, who lived in Monmouth House, Lawrence Street; later the painters Turner, Whistler, Rossetti, Sir John Lavery, and the writers Oscar Wilde, Carlyle and Leigh Hunt; Brunel the engineer, and many others.

Sir John Danvers introduced the Italian method of gardening so admired by Francis Bacon, in 1630, and later it was Sir Hans Sloane who gave the land to the Apothecaries Company for the Physick Gardens in Swan Walk.

All over this small part of London, street names commemorate the famous inhabitants: even the telephone exchange was Flaxman, named after one of Josiah Wedgwood's designers.

It was through Derek Chudleigh that I first knew Chelsea, for it was natural that we should be attracted to each other. We were both personable young people with similar interests. He knew a lot about the theatre, and encouraged me. With him I strolled about the pretty streets, past Don Saltero's, the eighteenth-century coffee house on Cheyne Walk, to Paradise Walk, up Tite Street passing Wilde's house, along the King's Road, sometimes drinking beer in pubs like the Markham, the Six Bells with its beautiful bowling green – the click of the woods as the Chelsea pensioners played their weekly game of bowls – down to Boris the delicatessen, a drink at the Cadogan, then across the road to Old Church Street, left into Justice Walk where, ironically, the notorious Judge Jefferies once lived, to emerge in Lawrence Street, with the tall lurching Monmouth House facing, and then to the right, the neat gardens with the statue of Carlyle in his square-topped shoes. Opposite, the spheres of gas-light, no longer lit in the blackout, on the tree-lined embankment; the fast flowing Thames, and the Battersea factories across the river. It had a grandeur and beauty such as I had only seen in Paris. Paris, and all that it had come to mean, I tried not to think about.

Yvonne and Derek made it possible, for indeed the flat was often so crammed with people that it was difficult to think at all. London can be a lonely city, and many residents in large blocks of flats never know their neighbours at all. This was not the case in Chesil Court, for very soon, through Yvonne it must have been, we knew quite a lot of people.

Arthur Barbosa looked like a Portuguese version of the man on the cover of *Esquire*, with shiny black boot-button eyes and a black curled moustache, always elaborately dressed in silk shirts, embroidered waistcoats, curly brimmed hats, and a long black overcoat. He had a vast knowledge of old military uniforms, and painted friezes and murals, using the uniforms in battle scenes. They were meticulous and exquisite. He moseyed about London, finding out what everyone was up to, and had the strange vice of having to start the day with brandy mixed with Moussec, a sparkling wine, sold in small bottles, popular at the time. He was sometimes known as 'King' Barbosa, for his knowledge of uniforms made him the instigator of the King Club. This very exclusive club met once a year: a King and Queen with an entire court were chosen, and all were dressed in the chosen period, when a ball was given. Some of the photographs taken on these occasions were used in Cecil Beaton's amusing spoof book, *My Royal Past*. Alas, the rigours of wartime put an end to this harmless but enjoyable annual entertainment. There was something very endearing about Barbosa.

Barbosa's wife, Rachel, worked in one of the ministries. We were all a bit terrified of her caustic tongue, but she did have good reasons, sometimes. She was called, unwittily, by us, the un-civil servant.

Mechtild Nawaisky was Polish and worked as art editor on *Lilliput* magazine. I unfortunately christened her 'no more whisky', which was shortened to Whisky. She hated this uncharacteristic appellation, and begged everyone to call her Mechtild, but Whisky she was and Whisky she stayed.

There was also James Dowdall, and his wife, Louise. James was a droll-looking Scot with enormous, drooping-at-the-corners brown eyes. I don't know what he did before he went into the Cameron Highlanders, but his father was a judge who spent his time rewriting the Bible, usually while reading the lesson in an Oxfordshire church. Jimmy was an excellent cook, and marvellous aromas of garlic and herbs came from the kitchen. He knew a lot about jazz and jazz musicians, and it is probably through him that we all got to know Arthur Young, whose band played at Hatchett's Restaurant in Piccadilly. Several members of this band had been with the Hot Club de France: Stephane Grappelli, the violinist, and the famous guitarist Django Reinhardt. Other members of this quintet were Tony Spurgeon and Chappie d'Amato.

Arthur Young, with his twinkling blue eyes behind small gold-rimmed spectacles, was more like a huge, blond, jovial doctor than a musician. His wife was an extremely pretty German actress called Karen Verne, who married the film actor Peter Lorre in Hollywood after the war.

Many times after the restaurant closed in the early hours of the morning, the whole band would come back to the flat and play a jam session until it was almost time for us to go to work. There were seldom complaints from the other tenants. That was the best of a penthouse.

Yvonne had a retinue of varied young men: from rugger buggers (her phrase) to elegant young officers, some on leave from France. For the first and only time in my life I lived the sort of existence that all only children imagine all big families do, but don't. We danced at nightclubs like The Nest, Coconut Grove and a gorgeous new one called The Suivi which had a pale-blue quilted satin ceiling. With the theatres still closed we enjoyed restaurants like the Café de Paris or Quaglino's, with a floor show, and particularly when it was the superb female impersonator Douglas Byng.

We used adjectives such as 'heavenly', 'divine' and 'marvellous'. We yelled at each other when the last drop of shampoo had been used, the last pair of someone else's stockings laddered, and when the frock *you* wanted to wear was staked by a friend who had come up from the country. The gramophone was on most of the time we were home. and it was always someone else's turn to put the record on

We played Jelly Roll Morton, Benny Goodman, Louis Armstrong, Jack Teagarden, Fats Waller and Red Nichols as we jigged about the flat to 'Honeysuckle Rose', 'Tiger Rag', 'Beale Street Blues' or 'Melancholy Baby'. The modern songs we liked best were 'O Johnny', 'Deep in the Heart of Texas' and 'Beat me Daddy, Eight to the Bar', which had the couplet:

Now Mr Paganini,
Don't you be a meanie . . .

Also an excellent song, called 'I Get Along Without You Very Well', which, for obvious reasons, was withdrawn.

The young officers on leave from France brought back presents of scent, or records of Tino Rossi, and of course Jean Sablon:

Vous qui passez sans me voir,
Pourquoi?

Derek was not in the least like his sister either in looks or personality: tall, dark-haired, with deep-set brown eyes which completely disappeared when he smiled, which was often; a loose limbed walk, as if he was double-jointed – not conventionally handsome, but attractive, and winning. He was a more introverted person than Yvonne, very even-tempered and extremely kind. He loved women and I think rather enjoyed having several around him. He was not in the least overwhelmed by us, and of course we behaved all the better for his presence. He could be quietly amusing, and we both spent quite a lot of time laughing at, and with, Yvonne. Despite the differences in all our natures, there were no personality clashes. Derek wrote very charming short stories of an allegorical kind, and often in the evenings when Yvonne was out he would tap away at his typewriter, whilst I read or caught up on my sleep. We both enjoyed the books of James Branch Cabell and Thomas Wolfe. Or we would have friends to dinner, and with food rationing becoming stringent, stuff and braise unrationed sheeps' hearts, or make mountains of spaghetti with a rich garlicky sauce. The big L-shaped room, with its balcony overlooking the rooftops of Chelsea and the river, was warm with central heating. The walnut wood piano and the period furniture gleamed invitingly.

Opposite this rather flossy block of flats was an excellent workman's diner. Bare well-scrubbed tables, dark high-backed settles to sit on, and a good solid meal of hot meat pie, or a 'cut-off-the-joint with veg' for a shilling; sausages, egg and chips, tenpence. It was unpretentious, friendly, and the food was well cooked and sustaining. There was the Blue Cockatoo on Chelsea Embankment when one was feeling flush and able to spend two-and-six on a three-course meal. Old Maggie, the waitress, missed nothing. A young man I knew, dining there with two girl friends he couldn't make his mind up about, lost both of them when Maggie appeared after the meat course, and said pointedly to him:

'Tart or Fool, sir?'

The small neighbourhood shops were usually staffed by their owners or members of the family. They were understanding, and willing to give credit up to a pound, but no more. They knew to a penny what the traffic would bear and didn't want us to get into debt. Vic, of Bullards, and Jack of Jax's Stores: kind, sad-eyed middle-aged men, who had been through the 1914–1918 war, and thought the Jerries still had something up their sleeve. The 'secret weapon' was much speculated on. They had a twinkle in their eyes, and often a rationed can of meat or a packet of cigarettes was smuggled across the counter and into one's bag with a wink.

A horse-meat shop opened in Chelsea Manor Street, called the Continental Butcher. At first it was hardly patronized, but later on when food was very scarce there were queues outside all the way past Jax's Stores, which didn't please Jack any.

Chelsea was still a place for artists to live. Many of the pubs were willing to take a painting they liked in exchange for drinks, and writers or painters were not treated with contempt, or as odd-balls, as happened in most parts of England, but were, in fact, helped and encouraged by the working man, who was proud to share, even vicariously, the traditions of Chelsea life.

At midday on Saturdays and Sundays we usually went to the Six Bells in the King's Road and drank gin and lime, or beer, according to the money we had. Friends knew we would be there and joined us when they felt like it. The saloon was a big, long, high-ceilinged room with the bar running two thirds of the way down. On the other side was the public bar and partitioned off, at the bottom, a billiards room, which had a small hatch through to the bar and the Saloon. Tall glass doors at the end opened out on to the velvety bowling green. There were stools at the old-fashioned, heavy mahogany bar, and small chairs and tables on the left-hand side. The clientele was mixed, but painters like Adrian Daintrey, Mervyn Peake, James Proudfoot, who painted me looking like a large tawny tiger, and the Royal Academician, Egerton Cooper, were nearly always there, as well as writers such as Henry Savage, musicians and actors.

On this Saturday morning we were with Barbosa, Rex Harrison and his agreeable first wife Colette, whom I liked on first meeting but had little chance to know better, as she was mostly with her small son and her family in Cornwall. Her younger sister was a friend of Yvonne's, as they came from nearby the Chudleigh home. Rex Harrison was a friend of Barbosa's. He was rather sleek in those days, with an interesting and distinctive face which somehow reminded me of one of those elegant pedigree cats one sees photographs of at cat shows but never encounters in real life. His conversation was easy, amusing and polished, and it is not difficult to see how the word debonair became the cliché for describing him. I think he certainly encouraged it, and the parts he played opposite Vivien Leigh, especially in *St Martin's Lane*, fostered this image. He gave women the impression that he was sizing them up and filing away for future reference. I only met him a few times, as I think he went into the air force shortly afterwards, but I enjoyed his company. I was also not in the least surprised when, some time later, I heard that the German actress Lilli Palmer had supplanted Colette.

On this clear, cold, winter morning the conversation

crackled and hissed like a well-seasoned winter log burning brightly. The war hadn't amounted to much so far, and for us it meant an earlier emancipation from family life. We were young, reasonably uncommitted, except for Derek who was expecting to be conscripted any day. Barbosa's boot-button eyes gleamed and glinted as we talked and laughed about whatever caught our fancy for the moment.

It was nearing closing time. Elbows were jostled, drinks spilt, the pitch of conversation raised, as the frenetic English onslaught on the bar for 'last orders please' took over. I was being pushed from behind, and as I turned angrily round, a pleasantly drawling voice said:

'Well, you do seem to be having a gay time, Pussy.'

Chapter Six

If this was a novel, it would all be plain sailing from now on, but in my experience nature seldom imitates art. Peter had arrived from Paris two days previously and telephoned my mother, from whom there was no reply. He was obviously pleased to see me, playful and teasing in manner, but preoccupied. It was difficult to find time to see him alone on account of my work on most days as a mannequin, until a merciful attack of tonsilitis gave me a few days off.

He was sitting by the fire in the Six Bells when I went in, and he sprang up, almost running to greet me. He was wearing a long charcoal-coloured riding jacket over dark corduroy trousers. I remarked that he was back in time for the hunting season.

'Hunting?'

'Your jacket. It's what is *de rigeur* for riding to hounds.'

He had no idea what it was, but was attracted by the deep pockets. He could almost go away for the weekend with it. It was somehow comic to see him in riding clothes.

The conversation was on a superficial, bantering level. He kept on saying how much he liked 'my young man', which was unanswerable and offputting. Anthony Powell in one of his *Dance to the Music of Time* novels writes that teasing is a sign of inner misery, and I wish I could have known that then. He inquired about the play I had been in, and I in turn inquired about his painting. Normally a chatterbox, I found it difficult to frame a sentence. He insisted that we drink the expensive Pimm's no. 4, as he said it was a celebration. It was suggested that we had a light lunch at his place. The pattern was the same as the first time I met him, yet I was much more uneasy.

The delicatessen shop was a bit of a disappointment, as all the good things were rationed and neither of us had our books with us. Boris, despite his name, had a very cockney accent, and showed bewilderment when Peter called the homely gherkin *cornichon*, and the black pudding *boudin*. We settled for the cornichons, some little squares of mystery called unattractively 'faggot', potato salad, bread and a carton of cottage cheese.

The room was on the top floor of one of the tall houses in Oakley Street. It was at the back, and looked out on to the large and beautiful garden of Crewe House. The leafless winter trees made intricate lacy patterns against the pinkish snow-cloud sky. There was a gas fire with a shilling-in-the-slot meter at the side. The room was neat and clean, and on the bed was a spotless, unruffled, heavy white counterpane. In the middle of the threadbare rug was what looked like an old-fashioned carpet-bag lying open, and from it spilled shirts, tubes of paint, several French paper-backed books and a bottle of brandy. On a long table under one of the windows a new, slightly different version of the multi-coloured room painting leaned against the window ledge. A copy of Huysmans's *À Rebours* was on the table. There were no knives or forks, so the meal was eaten by means of a penknife, and the tops of the cartons containing the gherkins and potato salad folded over to form a scoop. The brandy was drunk neat out of a tooth glass. We sat on hard wood kitchen chairs: the gas fire hissed and warmed the room quickly. It was all a little bit eerie, doing similar things in such different surroundings and behaving as though we had just met.

He had come back to England for just so long as it would take him to arrange that his money be sent to France, and to see his friends. Why didn't I come back with him? Hesitantly, I mentioned the war . . . Oh, that made no difference; if one had been living in France, it was quite easy to get back.

'Germans?'

They would never come into Paris. There was the Maginot Line, and everyone knew that they would have done so by now if they were going to. Of course, I did have that young man . . . he could offer me nothing, whereas the young man might marry me.

But I didn't want to marry anyone.

In that case, why not come back? It would take a little while for the bureaucrats to sort things out, and I could think it over. The phrases were said dispassionately, but even so I might have agreed on the spot had I not turned my chair slightly to avoid my legs being burnt by the gas fire. On the back of the door we had come in through hung the most beautiful blue, purple and chartreuse-yellow woman's tweed coat.

Why it should have had such a sudden chilling effect on me I shall never know. But it hung there like a warning signal. Naturally impetuous, it stayed me. What friends? What money? Why hadn't he written? Recriminating, insinuating thoughts crept into my head, but never once did it occur to me to ask to whom the coat belonged. My head ached, and for the first time that day my throat was sore again and my voice husky.

Back at Chesil Court, Yvonne chided me for going out, and made me go to bed. Derek came home and brought me bowls of hot soup. For two days I had a high temperature, and then Yvonne and Derek succumbed. We three groaned and shivered, dragged about in dressing gowns, occasionally administered to by Barbosa, and once surprisingly by Peter, who came and made us some tea, a beverage he heartily disapproved of, and said so. Yvonne's malady turned out to be German measles, so we were all in quarantine. It was one way, for me, of not facing up to the situation.

When we were all better Peter and I met almost every day, usually in the company of other people, but not always. Once or twice he kept apart with a very pretty dark-haired woman, and I thought of 'I like dirty, black-haired women.' This one didn't seem dirty enough, but one never knew. I was always depressingly clean-looking, no matter how hard I tried – like William Blake the poet and painter, whose wife once sharply reprimanded someone for saying that Blake should take more baths by commenting:

'Mr Blake don't dirt!'

It was extremely difficult for a young woman used to a

certain amount of adulation from men to understand someone of Peter's temperament. He never made an overt gesture to give me the confidence that he really wanted me. Most of the time I spent with him, I was teased unmercifully, and only when I had lost my temper, and was going, did he say something affectionate as a parting shot. My mixed Irish, Cornish and Russian ancestry didn't understand it, and this made me uncharacteristically shy. Also, although I had lived a lot in England, I was not conversant with Englishmen in love. The banter and the teasing were his version of the 'stiff upper lip', and foreign to me. My roaring ranting crew of a family had few sexual inhibitions, and followed their hearts sometimes to the point of eccentricity.

Peter still fascinated me in many ways, but no matter how close one got to him, he was yet elusive. With his curious nature, it seemed that the ordinary emotions which many people experience were side-tracked, or put aside for a further investigation which might never take place. It could have been that subconsciously we knew, for this particular time in our lives, that we needed each other. We were linked, not by *une grande passion*, but by something that would hold us, even tenuously, together for the rest of our lives.

Perhaps it was that all the old bureaucrats had been sent to the West Country or Wales, for the new bureaucrats didn't take long in making up their minds that it was all right for Peter to go back to France. Quite casually, one day in March 1940, he announced that he was leaving the next day, and that he expected me to follow shortly.

Soon after this Derek was called up and went into the King's Royal Rifle Corps, the Sixtieth it was called, as a rifleman. Quite often I made the depressing, slow train journey down to places like Tidworth, Luggershall, Andover, and Middle Wallop to see him – endless army huts; thick, chipped china, and Naafi food swimming in grease, which Derek seemed not to mind, so hungry was he from unaccustomed route-marches and other strenuous army training.

Thousands of young men filled these camps, all looking enviously at the ones who had a girl with them. It was a myth of the time that saltpetre or bromide was put in the tea to stop them feeling sexy.

Was it?

Did it?

The small country pubs nearby were filled to standing room only, pints of beer awash on the floors and tables. The anxiety of getting a late pass or, if lucky, an all-night one . . . disagreeable landladies who demanded ration books or identity cards to make certain that 'no immorality was going on under their roof' . . . the smell of sweat; the stench of urinals; rough wool of new uniforms; the noise of army boots walking along the street. Barracks called Jellahabad or Allahabad, so far removed from their musky Eastern counterparts.

'Did you know that the Sixtieth march 120 to the minute?'

'What does that mean?'

'One hundred and twenty paces to the minute.'

'It seems very fast.'

'It is.'

The long journey home on Sunday night, the train filled with twittering girls, giggling about what Charlie or Jack said; women and children, tired and unhappy at leaving their loved ones, wondering how to make do on the curtailed army pay; and the let-down feeling after spending the weekend in such alien and uncomfortable surroundings. What a sigh of relief they must have given when they got home and settled down in an old but comfortable armchair, to listen to Tommy Handley in *ITMA*, or the late news on the wireless.

For the news had become more and more disquieting. Finland had been invaded by the Russians, but on 21 March she conceded to Soviet demands and made peace. 'Arms for Finland' was dropped in favour of an expeditionary force to Norway and Sweden. Chamberlain announced that 'Hitler has missed the bus', whilst Hitler was in fact planning a full-scale invasion of Denmark and Norway timed for 8

April. The recovery of Narvik, the Norwegian port, from which iron ore was shipped to Germany, was the current open secret. Chamberlain's government was uneasy: there were speculations as to whether the Labour and Liberal parties would serve under Lord Halifax or Winston Churchill. On 9 May, Churchill became Prime Minister. The next day Holland and Belgium were invaded by Hitler. On 13 May, Churchill made his now famous speech combining and paraphrasing the words of both Garibaldi in 1849 and Clemenceau in 1917, in which he said:

'I have nothing to offer but blood, toil, tears and sweat . . . What is our aim? I can answer in one word: Victory . . .'

Around 14 May the Germans broke through the allied forces in Belgium at Sedan, which cut off the British Expeditionary Forces, and on 15 May the Dutch army surrendered. Queen Wilhelmina came to England, with her bicycle, and set up her government here.

The war had truly begun: the days of the jam sessions were over. The penthouse was quiet, for the elegant young men were far away, destination unknown, some never to return. Yvonne had fallen in love with a naval officer whom she subsequently married. By then I had already taken the long road back.

In France, Daladier had been replaced as Prime Minister by Paul Reynaud: France and England had agreed not to make a separate peace as the German panzer divisions prepared to launch their attack on France, but there was little to stop them. On 16 May, Churchill was in Paris for one of the many consultations with General Gamelin, who three days later was replaced by Weygand, an elderly general who had served under Marshal Foch. Calais fell after a fierce battle, and Belgium capitulated, thus trapping almost a third of a million men and their equipment. Operation Dynamo, the evacuation of Dunkirk, began on 27 May, when nearly nine hundred British ships of all descriptions, from destroyers to river pleasure-boats, rescued the BEF and many French soldiers. The last men were brought away on 3 June, but fog prevented evacuation from St Valéry, where the entire

Fifty-first division was lost. Spirits were low, for there was little force left to defend France: Weygand and the elderly General Pétain talked of an armistice. On 9 June the French government left Paris for Tours and Briare; the next day Italy declared war on France. On the 13th Churchill was again in France, and the French government left Tours for Bordeaux. On 14 June the Germans entered Paris, and Italy invaded the south of France.

The ordinary citizen knew only the barest of these facts, for newspapers were but a single sheet. To many French people it appeared that the British had saved themselves at Dunkirk. That nearly 140,000 French soldiers had been taken off, who formed the nucleus of the Free French army in England, was not known. Rumours slithered about like snakes, and the blazing summer sun, instead of inspiring leisurely holiday thoughts, only increased the feeling of oppression and fear.

Fear affects people in different ways. It is easy afterwards to say, 'I was not afraid' because one acted calmly, but it is surely only the statement of a very insensitive person or a moron. Fear is not cowardice, it is one of the most natural human emotions and manifests itself in many ways. For most people, death is less fearful than, and preferable to, torture or total disablement. Fear is many faceted: it makes the young old, and the old younger; it can cause betrayal, separation and incredible bravery. Physically, it can produce sweating with heat or shivering with cold. Fear is the unknown, and it may be said to have had Paris in its grip on 14 June 1940, when the German army entered that city.

It was through a misunderstanding, and the chaos on the roads outside Paris, that Peter and I were separated. Events happened too quickly for us to know what was going on, and all I knew was that he had gone to pick up his money in Tours. Then we would make our plans when he came back. That the government and other official bodies had left Tours was still a secret. Even early that morning the heat was intense, the pavements shimmering, the air stifling. Everything was closed: no bread or milk, the café on the corner locked up. That huge humming city shuttered itself up and was silent, for even the small amount of traffic seemed noiseless.

Telephone calls; always with no reply. As I was walking along the street to contact some friend, a strong arm covered in black hairs pulled me into a doorway, and a voice muttered, 'Les Boches . . .' as an armoured car drove in the middle of the street, its smiling passengers dressed in field grey. I didn't recognize it as German, never having seen one before, and thought it was a new branch of the French army. All morning I walked like a skulking dog across that city, keeping to the walls or shop doorways. Always the same answer from the concierge:

'They have left.'

K. had also left, but his half-German boy-friend had stayed. In the hallway of the magnificent house on the Ile de St Louis were two bicycles. Upstairs we drank delicious brandy from exquisite glasses.

'We must get away. This morning I saw an armoured car . . .'

'I can't. K. has left me all his belongings. I have never had anything of my own before. Look around at the beauty, the comfort. I can't leave it.'

'But if they arrest you, or shoot you? There are bicycles downstairs.'

'No. I will be safe. I speak German. You go. I have maps and some money for you.'

'Oh, come with me, please, please . . . you won't be safe.'

'Where could we go?'

'Anywhere, away, to Tours, further south; we could perhaps come back.'

'No, I can't leave it all. I will be safe. K. and I were going to take a trip together. I have all the maps and equipment. You take it.'

'Come with me for a few days, and then see . . .'

'No. I will stay and look after his things.'

He produced a light canvas bag and insisted on packing it for me. Had I gone back to my rooms I would have found Peter's message. He came with me on the other bicycle to the Porte de Versailles, and we had a final drink at a café there. Again I tried to persuade him. No. Dear, brave little blond figure, smiling and waving as I set off. Did he live to enjoy his luxury? Who knows?

The city streets were empty, but the country roads were crammed with every available vehicle: hand-carts laden with bundles, old and new cars left on the roadside without petrol. All faces showed anxiety, and sweat poured down people's cheeks like tears. Get out of this confusion, take small roads, go across fields, hurry, go south, anywhere, away from crowds and confusion.

'The world is in a state of chassis': why suddenly think of *Juno and the Paycock*? Why not? Try to remember the names of all the characters. Juno and the Paycock, that's easy. What was the Paycock's name? Doyle, Boyle? Joxer Daly, Mary, Johnny the boring one, Maisie Mulligan–no, something like it, begins with M; Jerry Devine, Mrs Tancred, funny name for an Irishwoman. 'The blinds is down Joxer, the blinds is down!' Maisie Madigan, that's it; Bentham: 'Take away this murdherin' hate . . .' getting too near the knuckle. Think of the lines of the last play you were in: 'Must we have the worst table in the room?' Mother of God,I can't go on talking to myself like this – but it helps, like waking up in the night in the middle of a bad dream, and saying 'think of something nice'. Think of the books you like: all rather depressing ones. Music then: Scarlatti, Vivaldi, Mahler, Mozart of course, except for *Don Juan*: makes me feel uneasy when he's in hell. Hum some of the melodies. Can't go on humming da-di-da-di-di-di-da to myself. I'm very hungry, but for God's sake don't start thinking about food. My bum's sore from bicycling. This damned racing bike's very tiring, all that bending forward. Should be easier if it's for racing. Take away this murdherin' heat. . . my skirt's like a second navy-blue skin.

That postman and his wife were very kind. I've still got some of the bread and sausage left. Their son's trousers fit me perfectly: a bit hot, but much more comfortable on this man's bike. Next time I get to a pair of scissors I'll cut them off and make shorts of them. It's so hot, and I'm so tired.

Must be the hottest summer on record. Always talking about the weather like the English. Slieve Kimalta, nice cold Hill of the Sorrows: *bas in Eireann*, death in Ireland: funny thing to have in a drinking toast. *Les anglais s'amuserent tristement* . . . the Irish as well it seems. Who said it? Talleyrand? No, he said about the English having three hundred religions and only one sauce. What sauce? Bread sauce? Mint sauce? That's two already. Bit of a cod, Talleyrand saying that about the sauce; I can think of at least six without trying. Brandy butter? Is it a sauce? Of course it is. One thing I wouldn't like now is Christmas pudding, makes me feel hotter to even think about it.

Where on earth did Peter get to? Not at Donald's flat or at Consuelo's. Hope to God he gets away, he wouldn't be able to cope, just put the Germans' backs up, even more than they are already. My darling, we seem born to be separated. If you were here now the time would go like magic, as we talked or argued. Proust for instance: can't get further than *Swann's Way*, means nothing to me. Much rather have gusty old Joyce. At least Bloom thinks about sex and pigs' kidneys; better than those bloody madeleines and duchesses. I wish T. had come with me. I feel unhappy at having left him. I did try, but he was so set on staying. Perhaps he'll find some German officer who likes him. Hope so. Wouldn't like to be an adolescent queer: bad enough being an adolescent anyway without extra complications tacked on.

I'm more frightened when night falls. Thank God the dawn comes early. The slightest sound is terrifying when it's dark. Why? Pain is worse at night too. Why are we scared of the dark? It can be very cosy and friendly if you're with someone you love. I'll go right on until the last minute of light, and then get up at dawn again. I can lie down somewhere in the heat of the afternoon. Can't cycle then, too hot. Noises all day, sound like cars backfiring: in the night they are always guns, no matter how hard I try to stop thinking so. Fear stops you feeling sexy. Good thing at present. Oh please dear Mother of God help me to get to Bordeaux soon. Don't pray just because you're frightened, it doesn't count. Think of all the millions of people praying right now: must be like a blocked telephone exchange. How peaceful it was lying on that old haystack staring up at the blue, blue sky, the colour of flax flowers, the sweet smell, and the friendly crackly sound it made when I moved. I felt safe for the first time when I saw that aeroplane fly over, until I saw the swastika painted on the side. Did I imagine it? Didn't wait to check. Couldn't see my arse for dust as they say in England. How many days have I been going? Nine, ten? I'm a lovely golden brown, for the first time ever. Suntan with tears. As long as I live I'll never forget the trees of France. Poplars, plane trees, and those trees pruned in that funny bunchy way. What's the word for it? Pollarded. There was a fat brown mare lying dead under one; she was just like dear old Dolly. A belly full of lead instead of a furry, gawky foal inside. That must have happened during the machine gunning which at first I thought was a hail storm.

Bordeaux, bordeaux, bordeau, bordea, borde, bord, it makes the wheels go round faster. *Enfin*, Bordeaux. Go to the biggest hotel, that's what your father always said, if you're broke or in trouble. Beautiful city: Place de l'Opera, not much activity, but a few people. What do I say? 'Ou est l'Ambassade de Grande Bretagne?' Sounds like a sentence from an old-fashioned phrase book. Wish there was an Irish Embassy.

'Ou est l'Ambassade . . .'

'Gone? But where . . . when?'

'Angleterre.'

Sit down and think what to do. At least you're not alone here but you must look odd: frayed cut-down trousers, sweaty, hair nearly white with sun, shoes white with dust which is burnt on. Ask more questions. Find out something. Go all over, make a nuisance of yourself. St Jean de Luz. What's there? A ship. How on earth do I get there? Find the road out of Bordeaux: look at T.'s map. It's like lavatory paper now with creases; wish they'd make them so they fold properly. Soldiers: smile – girls are supposed to smile at soldiers.

'My papers?'

'Yes, here . . .'

'Wait.'

'Why? I have to find my husband – no, lover, father, son, brother. Please, please.'

I thought he'd never let me go. Kept staring at my passport as though it held the key to hidden treasure. Expected to have the red carpet laid out for me in Bordeaux. Thought Donald Maclean and I would have that blow-out at the Chapon Fin, and I'd be treated like a bloody heroine. Instead of which sore bike bum again. At least I'm away from the Germans – didn't realize I'd been just that bit ahead of them. Good thing I didn't know. When you get to St Jean de Luz make straight for the port. Not far now.

Oh the joy, the exquisite joy of having arrived. The quay is crowded. Comforting blue-suited officials actually worried about me. Park your bicycle, go and have a drink, but for heaven's sake don't miss the boat. Talk to someone, instead of to yourself.

People hung about in groups, standing up, holding their limited possessions. They seemed hardly to talk to each other, so weary were they. Weary from worry as much as physical tiredness, and many were English: middle-aged couples who had probably retired and come to live in France. There they stood under the scorching sun waiting to be told what to do. Conversation was limited to polite replies to unanswerable questions, for no one knew anything for certain. I wandered about with my hold-all slung over my shoulder feeling lost and alone without my bicycle. It had become my friend, the recipient of many confidences during the long journey. It was difficult to see through the knots of people, so I weaved through them towards the sea. Occasional phrases in English made me smile:

'Oh, Jennifer, you can't want to go again . . .'

'Yes I do, Mummie.'

Anna Wickham's poem which starts 'O give me back my rigorous English Sunday' flitted across my mind. Well, they would soon be enjoying it.

A group of Basque fishermen, strong and sturdy like bronzed Welshmen, stood talking and gesticulating by one of the bollards. I moved nearer to avoid the glum groups. A large red-bearded man was sitting on the ground, his back resting against the bollard, waving a bottle and laughing. This seemed more jolly, so I went closer. I edged round the fishermen and approached him from the side.

'Well, you do seem to be having a gay time, Peter.'

He jumped so, that I thought he would roll off into the sea. He beamed, the red whiskers twitching up like a pleased tom-cat.

'Oh, Pussy, you are clever to arrive on my birthday.'

It was 26 June.

Later that night we embarked. The smell of kippers and boiled cabbage on the ship was as strong as in an English theatrical boarding house, and never was it more welcome. With three bottles of Pernod exchanged for our bicycles, we sailed early in the morning, after a terrifying strafing by German planes, on the perilous journey back to the comparative safety of England.

Chapter Seven

We arrived at Southampton looking like a road-show version of Svengali and Trilby, with a smack of an out-of-season *Peter Pan* thrown in. There were two queues: one for British citizens and one for aliens. Peter, as a French resident, went in the aliens' queue and I the other. He got ten pounds and a camelhair overcoat made for a giant, for even with his six feet three inches it came down to his ankles: a curious gift with the temperature in the eighties, but it was to come in useful later on. I got my passport stamped and a push in the backside from Jennifer who was behind me. No doubt she wanted 'to go again'.

At Waterloo I swapped a few French cigarettes for the twopence to phone my mother. After a preliminary remark to the effect that bad pennies usually return, she was glad to hear from me.

'Are you alone?'

'No.'

'Well, I suppose you'd better both come out. If Rita isn't there, the key is in the usual place.'

As we had no English money we took a taxi, stopped at a bank near my mother's house, and tried to change our francs. There wasn't any call for them, so we got rather short shrift until I got the manager. On promise of repayment, he lent me ten pounds, a large sum in those days, which was very kind of him, especially as at that particular moment I had no way of repaying. But I didn't bring that up.

Jason, the dog, was delighted to see me. He sniffed suspiciously and growled around Peter's ankles, but then he was that kind of dog. Even the cat stretched, yawned, winked at me and extended a condescending paw. Boy Boy was the nicest cat we ever had. Rita was out. I rang my grandmother, who said she would send my aunt's housekeeper Mrs Hayhoe over with a bottle of whisky. My grandmother was a great believer in the powers of a bottle of whisky. Mrs Hayhoe went back with the story that my mother had someone staying there who 'put her in mind of Edward VII'. Peter seemed very nervous. I suppose it was the idea of 'mother': everyone's dumpling, apple cheeks withal.

My mother was in her middle forties, but looked much younger. Her great asset was that she was unshockable and loved being amused, especially by men. For something over twenty years she had worked at a clinic founded by my grandmother at the turn of the century in the slums of London, and she said that nothing that human beings did, either good or bad, could surprise her. At this time she was also working several nights of the week at a first-aid post, after which she had a long journey home. No wonder she wanted to relax and be amused when she got there.

Peter thought she was very beautiful and said so frequently. For some time I thought he was going to make the remark that had dogged me since I was six: 'She'll never have half the looks of the mother', but thank God he avoided it. They got on well together, despite the difference in their outlooks. In an attempt to find Peter some clothes left by former male members of the family, I unearthed several sequined or beaded shifts – the only word I can use – worn by my mother in the early twenties. Peter insisted we put them on, and on a hand-wound gramophone we played scratchy records of 'Bye Bye Blackbird', 'Black Bottom Stomp' and 'See Me Dance the Charleston'. My mother's attempt to teach Peter the Black Bottom and the Charleston made me laugh so much that I had to go and stand in the hall. Even today the thought of it produces that giggly feeling in my stomach. Rita Mayer's huge sad eyes, with the tragedy of centuries in them, boggled as we jigged and Charlestoned around, carpets flung back, until we were exhausted. One day Peter started to mow the grass. My mother said:

'Do stop him, he doesn't look right doing that.'

Friends called when they heard I was home, and of them

all Peter liked Sophie the best. Sophie was not her real name, but Peter called her that, as he said she had a face such as one would find on a Victorian cameo, and Sophie she still is. We had known each other since we were five years old, and she liked being with me because, as she said, 'there was always trouble about'. We were both brought up by our grandmothers, but Sophie also had to contend with two maiden aunts, one with the glorious name of Zenobia, and a maiden great-aunt, in the same household. It was a bit oppressive for a young child, which is no doubt why she liked my trouble-finding proclivities, for by herself she had a passive nature.

Her grandfather, Mr Warren, and my grandfather Theodore Andrew, dressed in morning suits, high hats and canes, went for a stroll with the dog, Mick, each morning. This was in the middle twenties. No one quite knew where they went until Mick gave them away. My grandmother and I were out shopping one morning when we saw Mick sitting outside a pub called The Haymaker, quite a distance from where we lived. It was beneath Grandma's dignity to go in, and unthinkable to send me. A beery customer came out. Quick as a trice Grandma said:

'Do you know who this poor dog belongs to? I think it's lost.'

'Not a bit of it, Ma . . . that's old Mick, Mr Warren's dog. The guvnor's inside as he is every morning, God bless him. Old Mick has his arrowroot biscuit reg'lar: won't give us no peace till he gets it. Good boy Mick.'

Mick wagged his tail half-heartedly and looked sheepishly at us.

My grandfather, when taxed with this outrageous deceit, said that it was the best place to discuss theological problems that interested them both. They couldn't do it at home, as there were too many women about! My grandfather never really liked dogs after that.

Sophie was still living with the maiden aunts: Mick, grandfather, grandmother and great-aunt Anna were all dead, but it didn't make the big old house any more cheerful. She was dying to get away and find some trouble of her own – at which, as it turned out, late-starter notwithstanding, she became adept. We decided to share a flat in Chelsea together, and in order to facilitate my finding one, Sophie being at work all day, Peter suggested we would meanwhile put up at the Cavendish Hotel in Jermyn Street. It all sounded rather grand, and I couldn't see how we would afford to live in such an expensive district, but with Peter one asked no questions.

Much has been written, and even more spoken, about Rosa Lewis who owned the Cavendish Hotel. She was unknown to me, and if I had read Evelyn Waugh's *Vile Bodies*, I did not for a moment think that the character of Lottie Crump had a real-life counterpart.

Jermyn Street, running parallel to Piccadilly, is narrow and discreet, and was then almost unchanged in outlook since Edwardian days. That is, it catered entirely for men: Mrs White still made the best men's hats (my father frequently sent from Tipperary for them); Paxton and Whitfield were the finest grocers for delicacies that men enjoyed, and had the largest stock of cheeses in London; there were various shops for boots, ties, cravats, socks, and silk scarves; expensive jewellers, and antique shops with *objets d'art* to please the most discriminating or exacting mistress; apartments, called chambers, for men only, and if all else failed, Fortnum and Mason's side entrance on the corner, where you could get kitted out for game-hunting in darkest Africa.

Strolling up from St James's, the Cavendish was on the right-hand side, a pleasant brick building with a front entrance like a private house, a discreet brass plate with the name at the side. Inside, the Edwardian atmosphere continued. The hotel was run entirely for men: women generally, unless they were titled, were only tolerated because men liked to have them around. I don't think Rosa thought much of modern girls: she said they only came in to have a pee and pick someone up. At this time she would have been in her seventies: tall, erect, with silver-white hair, a ruddy complexion devoid of any make-up, and penetrating large blue eyes with as much warmth in them as a seagull's. She was always dressed in a long-skirted suit, cut like a riding habit, in various colours, with a white cambric man's handkerchief knotted around her neck.

Stories about her were copious and conflicting. She had been Edward VII's mistress – or was it her mother? – Lord Ribblesdale's, or Sir William Eden's; or a French duke's. Her mother had been cook to a French nobleman, and Rosa as a pretty girl, in this aristocratic household, had . . . The most likely was that as a young girl she had married a dull Welshman called Lewis, and they had separated. She then trained a troupe, if that is the right word, of pretty girls to serve at the tables of the rich, she being responsible for the food. The truth does not matter. Whatever Rosa's early life had been, it had given her an undying love for the aristocracy and their way of living. Champagne was drunk all day long, and most of the night too, for Rosa never went to bed if there was a party on. When she slept is a mystery, for she was about first thing in the morning. There were always at least six or eight 'regulars', one usually being a rich American of impeccable family, whom she had met, or his father, at one of the grand houses before the 1914–1918 war, or on her visit to the United States in the 1920s.

Ex-kings were especially welcome, as were dashing young blades of good, preferably noble, family. In fact 'blades' were expected to be dashing and were cold-shouldered if they were not. After Evelyn Waugh had immortalized her in *Vile Bodies*, a portrait which did not amuse her, writers were allowed only under scrutiny, and anyone she disliked was referred to as a writer and usually asked to leave. Painters, on the other hand, were both liked and encouraged, and if they were knighted or honoured, like her special friends the Irishman William Orpen, Alfred Munnings or Augustus John, so much the better.

It was not an hotel in the ordinary sense of the word, although there were many innocents who haphazardly chose it to stay in. I often wondered what they made of it. For Rosa was a Robin Hood of hoteliers. The rich got very large bills, and the poor none at all. Rosa decided who could pay and who couldn't, and there was no use arguing with her for you would be told, in the fruitiest cockney, to get out. Like a true Edwardian, her conversation was pungent and spiced with references to tarts, backsides and chamber pots. The servants, if such they can be called, were varied, and led by Moon, an extremely old, bent headwaiter, porter, odd-job man, who was reputed to have been the Duke of Blank's butler in former days. He was so slow and so deaf that it was pointless to ask for anything. You got what he thought you should have. I once asked for some brown bread and butter and after half an hour was given a large brandy. There were several elderly, bearded housemaids, dressed in nineteenth-century clothes, and a young boy, his face shining like lard, wrapped in an enormous green baize apron. He had no name, but answered to 'Cheeky'. The one who did most of the work was called Charles Ingram, and he was unmercifully teased by Rosa. There was also Edith, or Edie. I didn't know quite what her function was: small, shy, brown-haired, with eyes like a partridge, she was usually to be seen carrying round, and consulting, a large heavy ledger – no doubt trying, with Sisyphean labour, to balance the books. Rosa for many years had a succession of West Highland white terriers, all called Kippy. There was a small marble slab low down on the wall near the floor, in the main room, known as the Elinor Glyn, commemorating the death of the last one. It had been the dog's favourite place for lifting his leg. There was another one of these slabs outside the front door. The main dish served went under the name of Game Pie, but the nearest it got to that in wartime was rook. This was always on the go, and served for breakfast, lunch and dinner. I only once had a change of breakfast diet: it was a chunk of smoked haddock, which tasted like fish flannel, and I was glad to go back to the unspecified game pie.

Having two very strong-minded grandmothers, I had had a little experience in handling self-willed old ladies. For several days we both watched each other, and although I was technically staying in the hotel, I was not yet wholly accepted by Rosa. One morning, grudgingly, she said:

'You're quite a nice girl, not like that saucy tart Francesca: go and put your name down in the hall.'

For there had been no signing of the hotel register on arrival. At the Cavendish you signed when you left, like a visitors book in a private house. I was very glad, for if Rosa took one of her unpredictable dislikes to you there was no way of getting round her. To put it mildly, 'you had had it'.

It was impossible at any hour of the day or night to creep in without Rosa spotting you, for her sanctuary was a medium-sized room just inside the front door on the right as you came in. This resembled the comfortable study of a man of varied interests but little intellectual ability: leather armchairs, Rosa's winged armchair, a desk, heavy pieces of furniture of mixed antiquity, the walls plastered with signed portrait photographs, sporting prints, caricatures by 'Spy', yachting pictures, vintage motor-cars, old and young men riding or leading in the winners of well-known races. The regulars spent most of the time in this room, only moving to the Elinor Glyn at the back of the hotel at night, if there was a party. This weird collection of an old lady's life interested me, and I spent some hours looking at it. I was, therefore, both surprised and delighted to see a photograph of my father leading in his horse, Victor Noir.

'That's Adam . . .'

Rosa was behind me, champagne bottle in hand.

'What's that to you, Miss Christabel?' Rosa always called me that, for she never bothered to remember anyone's name, preferring to christen them herself.

'He's my father!'

Rosa was delighted to be able to give me a label. Most of her introductions were in the nature of Lord Whats-his-name, Lady Thingummy, Pullman (Pulham) who-takes-all-the-photographs; Lulu Waugh (Evelyn Waugh) who-writes-all-the-books. Now it was Miss Christabel, whose father-owns-all-the-horses. Elderly mahogany-faced gentlemen would sidle up and ask me for racing tips, for most of the regulars were great gamblers. Rosa too liked her daily flutter. I hated to think that their fortunes were made or lost by my haphazard predictions, but they were so insistent.

Once Rosa had been able to place me I was guarded like an Infanta. For Miss Christabel, although I did not know it at the time, was not a very friendly appellation. There had been a lawsuit regarding paternity in the 1920s, and one of the protagonists was Mrs Christabel Russell. A jingle of the time was:

I'm Mrs Russell's baby,
Blue eyes and curly hair,
I'm looking for my Daddy,
All over Leicester Square.

This rhyme I learned subsequently from my father, who was enchanted to hear of my brief connection with Rosa Lewis. For all the high jinks at the Cavendish, Rosa had quite a strict moral code. It was all right to 'carry on' if you were unmarried, but any sign of rumpling the 'sanctity of the home' was treated very roughly. A newly married young Guards officer on leave, with his young wife pregnant in the country, was pursued by Francesca, or someone like her. She was told loudly and firmly in front of us all:

'Get your fat tart's arse out of my house.'

On another occasion, hearing one man say to another, 'May I speak to your wife?', Rosa misheard it as, 'May I sleep with your wife?', and the trio were out sharply, without realizing why.

At this stage of the war, after Dunkirk and the fall of France, anyone whom Rosa liked was given the kindest of welcomes. With vivid memories of the earlier, bloody war, she became hostess to endless children of the fathers and mothers she had known in the past. Frequently she mixed them up, and addressed them by their parents' names, but there was a jeroboam of champagne, called a cherrybum by Rosa, to speed them on their way. Edie usually retired to bed about midnight, taking the ledger with her. One morning at about three o'clock, Rosa went off to the dispensary to get another cherrybum. Her old handsome face was flushed, and she looked tired, so I followed, thinking I could at least carry back the wine. In the dim, torch-lit dispensary she was bending over with her back to me, pouring one bottle through a funnel into another. A harmless enough deception in the early hours of the morning, especially as the source of champagne from France had been cut off. She turned, saw me and spat out:

'Get out of here, you bloody little spy.'

'Rosa dear, I only came to help you carry back the bottle. I promise you . . .'

'All right, all right, don't make a song and dance about it. Hold this bloody torch.'

From then on we were in league, and many times thereafter I heard the crisp voice saying:

'Come on, Miss Christabel, get off your backside and fetch another bottle.'

For Peter and me it was like being on leave, after the gruelling journey through France with fear and apprehension as travelling companions. Although we were outwardly gay, there were times of deep depression. Peter had only the rag-bag jumble of clothes he stood up in. All his possessions and paintings he had had to leave behind, and the sole prospect was conscription into one of the forces, to which he was violently opposed. The only sure work for an actress was with ENSA, entertaining the troops. I would willingly have done this, but my talents did not lie in singing or dancing, which were what was wanted. Peter worried about his friends in France, especially those who had already been pronounced 'decadent' by the Germans, such as Max Ernst and Giacometti. For this reason he was always delighted when English people he knew turned up, which they often did in the evenings at the Cavendish, for entertainment was limited at this stage of the war – all cinemas being closed by nine o'clock at night (there was just time to see *Gone with the Wind* if one went in after lunch), likewise the few theatres like the Windmill which ran a non-stop girlie show. They were a marvellously assorted mixture of people: amongst them the handsome Hamish Erskine, soon to be reported missing; outrageous, delicious, homosexual sauce-box Brian Howard, on whom

Evelyn Waugh modelled his characters Ambrose Silk in *Put out more Flags* and Anthony Blanche in *Brideshead Revisited.* Brian joined the air force in his forties, as an aircraftsman, and when asked by a pompous air force officer in the Ritz Bar for his name and number, replied:

'My name is Mrs Smith!'

I was always very fond of Brian, also his young Irish friend Sam Langford, who came from Tralee, and I delighted Rosa by calling him 'The Rose of Tralee'.

Dashing Lord Shimi Lovat – who, kilted, and with bag-pipes playing, led the commando raid on Dieppe in 1942 – was another of the regulars.

Witty Daphne Bath, gentle and tender as only big women, in every sense of the word, can be, seemed goddess-like to me. She was one of Rosa's 'specials', for Rosa had cooked for her grandmother, Mrs Harry McCalmont, when she entertained the Prince of Wales, later Edward VII, at her country house. Now Daphne Fielding, she has written an enchanting book, *The Duchess of Jermyn Street*, about the life and times of Rosa Lewis.

And there was Crabbe: his first name was Lionel, but he was always called Crabbe. He looked like a younger, more genial version of the sailor on the Player's cigarette package. He was at this time an AB in the navy, dressed in bell-bottomed trousers, and was most engaging; quite small, but so perfectly in proportion that he didn't look a short man. He seemed delighted that Peter had a girl who was looking after him, as he put it, and kept telling me that he had bought an early Pulham painting of which he was very proud. A little before this he had come into a small inheritance which he had decided to blow on a celebration at the Cavendish. Of course, he well overspent it, and Rosa in one of her unpredictable moods had made him seriously work off the debt. This he did for several weeks with good humour. Many times later he came to Chelsea to visit us, and it was always a special treat to see him, for he was bold, brave and amusing. He survived the war, but disappeared in April 1956, when he was last seen diving as a frogman under the *Ordzhonikidze*, the Russian cruiser, during the visit of Bulganin and Khruschev to England. The Cavendish was a very romantic house. There were endless passages all leading to the same place, and many suites (I never saw a single room), which were very charming. Besides the old-fashioned huge bath-tubs, where the supply of hot water was capricious, the rooms were crammed with furniture of all descriptions, for Rosa was a great collector. She had a large Daimler motor-car, and for many years had resolutely attended auctions of the houses of the nobility. She was an emotional buyer and bought indiscriminately. With the war on, and many rich families abandoning their London houses, which were often used as offices, Rosa felt it her duty to buy up as much as she could. She was always delighted with her purchases.

As my main object in moving into central London had been to find a job and a flat, I was out most of the day, on those days when there hadn't been too many cherrybums the night before. As often happens, on this particular day I had found both, was utterly exhausted, and crept past Rosa's parlour to my room. At first I thought I must have mistaken the number, for as I opened the door it only went halfway. I groped for the light switch, and was confronted with a staircase. For a moment I thought I had lost my reason and went out to check the room number. I sat down in the corridor, wearily wondering whether I had the energy for the Elinor Glyn that night. Dammit, no, I said to myself, walk up the stairs and see what happens. So I walked up the staircase, round the corner, down the other side and eventually found my bed. The next morning when I awakened, there was Rosa sitting on the top half of the staircase with my breakfast tray (game pie again) on her lap.

'What d'you think of it? Beautiful carving isn't it? Got it cheap from Lord Whats-his-name's town house.'

Dear Rosa, how many hundreds of people she must have cheered in her life. Given them a welcome taste of lotus-eating and gaiety, even the grandchildren of her original friends. She stayed at the Cavendish all through the war, leaving only for a few days to stay at a nearby hotel when the Cavendish was twice badly bombed during the Blitz. On each occasion a hamper of champagne accompanied her. A few times she went to the air-raid shelter at the Ritz Hotel, but generally, as did many elderly people, she preferred to stay in her battle-scarred home, until the last year of the war, when severe illness made her go to a nursing home. But this was not to Rosa's liking, and she was back in a few weeks, with a new 'Kippy', the fourth terrier in succession. She died peacefully in 1952, aged eighty-five, at her beloved Cavendish.

When I unpacked my small amount of luggage in the new flat, there was, snuggled in a spotless white napkin, a cherrybum.

Requiescat in pace.

Chapter Eight

The flat was in King's Mansions, Lawrence Street, Chelsea, a block built about 1910 which ran from Justice Walk to a small pub with a garden, the Crossed Keys. It had four medium-sized rooms and was fully, if drably, furnished. Rents had dropped considerably owing to the evacuation of many people to the country, so for this 'mansion' flat we paid two pounds a week. Reasonable enough – but the most Sophie or I could hope to earn a week, working a nine-hour day and Saturday mornings, was four pounds in a regular job. Temporary work was slightly better paid, but it was chancy. Photographic modelling at two to three pounds a day was almost non-existent, as all paper was rationed: the few magazines published were extremely slender, and newspapers consisted of a single folded sheet. When this temporary work turned up it was always a great temptation to take it and plead illness, but the day's pay was docked from the weekly pay packet unless you had been working with the firm for a year.

Peter couldn't paint as he had no money to buy canvas, brushes or colours. Sophie and I would go to Green and Stone's, the artists' shop, in the King's Road on Saturday afternoons and buy him a tube of paint or a brush between us, so that he could build up a little stock. For this reason many of the pictures he painted then are in monochrome. Once he took some money from the joint housekeeping to buy a tube of viridian green. He said he couldn't resist it, and would live on bread and garlic until he had made up for it. The garlic was the remains of a large bulb he had brought from France. The last clove I planted in a wooden box: it flourished, so for the rest of the war we had a small but continuous supply. All available pieces of wood or hardboard were commandeered to paint on, and two rather gloomy Victorian paintings already in the flat were treated and painted over, as were second-hand pictures bought for a shilling or so in one of the many Chelsea junk shops. Canvas was both expensive and scarce. My mother bought him a second-hand easel which lasted for over twenty years.

At this time we were told to expect an invasion and to stock up our larders accordingly. This was difficult for people with limited incomes like us, for tinned food was expensive, often at black-market prices, when unrationed. We were always hungry for the rations were meagre. One person's weekly rations consisted of one ounce of butter, four ounces of margarine, one ounce of cheese, and between one shilling and one and threepence worth of meat, with a few rashers of bacon. One egg weekly in summer; the winter was unpredictable. Egg powder, that is dried powdered egg, was expected to make up the deficit. The small amounts of sugar (½ lb) and tea (¼ lb) we often swapped, illegally, for cheese which was of the uninteresting 'mousetrap' variety, and best made into Welsh rarebit with a little beer. Tinned fish and meats were on a points system, so many points being allocated each month. A tin of stewed steak or corned beef took two thirds of the allowance. Unless you were pregnant, or a child, milk was only two and a half pints per person a week. Vegetables and fruit were ration-free, but limited and seasonal (in 1941 I queued for an hour to get onions from the greengrocer). Fish was also unrationed, but with mines and U-boats at large it wasn't plentiful, and sometimes didn't seem all that fresh. Chicken was expensive and kept 'under the counter' (a current phrase) for good customers. Technically all offal was free, but as the war progressed it was difficult to find. When I remarked to the butcher that all the animals seemed to be born without tongues, tails, hearts, kidneys, livers or balls, he winked at me, a great arm went under the counter, and he flung up a half-frozen oxtail. I had never cooked one before, but even today I can taste the thick gravy and see our grease-spattered lips as we chewed on the bones. Unrationed rabbit was the salvation for many people in a low-income group. I made big jellied pies with a scrap of bacon and onion; braised rabbit in dark beer with prunes, which made it taste vaguely like pheasant; or with cider and tomatoes; or with curry spices or paprika; or stuffed and baked rabbit, when we would pretend it was chicken; and if it was very young, Peter would joint it, and we would fry it in a crisp batter. Frying was quite difficult, as lard was rationed and olive oil only obtainable at a chemist on a doctor's prescription, so sometimes we were reduced to liquid paraffin. At least we didn't suffer from constipation! Another 'filler' was pasta, which could be bought freshly made in Soho; rice disappeared as the war went on, and even in Chinese restaurants spaghetti cut to look like rice or pearl barley was served. Housekeeping was made more difficult by the hours spent in queues. Local shopping was done by Peter, who became very good at it – except for the butcher, who gave me bigger cuts, so I bought the meat on Saturday afternoons. I also spread the ration books over different shops, for each one would give a mite over, which added up on three books. Indiscriminate shopping where you saw the best food was not allowed, for you registered at a certain shop, and it involved great bureaucratic difficulties to get the book changed. Soho was still well stocked, and Sophie or I would dash down in our lunch hour for coffee beans, smoked fish, pasta, or herbs and spices with which to dickey up the monotonous fare.

My mother would come over some weekends with tins of food 'for the invasion', also packets of dried milk powder. Little did she know we were so hungry that often she had hardly got to the top of the road before we had eaten them, usually out of the tins. The milk powder we didn't quite know what to do with, so that was our only invasion hoard. We didn't complain, because it was the life we wanted to live, and we had hardly known about housekeeping under any other circumstances. For those who took the challenge, it produced good, imaginative cooks who, once the war was over, felt they were in clover.

Even with these limitations we entertained frequently. Peter's heart was still in France, so he would describe French dishes vividly to Sophie and me and we would try to emulate them from his description, for at that time he was no cook himself. One of our first guests was the young diplomatist Donald Maclean. Until the fall of France he had been a secretary at the British Embassy in Paris, and enjoyed the company of the writers, painters and their friends who met regularly in the Café Flore. He was particularly kind to Peter, for when the Embassy moved from Paris during the German advance, and Peter was undecided about leaving, he left him his apartment in the rue Bellechasse, the rent having been paid beforehand. He had found us again through Isabel Delmer, later wife of the conductor and composer Constant Lambert, who sometimes referred to her as 'barmaid at the Mermaid'. Isabel was extremely striking to look at, with a strong, beautifully moulded face, large brown eyes full of mobility, and long dark hair worn straight. She was the model for Epstein's *Isabel*, which portrait bronze is like her in both character and looks. She had verve. Peter had a lot in common with her, for they were both painters. Isabel was married to the journalist and writer Sefton Delmer, but I think by this time they had separated, for I never saw them together. Constant Lambert's description of Isabel sums her up succinctly: 'drawing corks, nudes, and conclusions'.

The hot summer had continued through August, so that Donald and Isabel were able to sunbathe on the roof of King's Mansions. I was still working, therefore Peter had asked them to lunch one Saturday. Isabel had a previous engagement.

Donald was then about twenty-seven years old, boyish looking mainly due to his slimness and immense height, for with his six feet five inches he dwarfed even Peter. He was not particularly boyish in manner, as he could talk well on a variety of subjects, and had a pleasant but not overpowering sense of humour. His excellent manners put everyone at their ease, and Sophie, who sometimes felt out on a limb with some of our friends, took to him at once, for his attitude to women was friendly and uninhibited. Light brown hair fell slightly over one side of his forehead, above the handsome face with a cleft chin and full lips, which nevertheless had a hint of Scottish doggedness about it.

He was delighted we had survived the collapse of France, and as pleased with our new flat as we were. The wine he brought went well with the meal, and we talked naturally and easily about all the things that appealed to us. For there was no need for Donald ever to hide his feelings in our company, and this he knew. We seldom discussed politics because we weren't particularly interested in them, but his outlook always seemed to be, at the most, humanitarian, rather than dogmatic. He wanted to know what Peter was painting: there was very little, owing to the difficulty of buying materials. This he sensed, without being told, and at some time during the day he pressed several pounds into my hand, to 'surprise Peter', as he put it. He was remarkably sensitive and thoughtful for a man of his years. Yet, for all his easygoing nature, he gave the impression of having strength of mind and tenacity.

This warm afternoon early in September as we sat over the luncheon table with our coffee, looking out of the window on to the clock tower of Chelsea Old Church, he talked of his young American wife, Melinda. Neither Peter nor I had at that time met her, for although they were married in Paris, she had (I think) gone back to her family in the United States when it looked as though France would become a battlefield. But she was coming back quite soon, and he was looking for somewhere for them to live, and then we must come to dinner. He waxed so enthusiastic over her that Sophie, who found him very attractive until then, could bear it no longer, and went and did the washing up, for he was obviously very much in love.

I brought out the coffee cups, and as I walked along the hall, there was a ring at the front door, which I answered. In the dim passageway stood a medium-sized, slightly pear-shaped young man, in a tweed overcoat several sizes too big for him, and a green pork-pie hat. He had prominent tawny-agate eyes like marbles, in a round cherubic face.

'Is this Mr Pulham's residence?'

It was said in a rather uneasy, plummy voice which

didn't suit the clothes, and the combination made me wary, for he had, or so it appeared to me, the plausible manner of a debt collector.

'What name shall I say?'

'Mr Thomas.'

Peter said it was a bore; he didn't know anyone called Thomas, but as he hadn't any debts in this country, he might as well see him. I went back to give Sophie a hand, and immediately Peter called us, and there were sounds of chuckling.

'Pussy, do hurry up, it's Dylan.'

I had not met Dylan Thomas, although I had heard about him from Peter, and was familiar with his poems in *Horizon* magazine. He had come, reluctantly, to London to look for work; Caitlin, his wife, had gone with the baby to stay with Dylan's mother and father in Wales. There was nothing like enough money to support them all in London whilst he found a job. How he discovered Peter I shall never know, for the idea of my taking the almost penniless Dylan for a dun obscured such questioning. Fantasies were built around the character of 'Dylan the dun', until eventually he became larger than life and burst, but by then we were all in a rollicking mood, for Dylan had that marvellous quality of being able to invest any character with comedy when he felt like it. He said it gave him fresh heart in his quest for work. We were very relaxed and happy; his fertile imagination had captured us all.

It was around five o'clock, the wine was all gone, and we began to think of going out for drinks at a pub. The air-raid siren had sounded a little earlier, but a warning about a week previously had amounted to very little, so we took no notice. It was, after all, still daylight. Out in the street, the sun was setting, and there was a faraway drone of aeroplanes and the sound of anti-aircraft guns. We decided to go to the King's Head and Eight Bells, a small pub on Chelsea Embankment, instead of the Six Bells. As we turned the corner there was in the sky a monstrous tower, looking like a giant puffball of smoke, away to the east. Even though it was too far off, the density of it made one's nostrils twitch with the imagined smell. We turned into the pub, normally empty at this hour, but the great menacing grey column in the east had brought many people out in search of news. The saloon bar of the pub had a long refectory table by the stairs, and several people sat there silently. It was old-fashioned in design, and over the bar, reaching almost to the counter, were panels of cut glass, with small windows on hinges which were swivelled open to give the orders. Through these foot-wide apertures the frightened eyes of the proprietors met one's own.

We decided to play a game of shove-ha'penny, a pub game of those days. It was convenient because both Peter and Sophie were left-handed, so we didn't have to keep changing sides as we spun the metal discs up the board. Men in tin hats, which we had all been issued with some time ago, came in from time to time with communiqués. When darkness came, the smoke had turned into a red bank of flames. It seemed as if they would flick out their fiery tongues and embrace the whole of London.

At about six thirty the 'all clear' sounded, and by then the sky was the colour of a blood orange, a seething, flaming mass. Donald said he would try to get home now; Dylan stayed quietly by my side. Against the now black sky, the fires shone doubly bright. After a year of the blackout it was weird to have light again, but it was an ominous brightness. It was not my night on fire-watching duty, but I thought I should report just in case. Donald walked with me to the post a few streets away. There we learned that the London docks and neighbouring boroughs had been pounded and set on fire. No, they did not want me, but would summon me if necessary. Donald brought me to the corner and went on his way.

Inside the pub, everybody was speculating as to what had happened on this sunny, Saturday, September afternoon. Jokes were made to relieve the tension; beer mugs were put down more noisily to shut out other sounds. We were glued together by dread. All our eyes were rounder, the pupils enlarged, and although we laughed, our lips twitched with alarm.

A little before nine o'clock the siren went again, and using the fires as beacons, the Luftwaffe sent wave after wave of bombers into the holocaust, until three o'clock next morning. Poplar, Bermondsey, West Ham and other places in the East End were bombed until they resembled desolate heaps of rubble, and at least a thousand poeple had been killed, many others trapped, wounded and made homeless. The planes flew up the Thames, which was lit up like a horrifying pantomime, past London Bridge, Victoria, Chelsea, dropping their deadly cargo indiscriminately. Nearby the flat, a gas main was hit, and a jet of white flame shot up into the darkness like a brightly lit geyser.

We did not know it then, but the winter of the bombs, or the Blitz as it was called, had begun.

Chapter Nine

The next day, Sunday 8 September, there was no gas to cook the breakfast with, so in a combined operation we made toast and coffee over an electric fire lying on its back, and cooked kippers on the flat part of an electric iron. For some time after this we smelt strongly of fish when we pressed our clothes, but at least we ate that day. Dylan had spent what was left of the night on the sitting-room sofa. The morning was bright with a hazy sunshine: the clouds low, and slightly oppressive. The government communiqué on the wireless said: 'Fires were caused among industrial targets. Damage was done to lighting, and other public services, and some dislocation to communications was caused. Attacks have also been directed against the docks. Information as to casualties is not yet available.'

'That,' said Dylan, 'is the understatement of all time.'

Sophie and I went for our customary Sunday morning walk in Battersea Park. Some of the trees were beginning to turn colour, and the swans paddled majestically downstream, looking more indignant than usual. The moonal pheasant strutted about the cage in the ornamental garden, its plumage shining and flashing like precious stones. The early autumn day was quiet, the air balmy, and it was difficult to reconcile the peace of the morning with the noisy, fire-drenched hell of the night before. Looking to the east, a pall seemed to hang just above the horizon. We strolled back across Albert Bridge, then up Oakley Street to join the others at the Six Bells. Everyone in the pub had theories: the invasion had begun; a great naval battle had been fought off Dover; the East End of London and the docks were finished, and this assault would be followed up by gas attacks. The cardboard boxes that civilian gas-masks had been issued in were slung over many shoulders, as were tin helmets. I telephoned my mother, who had been up all night tending to the wounded, organizing food and housing, for there had also been a smaller raid on the East End on the Friday. No, although the suffering and desolation were heartbreaking, they were far from finished. It was impossible to feel really frightened because it was all on such a vast scale. She was catching a few hours' sleep at home before reporting again that night. The East Enders who had implicit faith in Lord Haw-Haw's broadcasts (a traitor who relayed details of raids to come, from Germany on the radio) knew there would be another raid tonight. I was to be sure to go to a shelter. She had too much to do to worry about herself, and anyway had survived the First World War in France. Now she must sleep.

I was able to scotch a lot of the rumours, but even so the outlook was not exactly cheering. We decided to forgo the belly-swilling beer and club together for a bottle of whisky, which at pub prices was about a pound. It was a good decision to have made. The Sunday was indeed rigorous, that afternoon, as we sat and talked, each listening intently, and carefully avoiding our true thoughts. Dylan had an appointment the next day with Donald Taylor of Strand Films, who was making documentary films for the Ministry of Information. This started us talking about the cinema, which had had an enormous influence on Dylan, as it had on me, and we both knew quite a lot about it – particularly the early silent cinema, where as small children we had been entranced in the wonderful world of imagery, in which anything could happen: *Der Golem, Dr Mabuse, The Cat and the Canary, The Cabinet of Dr Caligari*, and in the thirties, James Whale's *The Old Dark House*. The latter we knew almost by heart, and during the afternoon we entertained Sophie and Peter by re-enacting large parts of it, squabbling for the best bits, which Dylan insisted on doing, because he said they were men's parts anyway. Thus was our fear sublimated into remembering, and acting out past childhood terrors, for on the far side of fear there is no fear, only endurance and hope.

The sirens sounded that night as darkness fell, and again we heard the throbbing, monotonous but unmistakable drone of the German bombers. Should we go to the shelter in the Embankment Gardens? We would go and see what it was like, and we weren't long in making up our minds. The long oblong concrete building was lit only by blue-painted electric bulbs, which gave an eerie light. Wooden benches were placed along the damp walls, and if they were occupied, you stood in the middle. People talked in whispers, and it was too dark to read or even knit. It was cold and dank, although outside the air was still warm. Peter made a joke, and someone 'shushed' him as though we were in church. I, for one, decided to take my chance outside rather than spend seven or eight hours under such dismal conditions. The others agreed with me, and it was the only time during the war that I went into a shelter. Out of doors, where you could see what was happening, or in a noisy distracting pub, was much better. That evening we took the latter course, and when the pub closed at ten o'clock we came home, finished the whisky, and did excerpts from *Der Golem* and *Dr Mabuse*. We did not, as it may seem, spend the war in a drunken stupor: we really drank very little, rarely more than a few pints of beer a night, for it was all we could afford.

Although the Blitz was to continue intermittently for eight months, the next ten days were the most intense in the Battle of London, for the city was bombed heavily both by day and night. The savagery of these diurnal attacks left no part of London unscathed. There seemed little to prevent annihilation, for the barrage balloons, in which so much trust had been put, only prevented dive-bombing. They did not stop high-level bombing. There were but few fighter aeroplanes, and only occasional gun-fire. The whole city reeked of smoke and the dusty plaster-like smell of rubble. For the first three days we had not adapted ourselves to living under a constant threat of death or mutilation: we followed our working lives as best we could with two or three hours' sleep, for the crump of exploding bombs, even in another part of London, was deafening and disturbing. But another more deafening sound was to occur towards the end of the week. All Thursday afternoon, bombs whined down through the sky, and it was impossible to clear the wrecked buildings of buried people before nightfall, when rescue work was brought almost to a standstill owing to the total blackout. The bombers came back to be greeted with a roar of anti-aircraft fire, which sounded like a mad Wagnerian orchestra. The preliminary shock to our ears was terrifying, until it was realized that we were in fact hitting back. For the first time that week, groups of people stood out of doors watching German planes caught in searchlight beams, and saw the twinkling shell-bursts like fireworks in the sky. That large, jagged, murderous-looking pieces of shrapnel fell around them did not matter. In fact they were collected like seashells and displayed on mantelpieces like trophies. It became known as the 'barrage', and the noise was sweet music to our ears. The 'barrage' did not stop the raids, but it prevented concentrated attacks. From now on the loads were more widely, therefore more thinly, distributed.

Dylan was the most frightened of us all and, once he was assured of a job from Donald Taylor, he sensibly went back to Wales. Henceforth when he came to London, our bell would ring at the most unexpected times, and we were always delighted to see him. For Sophie and me, Peter was the bulwark, for apart from hunching his shoulders and occasionally glaring with rage, he never showed his fear. He was determined not to let the bombing interfere with his work, and used backgrounds of fire for his still-life paintings. The air raids had the curious effect of making me hungry, violently so, and if there was nothing else I would wolf down slices of bread, or cold potato, after which I fell fast asleep no matter how much din was going on outside. This reaction infuriated Sophie and Peter, so much so that Peter started my 'instruction course' again, in an attempt to keep me awake. Vasari's *Lives*, and Leonardo da Vinci's *Journal* were pushed into my hands, usually to little avail. But whether we liked it or not, our lives were changed for us, and such is the resilience of human beings that it happened quite gradually in the space of a week or two.

In the First World War large numbers of the population

felt safe from the Zeppelin raids in the newly built underground railway stations. Many of the now homeless people, and thousands with homes, who left them during the afternoon, camped on the platforms of the London Underground. The railway authorities at first discouraged these squatters but, as the raids fanned out to envelop the whole city, the operation was organized by voluntary helpers, and this troglodyte existence, immortalized by Henry Moore in his shelter drawings, became the normal life of many Londoners. Seats and bunks were booked with foresight, like a permanent box during the opera season: deck-chairs, meals cooked on paraffin stoves, men and women wrapped in shawls, or with newspapers over their heads, like a surrealist picnic party; perambulators filled with clocks and vases won at funfairs, and bundles of old clothes which, when one got close to them, were people. The trains came rapidly out of the tunnels like snub-nosed centipedes, passengers got in and out before the centipedes vanished again, whilst the private life of large numbers of people was enacted on the platform. Several hundred families lived there rent-free permanently, enjoying the light, heat, medical attention, and cheap meals from the canteens. This was known as the 'deep-shelter mentality'. It was both depressing and fascinating; also rather horrible. But for the long diversions taken by buses to avoid craters or delayed-action bombs, which could be triggered off by a heavy vehicle passing, I would not have travelled by tube after the first weeks, for the smell alone was off-putting.

In big cities the moon is hardly noticed amidst the tall buildings, yet we became moon-conscious. A full moon, previously welcome in the blackout, as it bathed everything in clear light, was dreaded, for it meant a raid with three to four hundred planes, and was known as a 'bomber's moon'. We learned to look at the heavens as well as the gutter, for both could be treacherous. Certain unusual sounds became immediately identifiable: the noise like iron bedsteads rattling as if thrown from a height betokened a canister of incendiary bombs, and the sound as of heavy surf breaking on shingle meant heavy lorries driving over a solid bed of broken glass. A whole new vocabulary opened up: UXBs, unexploded bombs; DAs, delayed-action bombs; canisters, not tea-caddies but containers full of incendiary bombs; an 'incident' was not a trivial thing any more, but a badly bombed building; rest centres, a euphemism for a bare room where you were given a cup of tea after being bombed; stirrup pumps; chandeliers, which were multiple flares dropped before a bomb; siren suits – one-piece garments zipped up the front, worn during raids, so that one was fully dressed; and blast, no longer a mild swear-word, but the shock-waves caused by detonation of explosives.

Despite all the horrors, the Blitz was not entirely destructive, for it produced a marked change in the attitude of British people to one another. Experiencing a common danger made for a friendliness, almost a love, amongst total strangers. People were concerned with helping their neighbours: there was a joke or a laugh to keep their spirits up, and a sharing of scarce commodities. The last pinch of tea, or a bottle of whisky, was offered by people one had never seen before and might never see again. Everybody was in love with life and living. In apartment houses, the owner of the basement rooms expected to share his or her bedroom with perhaps five or six people of mixed sexes. Once you have lain on a bed, even platonically, with someone for several months, it is impossible to ignore them thereafter. A painter friend of mine, Francis Butterfield, told me he would miss his oddly assorted harem when the bombing stopped. Men felt masculine for, whatever some women might say, it was with the male sex they felt safest.

Social and sexual distinctions were swept away and, when a dramatic change such as that takes place, it never goes back in quite the same way. Whatever dreariness and anxiety the middle-aged and old people felt, for the young it was undeniably exciting and stimulating. It was God's gift to naughty girls, for from the moment the sirens went, they were not expected to get home until morning when the 'all clear' sounded. In fact, they were urged to stay where they were. When it came to the pinch, where their parents were concerned, fate was far preferable to death. Certain restaurants, such as Hatchett's and the Hungaria, and all hotels provided beds for their customers. Girls went out for dinner with their night attire, toothbrushes and make-up. Young people were reluctant to contemplate death without having shared their bodies with someone else. It was sex at its sweetest: not for money or marriage, but for love of being alive and wanting to give. Many married hastily when love was kindled by flames, and many of those marriages are today still snug in their happy philo-progenitive cocoons. An interesting point is that crime and nervous disorders actually declined throughout this tense period.

Instinct or intuition played a singular part in one's daily life, and it was unwise to ignore it. If you felt 'safe' in a certain place, you went there regularly. During a bad raid I usually had this feeling in the Six Bells and, when that closed, in a basement drinking club called The Gateways in Bramerton Street. There were several of these late drinking clubs in Chelsea (late meant until 11.30pm): The Studio, next to the Town Hall, the Pheasantry, and one in a private house in Upper Cheyne Row called, appropriately, the Crater Club! The raids were very bad in Chelsea before and after Christmas: the weather was beastly cold, food scarce, and what festivity there was took place in the pubs. But this after-Christmas night I wanted to stay home, read by the fire, and finish the remains of the meagre Christmas food and drink.

The anti-aircraft guns rattled the windows and the clear, frosty air intensified the whine of the bombs, which were very close. The German bombers liked clear, frosty nights. Although not heavy smokers, when a raid was bad we chain-smoked, and by ten o'clock were down to our last. The pub next door was shut, for it was closing time, and the old couple who ran it never gave a moment overtime, so there was nothing for it but to walk up to the slot machine in the King's Road. Peter offered to go, but on those nights I preferred to be with him. Luckily we had a shilling, for twenty Player's cigarettes were 11½d, the halfpenny change being enclosed in the packet. The night was bright with a full moon, searchlights and the now customary glow of fires. Large pieces of shrapnel were clearly visible on the pavements as we walked up Glebe Place. The King's Road was full of activity: clanging ambulances, fire-engines and wardens racing up towards the Town Hall. We hurried on to find a cordon around the Six Bells, and massive chunks of heavy masonry on the ground. The front part upstairs had been hit, and toppled into both the road and the garden a matter of minutes before closing time. People were trapped in the back. We helped to clear the rubble and brick; it was hard work and made us hot, despite the cold. A small entrance was made and the stretchers bearers, wardens and war reserve police went through. The lights still blazed, and someone yelled, 'Turn that bloody light off!'

Several dazed but unhurt people were led out by torchlight; one had a bottle of brandy which was passed round, and we all had a swig. Some were 'regulars' who recognized us. The one with the purloined bottle said jauntily:

'What happened to you tonight that you didn't cop this lot?'

There were more inside, trapped, probably dead, as they had been sitting near the front door. Curly, the Irish barman, had gone down to the cellar and was found, his rimless spectacles still on his snub nose, but he was stone dead, an unbroken bottle in his hand. Almost-full pints of beer were standing unspilt on tables in front of customers who stared at them with unseeing eyes, for they too were dead from the blast. Similar occurrences happened every day all over London, and one learned never to persuade anyone against their will to go to a certain place.

It was towards the end of this same Christmas week that the great fire and bombing raid on the City of London took place, when the Guildhall, eight beautiful Wren churches, Guy's Hospital and hundreds of office buildings were hit, but as it was on Sunday, the latter were mercifully empty. Fire watchers saw twenty-eight incendiary bombs fall on the roof of St Paul's Cathedral, and bounce off the dome. One was blazing, and miraculously fell outwards, where it was extinguished. Indeed, amidst the wall of flame and smoke the only clear sky was around the cathedral. Londoners with a new-found love of their city watched its survival from rooftops both near and far away. With tears running down their cheeks, they said in one voice:

'The old church stood it . . .'

There was also a macabre sort of humour: a government notice told us to beware of toffee tins with a tartan design bearing the name of a well-known caterer, and also to look for a bomb with a spring which jumped out like a jack-in-the-box, and could blow off a limb. It had the delicate name of 'butterfly bomb'. One windy night, Arthur Mallett, a helper at my fire-watching station, told us of a weird, scraping, dome-like 'thing' which had chased him up Old Church Street. As he ran, so did it, faster and still faster. He turned the first corner he came to, and saw it race on about fifty yards, then stop in the middle of the street. He waited for some minutes to see if it exploded then, curiosity getting the better of him, he cautiously approached the demonic device. In the clear moonlight, he saw it was a dustbin lid.

'You can laugh at it now,' he said, 'but by Christ, I never did then.'

Chapter Ten

The winter was as cold as the summer had been hot. Peter had no warm clothes except the camelhair overcoat given to him when we landed at Southampton in July. Coal was expensive, and the ration wasn't enough to keep a fire going all day. It was too cold for him to sit and paint with no heating. Sophie had a large soft dark brown blanket, and one evening when she was out I made it into a sort of monk's habit for Peter to wear over his clothes whilst painting. She was very cross at first over the loss of her blanket, but in a mysterious way she acquired two more, and asked me to make one for each of us. We must have looked like a queer religious order when callers came to the door. Twenty-five years ahead of fashion, my go-ahead grandmother knitted me some brightly coloured woollen stockings. Peter was delighted and said they were just the thing for an intellectual's moll. Truth to tell, although they were gorgeously warm, I felt a bit like Minnie Mouse.

The day came when I arrived at work to find a police cordon around the area; they refused to let me pass, because it was unsafe with UXBs. The place was like a wilderness, with craters and the usual mounds of stone and broken glass. This was serious, for not only did I have no job but I never got paid for that week nor, more important, could I retrieve my insurance cards. To get new ones entailed endless waiting in queues, doctor's certificates and other hocus pocus. We were truly hungry that week, trying to eke out Sophie's wages, until I pawned a family ring I had been given for my twenty-first birthday which seemed much longer than two years before.

The next job was quite horrible, with a wholesale dress firm. The owner was appallingly sex starved; no doubt his wife was safe in the country, and he made grabs at me, usually when my head and arms were trapped in taking off some of the horrible clothes I had to model. I left after three days, and then worked for someone called Wally Craps. The least said about that the better.

We were right down to our last sixpence, for youth pays in the present. It is only in middle age that you pay in arrears. The rent was owing, and the only cigarettes we had were rolled from butts. On a desperate last chance I tried calling on my theatrical agent: 'No, nothing suitable . . .', but as I was leaving the office, Anatole (Tolly) de Grunwald, whose first play I had been in just before the war, came in. Miracles do happen, for the next day I was at one of the out-of-London studios, with a small but good part in a film about Nazi Germany called *Freedom Radio*, scripted by Tolly, and directed by Anthony Asquith. They had worked together previously, on *French without Tears*. Diana Wynyard and one of my childhood heroes, Clive Brook, played the leads.

The outdoor scenes were shot in a replica of the stadium where Hitler gave his rabble-rousing speeches. During the shooting the air-raid warning went, and we looked up to see a solitary German plane above. What can the pilot have thought when he saw hundreds of swastika banners flying in the remote English countryside?

With all the high drama going on in real life, I had almost forgotten how much acting meant to me. It seemed such a long, long time since I had watched Louis Jouvet and Madeleine Ozeray with such fascination. On account of the difficulties of even a simple railway journey, I stayed at a nearby hotel, yet still managed to come home with what seemed a fortune in good folding money. Film money is always like fairy gold, and like fairy gold it melts away, but this didn't before we bought sweaters, silk stockings, paints, canvas, food, coal, redeemed my ring, and I also managed to hide five pounds against the wettest of rainy days. This action, when that day turned up, I was never allowed to forget. For ever after Peter was convinced I had something stashed away. Alas, it was often only shillings.

The film business is not known for its high moral standards, but after the grabbing garment-men, it was like a

Trappist monastery. My agent bucked up a bit after my getting that part, but there was pathetically little work going. A Midland repertory company I had worked for earlier wrote and said they were inviting 'guest artists' to act in well-established successes such as Robert Sherwood's *Petrified Forest*, *Idiot's Delight* and an excellent spine-chilling thriller called *Black Limelight*, and would I like to be included?

There was a lull in the London bombing, otherwise I wouldn't have accepted, and I left Peter and Sophie. What I didn't know was that there was a lull because the bombers had switched to the provincial cities, but they were scattered, often isolated raids and not comparable to those on London. In several cases I had played the same part a few years before, but I was a very quick study, so a bare week's rehearsal was enough for me to be word perfect. It was hard work, for in those days repertory theatres played two houses a night: one at 6pm and the second at 8.30. The contract was for two weeks playing at a time, in various cities.

The lodgings varied, but I can never forget Mrs Pigg, a kindly woman who resembled her namesake but slightly. The sparse meat-ration was eked out by massive helpings of glutinous tripe and onions which, when served to us cold after the theatre, emitted a loud farting noise as it was cut up.

At the end of the first two weeks I intended to go home after the late performance on Saturday night, coming back for the first house on Monday. Provincial cities in wartime are not the ideal places for spending leisure hours. The so-called milk train would get me to London at about 4.30am. It all sounded perfect. However, Birmingham was heavily bombed that night, and our train sat just outside the city until the 'all clear' went at about 4am. There was no heating, nothing to eat, dim blue lighting, and the bombing made it too noisy to sleep.

Sophie and Peter were particularly pleased to see me, for it transpired that Sophie's firm had closed down. She had fallen in love with a soldier, and was behaving disgracefully according to Peter. They hadn't eaten anything for two days except the 'invasion' dried milk powder, made up with water.

'I not only feel like a baby,' said Sophie, 'but I'm beginning to smell like a baby.'

We all went out to a slap-up lunch at the Queen's Restaurant in Sloane Square and afterwards slept like babies. It was lovely to be home, if only for a little over a day.

There was a limit to the length of time one could live so strenuous a life: I stood it for about another month, and when I finally arrived home Peter said dramatically:

'Sophie's disappeared. I hope she hasn't gone to the bad.'

'Why couldn't she go to the bad here?'

She had actually gone back to Aunt Zenobia until she found another job. I don't think she could stand Peter's forcible feeding with the dried milk powder.

During the following months, Peter and I were closer together than ever before. We had become adjusted to each other, and he showed great tenderness towards me. On 14 February he painted a valentine which he left on my pillow, an unusual gesture for him to make. Small household tasks were done to save me trouble. We bought loose tobacco, and Peter rolled the daily cigarette supply. He made me a window box for the garlic and a few other herbs I was growing. He did whatever he thought would give me pleasure. When Crabbe came down for the evening and bought a painting, he kept only a few shillings for himself. If I had early film calls he would waken me with coffee and come to the station with me. Often he was waiting at the bus stop when I came home, standing in the cold and reading a book, for the time of my arrival was uncertain. Then we would sometimes go to the Lord Nelson pub, since the Six Bells was closed after the bombing, and have a few pints of bitter beer, which at that time was eightpence a pint.

The Nelson was not as pleasant as the Six Bells, but we were sure of seeing our friends there amongst the many strange faces. It was at the Nelson that I met Neville Heath, the multiple sex-killer, dressed in his phoney air-force uniform on phoney leaves. Full of bonhomie, he seemed: the epitome of a fighter pilot, yet he was not attractive to me, for which one can only be thankful! Barbosa was often there, as was Peter's friend Adrian Daintrey, the actor Basil Langton when he was home on leave, and Dylan when he was in London, and there were pretty girls and plain girls with the painter Raymond Myerscough Walker. We all crammed in, standing room only if you were late, the barman, who had a very large head, shouting at closing time:

'This is a pub, not a club!'

Or, otherwise in the evenings, Peter would rehearse the lines of my part with me, sometimes commenting:

'Goodness me, this dialogue is bad! I don't know how you can say it.'

He suggested that for every bad play I did, I should learn one good one, which he chose. It was an excellent antidote to the bombing which had now started again even more viciously than before. Apart from the war, life was seductive during this strange springtime.

'"But I, who never knew how to entreat, Nor never needed that I should entreat – Am starved for meat, giddy for lack of sleep; With oaths kept waking, and with . . ."'

'Oh do put a little more expression in it, Pussy.'

'I can't, I'm hungry, and so tired. You know the air raids always make me hungry, and the raid's been on for four hours.'

'Well, read to the end of this part, then we'll see what there is to eat.'

'"What say you to a piece of beef and mustard?"'

'"A dish that I do love to feed upon . . ."'

'"Aye, but the mustard is too hot a little."'

'"Why then the beef and let the mustard rest. . ."'

'"Why then the mustard without the beef—"'

'Peter, this is torture. And it's like our bread and mustard in Paris, I didn't know it was in Shakespeare.'

'Everything is in either Shakespeare or the Bible. Just go on until Petruchio comes in.'

'"Go, get thee gone, thou false—"'

There was a thud as if a gigantic sack of coal had been dropped, making the room shudder. almost immediately another thud, and a tremendous explosion. The window blew in and a dense cloud of greenish dust moved slowly through the gaping hole, forming into the shape of a weird monster. Peter flung himself on top of me on the bed, his eyes wide and dark with fear. His face and lips, pressed on to mine, tasted gritty.

'Dear Pussy, dear Pussy.'

There was a noise like exceptionally heavy rain, and his weight became almost unbearable. The bedside light was still on: the clock said twenty-five past one. All the furniture had moved, not far, it had all just moved round about a foot, except for the chair with my clothes on which had been under the window. There was no sign of that. I could move only my head, for the bed was covered with lumps of plaster, broken glass, wood and what looked like small stones. Peter's face was thickly covered with greenish-white dust, his eyes luminous, and large by contrast, like a clown's. Puffs of dust came out of the monkish habit as he clawed furiously at the rubble to free me. Sweat formed on his forehead, making the dust look like stale, clotted, theatrical make-up.

'I'm all right, darling, I think. But what happened? There were those thuds, it didn't sound like a bomb.'

'Well, if it wasn't a bomb, I don't know what has brought the ceiling and walls down. You're right, though, it wasn't the usual long shriek.'

'Should we turn the light out?'

'In a minute, when I've got you free.'

'Find me a coat or something, all my clothes have disappeared. There's a torch under my pillow.'

Through the open window came the sound of excited voices. I turned my head to look out, and saw leaping flames quite nearby.

'I can see fires.'

'That's not unusual.'

'But it is. Normally all I can see is the church clock tower.'

He framed his face in his hands and peered out through the fog-like dust.

'I can't see the church either. I think it's gone. There are fires everywhere. I must get you out, Pussy.'

Dressed in a long orange chiffon nightdress, brown brogue shoes and my top-coat, I switched off the light and by torchlight we crept along the corridor. Peter picked up his overcoat from the bathroom floor, where it had been blown. It was like walking on a shingly beach. There was no front door, just a frame, and a pile of glass and wood.

'Cigarettes. Damn, look in the sitting room.'

From the first floor somebody shouted up:

'Come down slowly by the wall, the stairs may not be there.' Peter went first and held my hand tightly. Ahead of us we heard footsteps on the stone staircase, which was littered with debris.

'Some of the banisters have gone. Go slowly, sit down if necessary, and come down that way.'

We sat down, slithering on our bottoms like children.

In the street were the occupants from the lower floors, wardens, ambulances, nurses, firemen and police, all lit by torchlight, the wardens with their log-sheets hanging round their necks. Someone tried to herd me into an ambulance but I pulled away, and Peter and I went into the Crossed Keys, which was wide open, the door and one wall blown into the bar. The elderly couple who ran it, never known for their generosity, were sitting down sipping brandy, covered in white plaster, looking dazed and very, very old, amongst the people gathered there. A local resident was in charge and gave us all a drink.

'The old church has gone!'

This was repeated frequently: that they were alive seemed incomprehensible.

We soon left, and went towards the remains of Chelsea Old Church to see if we could help. The nurses' home of the Cheyne Hospital for Children had the top floor blown off: a neat nurse's bedroom, the ceiling light still shining, looked like a stage set. A warden perilously climbed up the bombed staircase and switched it off, although there was a flaming gas main burning around the corner which floodlit the entire area. The church was nothing but an immense heap of timber and stone, flames licking through it; a large vaulted tomb with a stone urn on top rose up undamaged in the front. The New Café Lombard and all the large and small houses at that end of Old Church Street had been flung together into a giant mountain of shale-like destruction, all lit by the fires and the gas main. Under that fantastic mountain were people, some still alive. Heavy stones were flung aside like pebbles: the local grocer of the street, Mr Cremonesi, put his hand down through a space and felt warm flesh. A naked unhurt woman was pulled up. An old lady appeared, staggering, from the far side of the mountain, having been flung at least thirty yards and then covered with glass, wood and bricks, from which she had extricated herself. She seemed unhurt. A curious rattling sound like a time-bomb made us cautious: a battered tin was moving on a piece of stick. Below, the young woman had forced it through the bricks to attract attention. She was rescued by a war reserve policeman. A sixteen-year-old girl, pinned, only her head showing, talked to a rescue worker: she was freed, but died several hours later.

Young and old brought buckets of water to supply stirrup pumps to douse the fires. The dust was like a great fog. Charred papers and smouldering wood choked the helpers. Still the raid continued with whining bombs, cracking, thudding guns, droning aeroplanes, both German and our own night-fighters. Huge chandeliers of flares hanging in the sky like Roman candles illuminated the bomber's targets. Our hands were cut and bleeding, and when I saw the blood on Peter's hands I felt suddenly sick and faint. He led me down to the Embankment. Although the day had been warm, a breeze came off the river and it was chill. He held me close to warm me. Several wardens, police and onlookers were there talking. Two land-mines had been parachuted down on the church, which was why the usual whining sound was absent. All the fire-watchers at my post had been killed except Arthur

Peter Rose Pulham in 1938, photographed by Howard Coster

A studio photograph of me, 1939 *right*; and wearing a Traquair model dress, 1940, photographed by Tommy Hepworth

Jean Cocteau, photographed by Peter Rose Pulham, 1939
(courtesy of Mary Ryan)

Pablo Picasso, photographed by Peter Rose Pulham, 1939
(courtesy of Mary Ryan)

‘The Muse’. Me at Rossetti House, 1942, photographed by Peter Rose Pulham (courtesy of Mary Ryan)

Peter Rose Pulham in his studio at Rossetti House, 1943, photographed by Bill Brandt (horse’s head in background)

Chelsea Old Church, shortly after its destruction, 1942

Constantine and me, shortly after our wedding in Chelsea, 1944

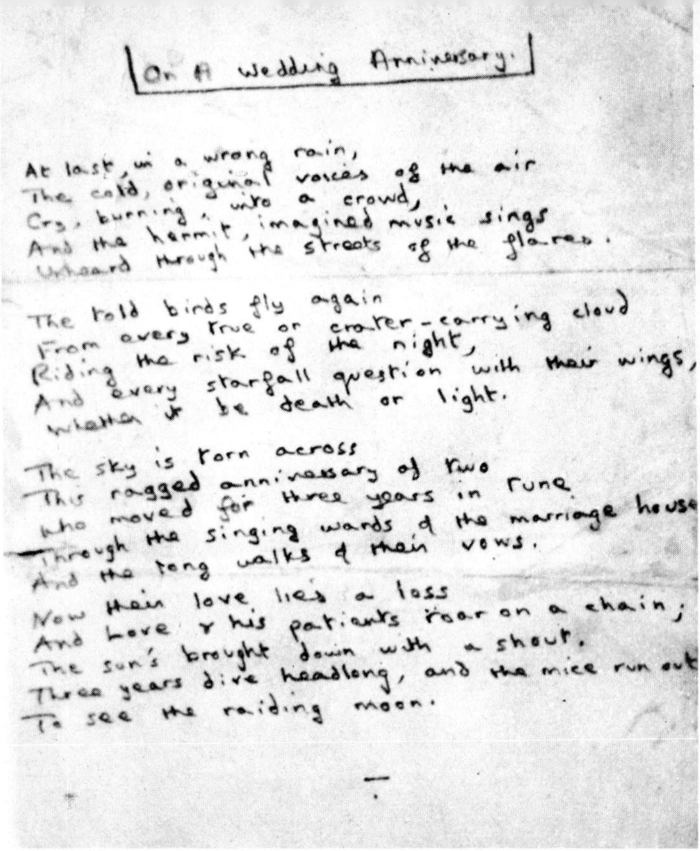
On A Wedding Anniversary.

At last, in a wrong rain,
The cold, original voices of the air
Cry, burning into a crowd,
And the hermit, imagined music sings
Unheard through the streets of the flares.

The told birds fly again
From every true or crater-carrying cloud
Riding the risk of the night,
And every starfall question with their wings,
Whether it be death or light.

The sky is torn across
This ragged anniversary of two
Who moved for three years in tune
Through the singing wards of the marriage house
And the long walks of their vows.
Now their love lies a loss
And Love and his patients roar on a chain;
The sun's brought down with a shout.
Three years dive headlong, and the mice run out
To see the raiding moon.

'On a Wedding Anniversary' – the original poem written by Dylan Thomas for Constantine and me, of which a slightly different version appears in Dylan Thomas's *Collected Poems* (courtesy of Caitlin Thomas)

Dylan and Caitlin, shortly after their marriage, 1937, photographed by John McNamara, Caitlin's brother (photograph by courtesy of Constantine FitzGibbon)

Norman Douglas, in the garden at the Crossed Keys pub, 1945, photographed by Sheila Curtis

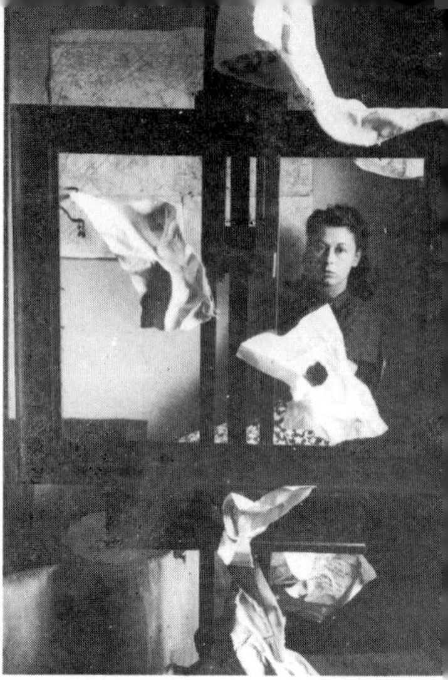

top left Mimi Mounsey, photographed by Francis Goodman

top right Mary Rose Pulham, photographed by Peter Rose Pulham (courtesy of Mary Ryan)

Constantine in Normandy, 1945

Mallett who had previously been chased by the dustbin lid. One of the mines had landed beside him and the other fire-watchers.

'For Christ's sake, run!' he had cried.

He had run so fast he couldn't stop in time to turn the corner into Old Church Street with the others.

'Bugger this, right ho, I'll carry straight on,' he had said to himself. He'd crouched behind a small iron post, seconds before the second mine landed, which also detonated the first one.

'Blimey,' he said laconically, 'that lot's gone.' All he had lost was the trouser on his right leg. Now he wanted a cup of tea, and to find his sister, so over the mountain he went, and met her halfway in that pitiful no-man's-land.

The Thames was at low tide, factories in flames opposite, as we smoked our cigarettes leaning over the wall near the steps leading down to the river. Bombs were dropping all round, but we were too exhausted to bother. So long as we could see them, we said. Down on the silty river-bank a man was walking about.

'There's a man down there, Peter.'

'Probably a fireman looking for an unexploded bomb.'

'Well, he's coming towards the steps. Let's go down and see. It's cold standing here.'

It was light enough to walk easily down the stone steps, and we were about halfway down as he was coming up. Over Peter's shoulder, I said:

'Looks like air force uniform. Hope it's one of ours!'

'Don't be so imaginative, Pussy.'

As they met face to face I heard:

'Leutnant—'and some German numerals followed.

Peter stood aside, and the German airman stood on the steps between us.

'Ich sprache Deutsch,' I said.

He repeated only what he had said to Peter, and we walked up in silence to the top.

The airman looked about twenty-three, the same age as myself; his face was pale with terror. He did and said nothing, just stood with his arm at his side, as is understandable when someone has just parachuted into an area which he has been bombing. Wardens and firemen came round, in fact one fireman had a hose ready in case he attacked us. Nobody knew quite what to do with this man who had dropped from the sky. The airman suddenly lurched forward, as a man who none of us had seen kicked him hard in the backside. The man then rushed to the front and wrenched a pistol from a pocket on the pilot's flying suit. Peter, usually slow-moving, quickly stretched out his long arms and wrested it away. It all happened so quickly, in the dim light, that only those close by realized what was going on. Two war reserve policemen materialized from nowhere, and quite quietly they marched off the German airman between them. Someone said: 'Like a drunk and disorderly on a Saturday night' – except that the captive marched firmly and erectly, and there was no disorder.

Without speaking to each other, Peter and I followed at a distance. We had been shocked by the pistol episode; death on the ground was more real and immediate than from the skies; and despite all our horrors of the long night, we both knew that the young boy was frightened too. In a funny way, he was 'our parachutist' and we wanted to see him in safe keeping. What can he have been thinking as he walked through the ruined streets, fires blazing in all of them, bombs still raining down?

The policemen marched him into Chelsea Police Station, and we were just leaving when other policemen came out and spoke to us. We went in, and reported as accurately as we could. At about four o'clock in the morning, two more parachute mines exploded nearby – one in front of the police station, and the other behind, but the block of flats, Cranmer Court, took the brunt. They gave us a cup of strong sweet tea, which tasted like nectar. The orange chiffon nightdress was in flitters up to my knees from the rubble shifting. We borrowed a pair of scissors and cut it straight. Even so we must have looked a comical couple, still covered in dust, blood and dirt. A few minutes before five o'clock the 'all clear' went, after eight hours of continuous bombing. It was the second heaviest raid on London, and became known as 'the Wednesday'. Eighteen hospitals and thirteen churches had been hit, one thousand people killed, and two thousand seriously injured. Many others were to have reactions later on. On the way back in the early dawn light women were sweeping away the glass and rubble from their front doors, as if it was snow. Everywhere there was the acrid smell of smoke.

Dressed in borrowed clothes I was half an hour late for work. Nobody was interested in my bomb story, they had become like fishermen's tales. I was the 'one who got away'. The day was interminably long, and I dreaded going back to our bomb-shattered home. There were large holes in all the walls, no ceilings in the bedrooms, no windows or front door. Everything when I had left was thick with plastery dust and shattered glass. With the curious illogicality of blast, two eggs in a bowl on the kitchen table were unbroken, lying amid a shower of debris. Peter greeted me like the *patron* of a good restaurant when wearily I came home. I walked from room to room with amazement: he had put the beds in the front, least damaged room, swept away the worst of the wood and plaster, and nailed some transparent material over the doors and windows.

'Not a flat any longer, Pussy, a bed-sitting room, but I can paint in the broken-down one in the back. There's nobody else in the whole block but ourselves.'

What we didn't know was that whilst we had been dealing with the German airman everyone else had been rehoused in a centrally heated block of flats for a nominal rent. Nevertheless, we felt a sense of achievement at having made something from what appeared to be ruins.

Three nights later the heaviest raid of the Blitz, known as 'the Saturday', took place, when seven hundred and twelve planes unloaded over a thousand tons of high explosives and four and a half thousand canisters of incendiary bombs in this area. That night as we looked at each other, standing face to face, we found our knees knocking together.

'I thought it was only a figure of speech, like hair standing on end,' said Peter.

Just after he spoke, I was suddenly lifted across the room

by blast. It was the most extraordinary sensation, as though one had acquired wings. I was gently deposited by the book-case, and we both sat on the floor laughing until the tears came out of our eyes. Peter said his first thought was that I had become holy and was levitating.

This was only a fraction, a few 'incidents' in one of the ninety-five boroughs that were bombarded that winter and spring in London, when over twenty thousand Londoners were killed. Although we didn't know it then, the Blitz, or the Winter of the Bombs, was to end as savagely as it had begun, on Sunday 11 May. On this night the Cavendish was badly damaged. When we heard about it several days later, Peter went up to find out what had happened to Rosa. He found the hotel shattered: her front parlour and large parts of the building a shambles. Rosa had gone off with her hamper of champagne to the Hyde Park Hotel for a few days; the faithful Charles Ingram was almost in tears, for Rosa's imperious parting words were:

'Everything has to be put back as it was by the end of the week... *everything*: d'you understand?'

There were but two days left to complete this Augean task.

Yes, the Blitz was over, but it was not the end of the bombing.

Chapter Eleven

Often in times of trouble, completely unexpected people come to one's aid. So it was when I was seriously ill, an aftermath of the bombing of Chelsea Old Church. Lady Mary Montagu had been no more than a pleasant drinking companion, in either a pub or the Crater Club. She was at this time in her thirties, small, plumpish, with a light melodious voice. She had very pretty well-shaped legs and hands, of which she was proud and pleased when one commented on them.

'They're American legs and hands,' she used to say, quite firmly, brooking no argument, although we had no idea what she meant. Later it was explained that she had an American mother.

Her high heels tapped on the stone staircase announcing her arrival, for with no real doors all sounds could be heard quite clearly. She took one look at my white face and the bomb-struck room, and tapped out again. When she came back, there were bustling noises in the kitchen, and eventually in came a tray with the most superb piece of fresh poached salmon and new potatoes, all swimming in butter. No salmon I have ever eaten since tasted so delicious.

'I've asked my doctor to call: you don't look right to me. Where's Peter?'

'He had to go to a tribunal about his call-up.'

'Golly, I can't see him in the army.'

'Neither can he see himself.'

The doctor was beautifully dressed, languid in manner, his skin paper-thin and as milk-white as a baby's bottom. He popped a thermometer in my mouth and then proceeded to ask me questions. It didn't matter that I couldn't answer them, for he walked about the room humming to himself as if composing a piece of music. He was clearly wondering how Mary, a duke's daughter, had got into such weird company. War made strange bed-fellows.

'M'mm, you'll have to go to hospital: beds are very scarce. I'll let Lady Mary know.'

He departed as languidly as he had come, never once having laid an examining finger on me.

Donald Maclean came to see me carrying a huge bunch of gladioli and some cigarettes: 'for me only'.

Forty white, perfectly made beds in the Women's public ward of a hospital was not Peter's style, or for that matter mine, but with shoulders hunched and eyes on the ground he strode in to see me, bringing a copy of *Horizon* magazine. When he had gone the woman in the bed on my left said:

'Made me feel all queer when he looked at me, lovely.'

The woman on the right said:

'Don't 'e talk nice?'

Although they had apparently kept their eyes straight in front of them, they hadn't missed a trick.

When I got home the gladioli were dead, their water stinking; the bed rivalled the Paris one, and the flat looked worse than the morning after the bombing. Mary found me in tears, said we must move, and she would set about finding us a place. In any case the landlord wanted us to go so that he could put in a full claim for war damage.

Although the population in Chelsea had fallen from nearly 60,000 to 16,000 people during the Blitz, there were few furnished flats to rent as most people had moved to the country or suburbs taking their furniture with them. We hadn't a stick between us unless you counted the easel, but again Mary came to our help. All her furniture was in store, and without a second's hesitation it was handed over on a long loan. For seventeen shillings and sixpence a week, we took the top half of a house in Oakley Street, and lived resplendent with the ducal furniture. Except for the basement flat, the rest was empty, although Matthew Smith the painter had a studio on the first floor, but did not live there.

It was difficult to express personally the kindness Mary showed to us, for she did not hang about waiting to be thanked or intrude in our life once she had set us up. She brought me back to health, took care of me when I needed it most, for which I can but simply write a few inadequate words with love and gratitude. Those who knew her then will know that I was not the only person whom she benefited during those lean years, and not only people, for stray or neglected animals were also fed and looked after. It was through Mary we met Shane Leslie (now Sir Shane Leslie), the witty conversationalist and writer, for she had spent part of her childhood with him in the north of Ireland, at her family's castle, Tandaragee, in Armagh. Shane Leslie, always kilted, was a full-time air-raid warden in London, and it was he who, when the bomb fell near the Cavendish Hotel, hurried round to find Rosa safe, sitting outside the hotel, enjoying a cup of tea with a bishop, as though she was at a garden party. He said he never thought to find her in such unlikely company, although he knew of her fondness for the cloth.

'A bishop in the Cavendish: the Day of Judgement must have come!'

By now we had all given up the Lord Nelson, and congregated in the small comfortable King's Head and Eight Bells, known to us as the Eight Bells, on Embankment Gardens. The long refectory table was usually 'held' by glares from Peter for us and our friends, and as the summer progressed we would take our pewter tankards of beer outside and drink by Carlyle's statue in the gardens. One evening Mary, who had great faith in Peter's knowledge of etiquette, said:

'How do you start a letter to a duke?'

'But your father is a duke, Mary.'

'Yes, I know, but when I write, I just say, Dear Dadda . . .'

It was decided that for someone who had met her father, 'Dear Duke' was the correct beginning. We none of us, including Mary, thought it sounded right, but that was how Mary's young man started his letter.

The imminent call-up was extremely unsettling. Peter had not become a 'conscientious objector' in the true sense, for he was prepared to take work not in the armed forces.

Having been through the Blitz, he opted for the Auxiliary Fire Service. This, however, the tribunal had to think over and would let him know. Naturally he wanted to get as much painting done as possible before he was drafted. He had almost finished for the time being with the crumpled pieces of paper, been through eggs and other spheroid objects, and now had a desire to paint not human, but animal skulls. Rabbit heads were boiled and washed: no, not the right shape, or big enough. I consulted my butcher friend, who clearly thought I had gone mad and didn't mind saying so. His carcasses came without heads, but he might be able to get me a sheep's head. When it came it was split down the middle ready for cooking, which rendered it useless for painting. However we had several meals from it, after endless boning, skinning and skimming. In any case Peter had decided that a sheep's head wasn't the right shape or size either. What he envisaged was something like a horse's head, and he did rather keep on about it.

The 'continental butcher' thought I was even madder than the other one.

'Orse's 'ead? No call for 'em, ducks. 'Ere's a lovely 'orse tongue for you.'

Thinking of Dolly, and all the other horses who had nuzzled my pocket for sugar, I felt quite sick when he slapped the dripping, horny tongue on the counter.

'Don't want to eat it? Blimey, surely you don't want it for decoration?'

Explaining as carefully as I could the reason for this strange request, a gleam of comprehension came into his eye.

'Oh, artists.' He drawled out the word so that it ended with a hissing noise. 'I've got yer now, ducks, fer one of them gruesome pictures.'

He gave me the name and telephone number of a knacker's yard near King's Cross Station.

Yes, they had one, and would clean it for me.

Never, if you can possibly avoid it, ever go to a knacker's yard. The stench of blood which sticks in the gullet, queer thuds and shuffling sounds, occasional shouts, even the slamming of a door combine to make the flesh prickle and creep. After a few minutes we came out and stood in the road, then went to a convenient pub.

'It must be awful for you. Pussy. I've never had any contact with horses, but my stomach's turning over. Let's leave it.'

'Well, we're here now, and I ordered it. I saw an office on the right as we went in. Go in there. I'll stay here . . . do make sure it's cleaned, darling.'

It was cleaned after a fashion, but bits of flesh and hair clung to parts of the jaw, making it look like something from a horror film. We could still smell the yard when we came home on the bus with our grisly parcel. We imagined that people were avoiding us, especially when a man changed his seat and moved further down the bus. The day was warm and humid, which didn't help any.

'Let's stop at a chemist and get some ammonia or something to soak it in. Then we can put it on the roof to dry in the sunshine. It's got a frightful gluey smell at present.'

During the course of this Saturday afternoon we soaked, washed, scrubbed, even cleaned the teeth, which we found lifted in and out, of the noble skull. It looked superb, like an unglazed T'ang head: the nostrils taut and almost quivering. One could imagine Ghenghis Khan having ridden it. I was standing on a chair, which was on another chair, preparing to spring up into the loft which led to the roof, when Dylan arrived. He was more goggle-eyed than usual when he saw what we were doing. Like many imaginative people he revelled in horrors.

'Pass me up those back teeth, Peter, we'll dry them before we put them back.'

Dylan made that characteristic sound of his: a cross between a snort and a snigger.

'Vernon would love this: it's like the Mari Lywd.* Most people bury their bodies in the basement, you put yours on the roof. You're like animal Burke and Hares. Payday yesterday, where shall we go? There's Tambimuttu at the

*Vernon Watkins, poet, who wrote *The Ballad of the Mari Lywd* about a ghostly horse's head.

Wheatsheaf, Ivan Moffatt at the French pub, or Augustus John round the corner at the Eight Bells.'

We settled for the Eight Bells, as we'd already had a long journey that day.

This summer of 1941, Dylan called whenever he was in London working with Donald Taylor and Ivan Moffatt for Strand Films, from whom he drew a regular income of between eight and ten pounds a week. He and Caitlin with their young son Llewelyn were staying with Frances Hughes, wife of Richard Hughes, the author, at Laugharne Castle in Wales. The wartime journey could take anything up to twelve hours in an unheated train, so sometimes he would spend as much as a week with us; other times he would spend a night, then disappear and reappear a few days later in quite different clothes, for he had the habit of discarding his own dirty shirts, ties, even trousers, and replenishing them with whatever of his hosts' took his fancy. Peter was almost the only person he couldn't do this with for Peter's entire wardrobe was more sparse than Dylan's. Once Dylan and I spent hours with Ivan Moffatt in the Swiss pub in Soho and, when Ivan was getting a drink, I suggested that we must get back to Chelsea soon. Dylan sniggered and said he couldn't leave until Ivan did because he had his trousers on. They must have reached almost to his chin, for Ivan was a much taller, slimmer young man.

Dylan as a dinner guest was like the Master of Hounds in *Handley Cross*:

> He will bring his nightcap with him,
> for where the MFH dines he sleeps,
> and where the MFH sleeps he breakfasts.

His favourite breakfast was ice-cream and a fizzy non-alcoholic drink as a starter. Once when there was no lemonade to be got, he put a dollop of ice-cream into a light fizzy beer and seemed to enjoy it. Peter would bring back the ice-cream when he went to buy the newspaper at the corner shop. Dylan always had a craving for sweets, and the only food or drink I ever had to dole out gradually was the chocolate ration, otherwise a month's supply would go in minutes.

Far too much has been written about Dylan's drinking. In those days he drank very little more than, if indeed as much as, all his friends and contemporaries. He had no capacity for strong drink, so less made him seem drunker. Also he had a vivid imagination, and was a born and brilliant actor. He would play the drunken young poet to perfection, and revert instantly to being as we knew him, once we were home. He could be drunk with words and images, keeping us enchanted until the early hours of the morning, with nothing stronger to drink than cocoa or lemonade. I was quite certain he had some sort of liver complaint, for he would be horribly sick some mornings, retching up a bright yellow bile.

'It's in good colour this morning,' he would say cheerily as he left the bathroom.

For someone like myself used to very heavy drinkers amongst my family in Ireland, what Dylan drank all day they would have considered a normal morning's drinking. And they were all men who worked well, rode hard and were not thought to be at all unusual. My father and his nine brothers always believed that when they drank beer or stout they were practically on the wagon, and that was Dylan's main tipple.

His magic, for that he had, lay in the ability to make both himself and other people laugh. We would perhaps be sitting gloomily wondering where to get a shilling to put in the gas-meter and, within a half an hour of Dylan's arrival, be laughing fit to bust, and not only superficially for he would have stimulated our imaginations. We might sometimes play my father's word game: a word was picked, say 'down', and rapidly going round the company each person said a word connected with it: falling, going, hanging, sitting, lying, eider, at heel, at heart, County Down. There it could stop, and we would perhaps talk of the beautiful neglected novels of Forrest Reid, who lived in poverty in County Down: *Peter Waring, The Bracknels* (now called *Denis Bracknel*), *Uncle Stephen*; or of Charles Williams, the Northern Irish don, whose book *All Hallows' Eve* had frightened the bejasus out of us, and the marvellous opening sentence from his *The Place of the Lion*.

'From the top of the bank, behind a sparse hedge of thorn, the lioness stared at the Hertfordshire road.'

The function of the game was not in the game itself, but in the way it cleared the mind and provoked discussion in a new field.

The resonance and beauty of Dylan's voice was, in itself, beguiling. His accent was not English, nor was it the sing-song Welsh of the music hall; 'cut-glass Welsh' he used to call it. Even though a cigarette usually hung from the corner of his lips, his words were clearly audible. The word 'always', which he used frequently, he pronounced 'oll-ways', and words like 'daughter' or 'laughter' he intoned on the first syllable. It is easy to see how the shilling for the meter was quickly forgotten for Dylan could enchant and 'put a girdle round about the earth in forty minutes'.

Outside the Eight Bells was parked a large, rather magnificent open motor-car. I think it was a twenties Bugatti for it had a long barrel-shaped bonnet and a shining exhaust pipe nestling along the running board. Such a car was a rare sight in wartime, because of its petrol consumption, and particularly in Chelsea. Inside the pub, the crisp, clipped, clean young man who owned it was sitting with Augustus John. They looked as out of place together, as did the shining old Bugatti outside the shabby pub. Augustus was staring in front of him, the keen blue eyes of the Celt watching everything and everyone relentlessly, his gingery-grey beard occasionally twitching in acknowledgement of the clean young man's remarks, for generally he hated small talk and would affect an even greater deafness than he had. He insisted I sit opposite him, and went on staring, now, at me. I began to feel like a giant species of butterfly pinned to the chair. Peter, Dylan and the clean young man were talking about Henry Green's novel *Loving*, which had just come out. It appeared that Augustus's deafness excluded him from the conversation until he boomed out, so that the whole pub was stunned into silence:

'I suppose he'll call the next one *Fucking*!'

Then back to the silence and the staring, for the next half an hour. He behaved and looked like a querulous old man of seventy: he was in fact fifty-nine. I told him about the horse's skull, now drying, rampant on our roof. This he liked, although between times he glared at Peter as though annoyed he hadn't thought of it himself. The pub had run out of their daily allocation of his particular drink so he wanted to go to the Chelsea Arts Club. The undauntable clean young man said he would drive us all there.

Augustus sat in the front, Peter, Dylan and I in the back. It was like being in a chariot and we behaved accordingly. Even Augustus was cheered by the expressions on the faces of the passers-by, and several times lifted his stick in royal recognition. We arrived at our destination only too soon, for it was a different situation at the elegant door of the long, low, white-painted club. Women were not allowed in: Peter said he would go in for ten minutes and join me at the Cadogan on the corner. As they filed past the doorman's arm came down like a frontier barrier, cutting Dylan off from the rest.

'You're barred, Mr Thomas.'

'Barred?' This was said in a hurt, full voice worthy of Sir Henry Irving. 'On what grounds?'

'A complaint was lodged by one of the members on the occasion of your last visit. I can't discuss it further.'

Peter wanted to come out too, but the official stood squarely between him and us. We said we would wait in the motor and make faces at the members through the window.

Dylan and I sat in the front seats like naughty children. We hooted the large old-fashioned rubber bulb horn, switched on lights, pretended to drive, and lit our cigarettes with the glowing gadget meant for lighting cigars. And like children we soon tired of our tricks.

'What did you do the last time you were there?'

'I called Sir G—a hoary blue-nosed old baboon.' He rolled the sentence around his mouth giving the simple words a spite they do not have on paper.

'Perhaps he thought you meant "whorey"?'

Dylan sniggered, and said:

'He's too deaf to hear anything, but so vain, and such a bad painter.'

The ten minutes were up and we were restless. Opposite the club was a row of beautiful five-storeyed Regency houses. Leaning up against one was a very long ladder, reaching to the roof.

'Wouldn't it be marvellous to be so brave that you could run up that ladder to the top?'

'It's easy,' I said, 'let's do it. Then they'll wonder where we are when they come out.'

We sprang out of the car and I kicked off my shoes before starting up the ladder at great speed, Dylan behind me. I got to the third floor past a small balcony, when I looked down. Dylan had retreated and was sitting in the gutter, his back to the ladder with his head in his hands. It was the looking down that did it, for not only did I get *vertige,* but the ladder appeared to be swaying outwards in an alarming fashion.

'Dylan, it's falling outwards, for God's sake come and hold it, I'm frightened.'

Still he sat there head in hands. I flattened myself against the ladder willing it to stop, but still it swayed, in . . . out . . . in . . . out . . . surely in a second it would go, and my brains would be dashed out on the pavement.

'You cowardly little Welsh swine, come and hold it,' I roared. Still he went on sitting. I tried to take one hand off and grab the iron railings just below me, but this seemed to make the ladder sway even more. I was quite transfixed, face pressed between two rungs, my bare insteps aching as they clung round the slippery wood for what seemed like aeons. It was far worse than bombs, for there was endless time for dreadful speculation and contemplation. At last I heard Peter's voice:

'But where is she?'

Augustus, Peter and the young man came over.

'Do come down, Pussy,' Peter entreated, as if I were a cat in a tree.

'I've got *vertige*, I can't move down, but hold the ladder, Peter, and I'll try.'

Even with the ladder being held, it still swayed at that height. Augustus advanced to the front door and knocked the knocker. An immaculate middle-aged man who looked like a general opened the door. Augustus said:

'There's a young woman up your ladder.'

'Dear, dear,' he clicked, 'we must get her down.'

I could hear them talking at the ladder's foot, making strategic suggestions. It was the 'general' who took charge, and at once suggested a solution for the situation.

'Well, the mountain will have to come to Mahommed,' he said briskly as they all went inside, leaving me, as I thought, to my horrible fate. Then the long windows behind the balcony opened, and out on the foot-wide shelf stood the 'general'.

'Well, well, m'dear, soon have you on terra firma. Hold on to this.' He produced what looked like a looped saddle girth.

'That's right, now lean hard against the ladder, and slip it over your head. That's a good girl . . . now, one arm, now the other.'

He gave me great assurance as I hooked myself into this harness.

'Now lean over towards me and give me your hand. I've got you, you can't fall . . .'

I was slung over the balcony by one strong pull and then lifted to safety. The 'general' led me downstairs like a pony, the harness still on me, to a superbly furnished drawing room where his elegant grey-haired wife was serving huge goblets of brandy and soda to the others.

'I've got her . . .' he crowed delightedly.

His wife in a sweet soft voice said: 'I'm so glad, the poor child.'

And I too was given a beautiful goblet of brandy.

Nobody, least of all the 'general' or his lady, thought to ask what I was doing up their ladder. I was just beginning to feel all right when I looked down and saw I had put a black footprint of what looked like paint on the off-white carpet. My feet too had got filthy climbing over the balcony. I sat with one foot on top of the other, pressing down on the black mark, but they were too well bred to notice, or to say anything if they had.

We spent the most pleasant hour there: seven strange and oddly assorted people, all conversing as easily and naturally as if by gold-edged white-carded invitation. I never heard their name and never saw them again, but their gentle kindness remains with me to this day.

Peter and I walked home after I had retrieved my shoes; Dylan said he would be back later. The clean young man and Augustus sped away in the metal chariot, waving grandly to our host and hostess. By the time Dylan came back to Oakley Street, the brandy-comfort gilt had worn off all of us. Stale beer tasted like rusty nails after it. Dylan and I glowered at each other. In his especially hurt voice he said:

'I didn't mind your calling me a coward, a swine, or Welsh, but I did object to "little". He pouted and looked deeply injured.

This incensed me, and made me say many more abusive things, so that we were almost in tears, both of rage and of misery. Peter wandered about humped up with despair, urging us to make up our quarrel, but we were word-locked with tantrum. Finally he made us laugh and broke it up by saying:

'What else could we expect when we'd been playing skulls and ladders all day?'

As a reconciliation he made me give Dylan half my chocolate ration, which we ate dipped into mugs of hot 'invasion' milk powder.

It was the only quarrel Dylan and I ever had; we never again played skulls and ladders. The next day my grandmother came to luncheon.

CHAPTER TWELVE

My maternal grandmother, then in her eighty-first year, had two favourite words. One was 'initiative' and the other 'go'. Women were expected to be liberally endowed with both these qualities; men at one time in their life should have had them, but were vaguely suspect if they displayed them too ostentatiously. Many of the men in her family had met sudden deaths at an early age, and I'm convinced Grandma thought it was because they had too much 'go' or 'initiative'. She was fond of saying that they 'warmed both hands before the fire of life', which as a child puzzled me, but then so did many other figures of speech.

She was Cornish, a descendant of Henry Fielding, the eighteenth-century novelist. *Tom Jones* was given to me to read when I was about ten years old, and I thoroughly enjoyed it. He too had warmed both hands before the fire of life, for he died at forty-seven. She herself not only had plenty of go, but was very go-ahead, for Grandma repeatedly said you had to 'go with the times'. In 1913 she went to Australia to investigate the sudden death of her brother, taking her own deckchair, which she brought back in 1914, and it is still in use. Whilst there, she shocked the polite Perth society by getting down from her carriage when out for a drive to assist an aboriginal woman through a difficult childbirth. The woman put a thin silver bracelet on my grandmother's arm, which was never to be taken off. Many times as a child I asked her to tell me the story of the bracelet, the aboriginal woman's most treasured possession, and how Grandma's grey taffeta frock was covered in dust and blood when she went on to the tea-party.

Contrary to most elderly people she thought modern life and times wonderful. Very soon after the First World War we had a motor-car with a chauffeur called George Deare.

Grandma called him George for, as she said, it would give a wrong impression if she said:

'Drive on, Deare.'

Not that she really cared at all for wrong impressions. Less than ten years later we were up in our first aeroplane at Hendon; goggles on in the open cockpit as we looped the loop with Alan Cobham's Flying Circus.

Every modern appliance or gadget was tried out, and many times if it didn't work to her liking she would set about redesigning it, and off we would go to the Patents Office. She must have registered more patents than most people had gadgets. She was a born inventor, mastered quite complicated electrical problems very early on, and studied architecture at seventy, when she wanted to build three small houses instead of her one large one. Some of it was done, I think, to annoy my antiquarian grandfather, whose idea of heaven was to sit alone in his room illuminating manuscripts or writing long treatises in an exquisite copperplate hand, for he hated any modern innovation and even circled round the telephone with a wary eye as though it were an unpredictable animal. He would never answer it when it rang.

Although a woman of the strictest moral principles, at the turn of the century she had opened her large house as a home for unmarried mothers and, later on after the 1914 war, worked almost exclusively for the poverty-stricken classes in the slums of London. Children were taken from Dr Barnardo's orphanage and given love, kindness and help, shared with her own children, and later with me – for, not only did she look after me from the age of ten when I was asked to leave my first convent, but she also took in two Jewish children whose mother had died. At this time she must have been nearly seventy. She firmly believed that if you could speak good English and Latin you could 'go anywhere'. When the Daniels children arrived they were being instructed in Hebrew so in our holiday classes we all learned Latin and Hebrew. Grandma was rather pleased when I did better in Hebrew than the Jewish children.

Quite early on I found that she liked to oppose the popular view, and the quickest way to achieve one's own ends with her was to be in a strong minority group. In fact the more factions were against you, the more Grandma was for you, for she loved opposition, even remotely. This showed in her political preferences: always for the side that was out of office.

Despite a firm belief in God, she tried and found all accepted religions wanting, arguing remorselessly with priests, parsons and even rabbis. When her youngest daughter died, she took up spiritualism, believing that if anyone could get through to the 'other' world, she could. But not for her the little medium round the corner. Off we went, starting on a pirate bus (buses run by private companies which were very fast and cheap), to see Sir Arthur Conan Doyle the writer, who at that time was one of the chief spiritualists. Me with a grubby copy of *Sherlock Holmes* in my eleven-year-old hands. Grandma thought highly of Conan Doyle, mainly I think for his championing the innocence of Oscar Slater, who had been convicted of a crime he did not commit. I never got around to asking him for my copy to be autographed, for on first sight I fell in love with his son, about five years older than me, who treated me with handsome disdain. I remember Conan Doyle as a large man with sad thoughtful eyes and a walrus moustache, giving us tea in the country house and tickets for the next large spiritualists' meeting at the Albert Hall. Much to my grandmother's annoyance, I was one of those picked out of the thousands of people present as having a Negro spirit guide with a message from the other world. She was convinced it was really for her: they had made a fatal mistake, and spiritualism was out.

If the thought of 'Mother' had induced nervousness in Peter, 'Grandmother' made him doubly so. Dylan Thomas on the other hand looked forward to the meeting and spruced himself up accordingly. A Muslim's Paradise is peopled with houris; Dylan's was a matriarchal Bardic society with ten grandmothers, several mothers, himself, his beautiful wife and children disporting themselves under their protective and watchful eyes. For he loved women of all ages, especially if they took care of him. The female pulchritude displayed in pub paintings by Alma Tadema or Fortunio Mantania made him groan with delight. He was amorous, and would make verbal passes at pretty girls and women as much out of affection or bravado as sex. His wife Caitlin was the princess from over the sea, his true love, then and always. When he became famous he was pursued by women who often mistook his love of women for love of themselves.

There were nearly sixty stairs to our part of the house, so Peter took the prettiest chair and put it in front of the window on the second floor.

'So that your grandmother can sit down and rest,' he said. Contrary to resting, Grandma remarked:

'Silly place to put that beautiful chair. If the window is blown in the upholstery will be ruined.' Whereupon she picked up the chair and proceeded up the remaining stairs, Peter tussling to get it away from her.

Her big red bag – she loved bright colours – was opened, and out came a bottle of whisky, fifty cigarettes and several tins of food. 'Just in case we had nothing decent to eat or drink.' Also a packet of her own cigarettes, Muratti's 'Lucky Dream', which were of different colours, gold-tipped and slightly scented. (The distinctive scent had given me away when I had tried my first cigarette many years ago.) There was no awkwardness at all; she behaved as if she had spent her life amongst penniless poets and painters, and she made it clear that she thought women who married too early without realizing their responsibilities were fools. When shown Peter's paintings she found them interesting and said one must go with the times. The horse's skull ones were much admired, and she liked the initiative shown in getting it. As I dished up the meal I heard her discussing Swansea, a town she knew well and didn't think much of, with Dylan. She told us the story of her sister's husband who had died near Swansea, and my great-aunt having all the floorboards taken up to see where he had hidden his money, since he distrusted banks. Alas, this treasure was never found and the farm never sold lest it should turn up. Dylan loved this tale of 'the rancour of years' as he put it.

After lunch I suggested a rest after the long journey, but the eyes as blue as larkspur petals flashed with contempt. Instead she glanced through the copy of *Horizon* which was lying on a small table. It was the July issue, with the first publication of *The Ballad of the Long-legged Bait.*

'This is by you; read it out to us.'

'It's very long,' said Dylan, 'over fifty verses, the longest poem I've ever written.'

'The longer the better, if it's good,' she said. 'I should like to hear it.'

The beautiful voice brought the smell of the sea and seaweed into the room: spray and salt and shells were outside the window. Any obscurities of modern poetry were hammered out on that 'mounting dolphin's day':

> Goodbye, good luck, struck the sun and the moon,
> To the fisherman lost on the land.
> He stands alone at the door of his home,
> With his long-legged heart in his hand.*

That evening we were to dine with Donald and Melinda Maclean at their flat near Regents Park. Peter found a rare taxi at the Albert Bridge rank, which we shared with my grandmother, but not before we had all promised to have lunch with her during the coming week, for as she put it: 'if she didn't see a bit of life, she would die of boredom.'

The Macleans' flat in Rossmore Court was small and rather characterless. It was the usual centrally heated box-like apartment of those days, with a combined dining-drawing room, and what could be termed a large larder, known as a kitchenette. A central table was laid for dinner, taking up what little space there was. Peter and Donald looked like giants in the cramped room. Melinda, small, dark, with a bird-like face, fluttered around us. Her features were a little too sharp for prettiness, but she had a charming, soft American voice, and she was a good hostess. It was a

*Dylan Thomas; 'The Ballad of the Long-legged Bait', *Collected Poems*, J. M. Dent, London 1954.

very conventional evening: dry martinis to start with and general conversation. Melinda spent some time in the kitchen, and from time to time Donald would uxoriously go to see if he could help. We were all brought out to see some dried onion flakes, the latest thing from America, and expressed our surprise and wonderment at them. When we got back to the sitting room Dylan said they looked like old men's toenails, which of course they did. However, when they turned up in the casserole which followed I don't think they were recognized as such. Good wine, salad, an excellent cheese, coffee and brandy. There were no explosions, conversational gaffes or over-drinking. A quiet, civilized evening which ended about midnight. Somehow we got a taxi home, and I remember Donald solicitously inquiring if we had enough money to pay for it.

At this time I had a very pleasant job with a firm I shall call Dorian Models. Mr Dorian, an erect grey-haired figure with a glass eye, was in love with his models. By that I mean the rather ordinary clothes he designed. He fondled them, gazed fixedly (the glass eye helped) at them, often making quick darts across the showroom to rub his hands lovingly down a sleeve or a skirt. To him they were animate children of his creation. I was something to hang them on. I don't think he could have described my face, for he never seemingly looked higher or lower than those parts of my body his clothes covered. He caressed his coats and dresses, cradling them over his arms when carrying them, and would never sell the models, only copies. What he liked best was to contemplate their beauty, on me, when there were no customers. So long as I was careful with his clothes, and showed them to the best advantage, my job was secure. Actually, it was rather hard work for me, as generally I only had to model when there were customers: at Dorian Models I was kept at it most of the day. Like all jealous parents he really wanted to prevent strangers coveting his clothes; accordingly, instead of displaying them in the window as was the usual, a discreet net curtain was hung from halfway up, to prevent prying eyes.

Dorian Models was near the comfortable, old-fashioned

Berners Hotel, which was filled with good mahogany furniture and chairs you could sleep in. The customers were elderly people of good standing who lived in the country, and the staff were like well-trained butlers or footmen. I often went there to make a telephone call, or to have a coffee after my sandwich lunch. One day as I was leaving, a taxi drew up, and out of it stepped a very dapper little white-haired man with a round face like that of a highly intelligent blue-eyed baby. I recognized him as being Max Beerbohm, whose cartoons and books, especially *Seven Men*, I loved. He was at that time giving some very amusing talks on the radio, one of which started with: 'Ladies and gentlemen, or if you prefer it, Gdeevning . . .' I admired him intensely, but felt quite impotent in his presence. All I could think to do was to hurry up to him and say excitedly:

'I think you're marvellous!'

Then stricken with every kind of embarrassment I went back to Dorian Models. The next time I went to Berners Hotel, Max Beerbohm was sitting in the lounge, looking even smaller in the enormous chair. He came over to me, bowed, and said:

'I think you're marvellous, too.'

From then on we would often meet when he was in London, have coffee together and talk. It was at Berners Hotel that I was to lunch with my grandmother.

On that day I was sitting talking to the packer at Dorian Models when Mr Dorian, face unduly flushed, ran into the room.

'Quick, quick,' he cried jerkily, for he had a faint foreign accent, 'ring for the police, there are some suspicious characters peeping through the window. I have locked the front door.'

Kenneth the packer was a typical phlegmatic working-class Englishman, who could never be made to hurry even during an air raid. He finished tying an elaborate knot then turned slowly to face Mr Dorian, who was incoherent with alarm.

'What harm if the suspicious characters are *outside*,

guv'nor?' he said laconically, 'All the stuff's inside. They haven't got a gun, have they?'

Mr Dorian was not placated, and became almost hysterical at the thought of a hold-up.

'They will steal our beautiful clothes at night. They are examining the place with searching eyes. Ring for the police and they will question them.'

'The place is well locked up at night, guv'nor, you do it yourself. The police couldn't question them before a burglary, it would give the game away.'

'All clothes are on ration now, they will make a fortune selling our models,' said Mr Dorian frantically.

'Well, let's have a look at these blokes,' answered Kenneth.

We three went through the workrooms of stitching girls to the showroom, Mr Dorian hiding one of his models displayed on a stand on the way. Sure enough, over the top of the net curtains two faces were pressed, noses squashed on the glass. One figure was very tall, and looked like a 1910 idea of a bolshevik; the other was quite small, so that only his cap, a bulbous nose and protuding eyes showed above the curtain rail. Kenneth and Mr Dorian were in front of me.

'Blimey,' said Kenneth, 'they are a queer-looking lot.'

I pressed forward, and indeed they did look villainous and rather intimidating with the light behind them. To my dismay I saw they were Dylan and Peter, who had come to pick me up before lunch. When Peter saw me, he waved.

'Now they are threatening us,' said Mr Dorian. 'I entreat you, Kenneth, ring for the police.' Mr Dorian was not going to let his beloved clothes out of his sight for an instant.

'No, no, they're friends of mine,' I cried out.

'Friends?' questioned Mr Dorian, clearly wondering if I was a fit person to employ with his treasured creations. 'Friends? Well what are they doing assessing my stock?' He said this as carefully as only someone who was unfamiliar with the English language would.

'I'm meeting them for lunch.' Then, feeling I had to offer an explanation, I said:

'One is a famous poet, and the other a painter.'

Unexpectedly the artist in Mr Dorian showed itself.

'Ah, la vie de bohème,' he crooned sentimentally, 'but what a shock they gave me. Open the door, Kenneth; no doubt they would find interest, especially the painter, in our beautiful things.'

I doubted it, but in they came looking like Rimbaud and Verlaine on an off-day. However they both sensed an occasion and rose to it. Peter muttered something about *Harper's Bazaar*, which was immediately seized on by Mr Dorian – '. . . and you think they would be interested?' – whilst Dylan, never at a loss for a word, rhapsodized about the very ordinary clothes. All in all it was very successful, for I was given an extra half-hour for my lunch. Mr Dorian's relief at the safety of his brain-children quite overcame him. From then on, too, Kenneth used to pump me about the 'carry-ons', as he put it, of artists.

We were a bit late meeting my grandmother in the Scotch House, a pub opposite the hotel, but she quite understood, and enjoyed the story, for neither Dylan nor Peter knew until then what had happened. Dylan sat very close to her, put his arm through hers and said:

'Lend us a quid, Grannie.'

She did, without any hesitation.

Chapter Thirteen

Dylan and I were cinema-crazy and our taste was omnivorous, We journeyed off to Classic cinemas in outlying districts of London to be terrified all over again by Léni's *The Cat and the Canary*, *The Old Dark House*, *des Dr Mabuse*, *Das Testament*, or Lon Chaney and Mary Philbin with the long golden hair in *The Phantom of the Opera*. We would re-enact our childhood memories of *The Lost World* or *Dr Fu Manchu* as the images remained fresh in our minds.

The cinema was true magic for many children brought up in the 1920s and early 30s, and Dylan and I were not exceptions. It was much more exciting than present-day television, it was an adventure in itself getting the few pennies together for the ticket, entering the darkened auditorium, to be entranced in a very real, often monstrous and also comic world.

Peter seldom accompanied us, only liking French or Russian films with the exception of Garbo. In any case he had a curious social life which took place mainly whilst I was at work and therefore I hardly ever took part in it. His engagement book, had he kept one at that time, would have read like a section of *Debrett*, and off he would lumber in his frayed, faded clothes, looking as Dylan described him in a letter in 1941, 'shabby, humped elegant Pulham', for he had an old nervous habit of hunching his shoulders when entering a room. He would tell me later about grand luncheons or dinners, and the participants became as real to me as if I had met them. In later years when I met some of these people I would, quite naturally, recall an incident, and they would say: 'But were you there? Funny, I don't remember you...'

At about this stage of the war a government order decreed that no restaurant could charge more than five shillings for a meal. If you had the money you could also have such delicacies as oysters or smoked salmon when they were available at a very high price, but the basic meal could not exceed the very reasonable price, even for those days, of five shillings. It was done to prevent black-marketeering, which it did to a certain extent. On account of this decree, many impoverished or elderly people took to lunching at the Ritz or similar hotels, as much as a return to prewar graciousness as for the meal itself, which was often disguised Spam or a similar product. And very pleasant it was, sitting on a well-upholstered banquette looking out over the verdant Green Park.

Lady Sibyl Colefax, a well-known hostess for many years – after Edward VIII's abdication the following lines were circulated in London:

The Ladies Colefax and Cunard
Took it very, very hard

– gave a weekly luncheon at the Ritz for friends, and it was to one of these that Peter brought me. As we were walking down the long hallway to the dining room, Peter stopped for a moment, put his hand on my shoulder, then tore off the flapping sole of his shoe. This he deposited amongst the potted palms framing the entrance, and we majestically sailed in, he with his sock meeting the thick pile of the carpet.

It was a remarkable gathering, with more women than men. Apart from myself they were well on in years with the curiously intense beauty of women who have accepted life and are long past youth. Ada Leverson, Oscar Wilde's great friend and champion both before and after he came out of prison, whom he affectionately called 'The Sphinx', Edith Sitwell, wonderfully medieval-looking, her face and body so attenuated as to be almost transparent, and Elinor Glyn, the best-selling novelist of the turn of the century, the originator of the 'It' girl, looking like one of her own heroines, startlingly, luminously beautiful with her abundant red hair curling from under the brim of a large hat, green eyes, and skin like fine rose-tinted marble. I sat next to her and found it difficult to stop looking at her and listen to what Vyvyan Holland, Oscar Wilde's son, was saying in his soft beguiling voice on my other side. Osbert Sitwell was at the other end of the table and so transfixed was I that I remember little about him. The bombs and barricades were far away, if they had ever happened: it was like dining with dinosaurs. I do not know what we ate or drank, it was not important, but I do remember at the end of the meal the magnificent red head of Elinor Glyn bending towards me; the crystal-clear eyes which had missed nothing in a long life fixed their gaze on me and a voice, almost ethereal so light was it, said:

'To preserve your skin rub it hard with a firm brush or loofah. All over your body, as well as your face. Do this every day!'

This segment of conversation, like a fossil caught in Baltic amber, has remained in my mind, and many times as I look in my mirror that beautiful face, and the voice like an incantation, is vivid to me.

It was no doubt when Peter was attending one of those functions (the word that comes to mind) that Dylan and I went to see *M*, the Fritz Lang film about the Dusseldorf child murderer. Dylan at that time looked remarkably like the young Peter Lorre, who played the child murderer, and it may have been that, as much as it was based on fact, that made us quite cold and quiet with terror. It was only when I realized that the film was about to start again that I spoke:

'Let's go now, quickly, I couldn't stand it again.'

Usually we chattered away after going to the cinema, making up sequels or acting out parts of what we had seen, but this time we clutched each other's hands and made our way to the French pub in Soho. It was crowded and noisy, which was just what we wanted to shake us out of our present mood. Old Monsieur Berlemont with his grey handlebar moustache and twinkling eyes greeted us and, when for the second time my drink was spilled by someone jostling me, he pointed to a small round marble-topped table which was empty at the back of the pub, near the bar, under his collection of signed photographs of Maurice Chevalier and other celebrities who had visited his pub.

Dylan and I were still very untalkative, itself an unusual occurrence, and when we did talk it was of serious matters like Caitlin wanting to come and live in London, for she and their son Llewelyn were still staying with Frances Hughes at Laugharne Castle. Mary Montagu had also indicated that she wanted her furniture back, so Peter and I were trying either to acquire some or get a furnished flat we could afford. For a few brief moments we thought of sharing a large flat or house together, but sensibly decided that as none of us had any money it would be straining our friendship too far. In any case paternity and Peter didn't seem to mix.

Opposite us at the further end of the alcove we were sitting in was a large man who sat looking like an angry tenant-farmer. From time to time his piercing brown eyes seemed to fix on us, trying almost to will us into looking at him, or possibly to engage us in conversation. Dylan was disturbed by this; he obviously recognized the man although he would tell me nothing. I thought of him as a 'pub bore' and was therefore not surprised when Dylan rummaged in his voluminous, magpie-cluttered pockets as a diversion and produced some dog-eared writing paper. He was in the habit of always carrying a pencil and paper with him, for not only did he jot down lines of poetry that he wished to remember, but he also drew very engaging little pictures or cartoons. This was to be a drawing in which we would both make contributions and see what turned out. A pleasant, distracting game which meant we weren't likely to catch the penetrating gaze of the angry tenant-farmer at the other end of the alcove. We started with a child's hoop which eventually formed the front plate of a large train engine, and so it went on.

We had completed, in so far as one ever completes, our doodle when the pot-boy came round emptying ashtrays, removing glasses and wiping the table-top with a wet cloth. He did the table in the middle, at which sat a lovesick pair of private soldiers, then on to the angry-looking man, who gave the lad a folded piece of paper, which he brought to us. Dylan unfolded the paper and laid it on the damp table. The cold terror we had known earlier that evening came back, for we were looking at a similar, very similar drawing to the one we had just completed. It was dominated by a large steam train engine as was ours. The effect on us was weird and uncanny; it produced an inner trembling in me; Dylan, almost white-faced, stood up and hustled me out. Outside, the summer evening seemed chilly, and Dylan shivered.

'We'll get a taxi if we can and go back to Chelsea at once.' He sounded unaccustomedly curt.

'But how did he . . .?'

Dylan's eyes like large tawny marbles widened as he said:

'That was Aleister Crowley, the Black Magician; he killed Betty May's husband in Sicily. He even calls *himself* the "Great Beast". Let's get as far away from him as possible.'

It has always annoyed me that in our hurry we left both the drawings on the damp table-top. No doubt they were screwed up and thrown away.

Peter laughed heartily at the whole story, which made us feel a little foolish but nevertheless reassured.

'Telepathy? What twaddle.' He said emphatically. 'It's done by mirrors.'

Dylan and I looked at each other by no means fully convinced. Peter on the other hand seemed immensely cheered up by our adventure. So much so that I thought something else must have happened to put him in such a good mood. His eyes had an amused, teasing look as he regarded the two of us, flopped out in the two armchairs, sipping flat beer.

'I've found us the most civilized place to live, Pussy. The drawing room is over forty foot long. It's Peter and Glur Quennell's old flat in Flood Street. You must go to the agents and fix up about it – I'm hopeless at all those business things.'

'What are we going to use for furniture?' Dylan sniggered. He waved his arm airily in the direction of his easel.

'We've got a bed and one or two things. Furniture doesn't matter unless it's very beautiful.'

'Won't it be very expensive?'

An annoyed look came over his face and he shrugged his shoulders, as he said that I must find out all those boring details. His enthusiasm had infected us for we spent some hours inventing a new and curious life for ourselves in a flat we would probably never live in. Yet when the time came to go to bed, we took the mattress from our bed and put it on the floor for Dylan, as he was still reluctant to go to wherever he was staying and to be alone after our strange adventure.

It was indeed the most spacious flat, taking in the two top floors of a small apartment block called Rossetti House. The entire building was empty, but in no way derelict, for there were recent traces of habitation as we peered through windows and peeped through keyholes of the flats on the intermediate floors. The drawing room was certainly at least forty feet long with superb parquet flooring; long floor-to-ceiling bookcases at one end, a large open hearth with a marble chimney-piece surmounted by a giant sheet of thick black glass at the other. It looked very swish and expensive. There were five large beautifully painted rooms, some with alcoves lit by concealed lighting, all with wall-to-wall carpeting.

'We can sit on the floor,' said Peter gaily. Upstairs, two more rooms, one with a dormer window in a deep recess almost the length of the wall. This recess was entirely filled with built-in cupboards and drawers on either side of a dressing table which had lights set into each side of the looking glass, as in a star's dressing room. This part shut down, so making the entire top a table about four feet wide. I envisaged myself sitting grandly at it as I put on my *maquillage*.

'H'm, a very good room for me to work in. I can use the top as a drawing table.'

'But it's a bedroom,' I said.

'There are plenty of other rooms to sleep in, but *this* is obviously the place to work.'

I said nothing for the time being, amusing myself by opening the many drawers, most of which were empty or containing small signs of occupation such as hair grips or safety pins. The contents of one drawer made me stop, determined to find the means of living there, for it was half-full of unopened jars of Elizabeth Arden's creams and unguents. When Peter wasn't looking I slipped one in my pocket; he had once made me bring back to the shop a large tomato I had taken when we were hungry. This was a real find for, apart from theatrical make-up which was only given to 'regular' customers, it was almost unobtainable and of very poor quality. We used Meltonian shoe cream for mascara (I had a brief week on moustache-wax which made my eyelashes look like furry spiders' legs), Trex or Spry cooking fat for cleansing cream (how many bearded ladies as a result?), calamine lotion as a powder base and sometimes even baby powder for face powder. Eye shadow was not fashionable then off the stage, but we put Vaseline on our eye-lids and lips to achieve that 'dewy' look. Often it trickled down if the room was hot, which looked as if one had been crying, and sympathy was often given as a result. We were far too sly to admit what in fact it was and sometimes pretended a sadness which did not exist. In an attempt to curl up the ends of my hair I was once surprised by Dylan as I was using a chunk of large macaroni, called *rigatoni*, with a hair grip. He was agog as he inquired:

'Are we going to eat it afterwards?'

I wanted to live in Rossetti House so badly that I became quite reconciled to moving there without furniture: surely we could get tea chests or strong boxes to use as tables and, as Peter rightly said, we did have a bed to sit or sleep on. But I knew without asking that even if the rent was reasonable the agents would want a month, if not more, rent in advance. If all else failed I would pawn my electric sewing machine, a twenty-first birthday present. When I saw the fat wooden case which housed it at the end of the book-case I felt reasonably secure.

Taking an hour off work to see the agents, I arrived home early to find Peter and Dylan just going out. It was too early for the pubs to be open, and Peter in front had a strange worried look on his face.

'We're just going up the road . . .' He hesitated and looked very guilty.

'All right, I'll come too. I want to tell you about the flat.' He shuffled about nervously.

'Come on, let's go. I can get the rations before the shops shut.' Peter's telltale eyes moved anxiously: he turned to Dylan.

'It's no good, I can't do it. I told you we shouldn't.' He moved back exposing Dylan, who was standing with his right arm behind his back.

'What have you got in your hand, Dylan?' My voice sounded shrill and school-mistressy to myself. He brought out his left hand.

'Nothing.'

'No, the other one.' I moved forward and pulled his arm. Out swung the fat wooden case, the weight swinging him round. In his hurt actor's voice, he said:

'We were only going to pawn it.'

'Pawn? You know I would never have seen it again. You, you thief!' I turned round to Peter. 'And you're as bad for allowing it.'

'Are you accusing me of stealing?'

'I most certainly am.'

Peter intervened: 'It was as much my fault as his, Pussy, I'm sorry . . . we had no money, and Dylan and I . . .'

I snatched the machine and ran up the stairs with it, not even noticing the weight. My relief at recovering my lifeline was so great that by the time they had followed me up I had quite overcome my temper. The episode was never referred to, and later that evening we went to the Eight Bells together as usual.

Dylan would disappear for three to four days at a time. We would assume he had gone back to Wales, which he did every week or so. I missed my cinema-going chum very much, but we were seldom alone for long, for once our friends knew that we were living in Chelsea, we had many unexpected callers, some on leave from various armed forces, which always underlined that we too would be called up before long.

As I came up the stairs one day I heard a woman's voice talking to Peter. Mary? Kenette? Isabel? No, when I got nearer it didn't sound like any of them. It had the quick phrasing and slightly rough intonation I associated with part of Limerick and Clare. My God, I thought, one of my Irish cousins.

Inside, Peter was standing up by the fireplace and Dylan was sitting by the window. A spruce tidy Dylan in a white shirt the colour of fresh snow, with a new, rather flamboyant tie. (So that was why he had attempted to take my sewing machine.) In the other chair sat one of the most lovely young women I had ever encountered. She looked as though she had been fashioned from wonderful wax, translucent and pliable. Her colouring was magnificent: pink cheeks, a creamy skin and a superb mane of golden curly hair. It shone and flashed like a beacon, now red, now gold and now the colour of ripened wheat. Tendrils, so beloved in certain literature, curled like filigree goldwork on her cheeks. She looked like the embodiment of all the heroines in literature, far removed from the sophisticated 'beauties' of the Paris days, the only truly natural beauty I had ever seen.

The beautiful head and body were set off by the rose-coloured velvet frock which had old and exquisite ecru lace at the neck and cuffs, so that she looked like a rich jewel nestling in a velvet-lined case. It was as though a seventeenth-century painting had come to life. Her manner was natural, it invoked no jealousy nor the feeling of competition common between good-looking women, for she seemed to me then far removed from the quirks of ordinary people.

This was my first meeting with Caitlin Thomas, and the beginning of an unforgettable friendship. In a few months' time, the winter of 1941 to 1942, they were both to live in London.

Chapter Fourteen

'Living in the style to which we are not accustomed. I must say I *do* like space,' said Peter as he walked up and down the long room in Rossetti House, whilst I sat on the floor watching the flames lick up from some salvaged wood burning in the large fireplace. I was sitting on the floor from choice, for there were several comfortable old leather armchairs my grandmother had rooted out of an attic. Several months before, we had solved the furniture problem by having my mother move in with us: it hadn't worked out and, when she moved to a smaller place a few streets away, quite a lot of her furniture had stayed with us. Even if we could have afforded it, there was almost none to be bought except horrible, cheap-looking new 'utility' (the government name) furniture which was allocated to young brides (marriage lines had to be produced) on a points system. A quarter's rent had been paid by my mother which was very welcome for I had been extremely ill and needed a few weeks' rest after leaving the hospital. Now all we had to worry about was food, and this problem was immediately solved in what seemed a miraculous way.

Mysteriously two barrels appeared outside the front door upstairs. They were there when we came back from delivering some 'samples' – I had temporarily become a commercial traveller, Peter volunteering to carry the heavy cases around for me. We rolled them in, poked, prodded and wondered about the contents. Beer? No. Whatever was inside was solid not liquid. How on earth did one open them? Peter went to the café opposite Chesil Court to borrow chisels, hammers and other tools; for what seemed like hours his strong arms levered and broad shoulders heaved.

'It's fish, Pussy, hundreds of fish all packed on ice. Who on earth could have sent them?'

Sure enough he was right – fish fresher than any we had seen for years, large, dark blue eyes staring reproachfully at us: herrings, plaice, gurnets, dabs, whiting and many smaller fish we couldn't name, all tail- and head-entwined in crushed ice. For three days we 'fished' extensively. We had them fried, baked, grilled and curried and Peter even tried salting and smoking some in the large chimney, for as he rightly said they would go bad before we could eat them all. Finally we bartered a few pounds from one barrel (the other we left sealed) for tins of meat with Vic the grocer, but not before we had given a large *fruits de mer* dinner party (fish knives not being admitted, there was the complication of having to borrow dozens of forks) at which Donald and Melinda, Dylan and I think Caitlin, Mary Montagu, Crabbe and Brian Howard were among the guests.

Ever since I had met Brian at the Cavendish the year before, he would appear, from time to time, like a genie. Brian and drama were synonymous: he was possibly the original one-man theatre for he resented other players. Having experienced this with prima donnas on the stage I knew just how to play to it, consequently we got on very well together. He was fond of calling me 'that wickéd girl' or 'that wickéd Madonna', although to my certain knowledge I did nothing in any way outrageous. Brian made it impossible to scene-steal, for then the curtain would be rung down abruptly. Most of the dramas had several acts of a tragicomic nature. He had the quality of making the simplest meal into a banquet: you could live a lifetime during one of them; eat, drink, laugh, quarrel, make up and still discuss ideas with gaiety and spontaneity.

When all the guests had gone, he declared he would stay the night, and he was shown into the room with pink-painted walls and ceiling. 'My dears! I should wake up in the morning like the rose-red cutie half as old as time! I couldn't possibly sleep a *wink* here.' We hurried around and made up a bed in a plain white room. He wasn't impressed and demanded another drink. Carefully we steered him away from truculence as the night lengthened. Even he was tired, wrung out by the evening's entertainment. The staircase up to our bedroom was narrow: we both stood on the bottom step close to each other to say goodnight. He stood there, a slim figure, his dark eyes burning in the handsome tortured face, the full petulant lips quivering, reluctant to be alone. With a last burst of energy he made a loud sobbing sound, his voice trembled as he blurted out:

'You're going upstairs to lie in each other's arms, and here am I, alone, just a silly old sissy.' He turned, slamming the door of the housemaid's bedroom.

When we got up in the morning his bed was empty. Carefully laid on the pillow was a note saying:

'My dears! the kitchen smells like Mac Fisheries on a bad day. Meet me in the downstairs bar of the Ritz at noon.'

Peter kept this assignation while I got on with my commercial travelling. As I opened the door on my return I heard Brian's voice imperiously saying:

'Where is that wickéd girl?' He rolled the word 'wicked' around his mouth as though it was an exotic edible stone. I looked down the long corridor to see Peter's large head peering round the corner. He looked put out.

'Thank goodness you've come,' he said tetchily, 'you can deal with that thing in the drawing room.'

'What thing?'

'Oh, I don't know what it's called, a chauffeur brought it, and said you knew about it. I can't understand why you didn't tell me.' These were quite sharp words for Peter; normally he accepted what I did. Since that day in Paris we had never quarrelled. I went into the drawing room, and standing forlornly, yet comically in the middle of the huge room was Gwladys.

Gwladys was a *rara avis* in the true sense, for she was an actress-penguin. She had starred in a film called *To Brighton with a Bird* and it was in a film studio I had first met her, and her owner. A few months previously I had met the owner casually in the street, who expressed to me her concern at finding a home for Gwladys for two weeks whilst she went away. Gwladys hated other penguins, preferring human company, therefore a zoo was out of the question. On the spur of the moment I said I would look after her. The fish should have warned me, but having been in hospital had put it right out of my mind.

Brian's large inquiring eyes opened even wider when I brought Gwladys into the kitchen in my arms. He sipped his gin and said:

'I do hope, you wickéd girl, you're not going to behave like your namesake Empress Theodora did with the geese!'

Gwladys wriggled when she smelt the fish, so I put her on the floor. She waddled over to the open barrel and very rapidly swallowed down several large fish.

'It'll choke,' said Peter. 'Heavens, it's already eaten as much as I could and it's only a fraction of my size.'

They were both fascinated by the behaviour and appearance of this comical bird, although neither of them would have admitted it. Peter had put his glass on top of the unopened barrel and, after the fish, Gwladys walked over to it; in a flash the beak was in and the gin gone. She looked up at us, turned round and walked, unsteadily it seemed, out of the room. We followed her along the corridor, as unerringly she went into the bathroom, hoisted herself up on to the side of the bath and tugged at the tap with her beak. As the water gushed out she chortled, rolled and splashed about with ecstasy. Brian turned to Peter and said:

'Fancy having a mistress with a gin-drinking penguin. It's going to cost you something, my dear.'

It was a tumultous two weeks for there were many times when, as Peter remarked, the flat looked like a second-rate lagoon. The gin (what little there was) had to be kept under lock and key as it was often broached; the bathroom door locked, for once we came back to find the place awash, the floors intricately patterned with wet webbed footmarks. There was but little painting or commercial travelling done, for she was a full-time job. Nevertheless it was worth it when she sat on my lap in the evening, her beak nestled under my ear as I read my book. Peter liked the surrealist 'mother and child' effect, saying that it almost made him want to take photographs again, had he possessed a camera.

In the unaccountable way that things happen he was soon to get a camera. Maitland Pendock, at this time with the

Ministry of Information, had been an ardent admirer of Peter's photographs for many years, and was distressed that he no longer took any. He had gone to the trouble of finding out from mutual friends where Peter lived, appearing one evening with a Rolliflex camera which he placed strategically on a nearby table. Before long Peter was fiddling with the case and looking inside.

'It's like my old camera,' he said; then putting the camera firmly back on the table, 'thank goodness I've given all that up.'

Maitland's thinning brown hair was blowing gently from the breeze of the open window. His kindly, round, blue-grey eyes glanced at me almost imperceptibly through his spectacles.

'I'll leave it just in case you feel like using it, Peter. I could sell any photographs you took, very easily. There's some film, too; it's impossible to buy these days. Now let's all go out and have a drink.'

During that summer Peter took in all about twenty photographs, mostly nudes of me, some of which were published in *Lilliput*, of which Mechtild Nawaisky ('no more whisky') was art editor. It was practically the only magazine at the time which had photographs. Later on they reprinted, at Mechtild's instigation, some of Peter's Paris photographs in a series called 'Surrealist Artists'. Inevitably the day come when he pawned the camera to buy canvas and paints. Maitland redeemed it, but it was seldom used. To be fair to Peter it must be stated that he was as painstaking a photographer as he was a painter. He always developed and printed his own negatives (he would tease Cecil Beaton by calling him an amateur when he sent his rolls of film to be processed) for he said that any fool could click a shutter but the true art was in the dark-room. Despite the blackout, fully equipped dark-rooms were not easy to find, as many were taken over by the War Ministry for printing photographs brought back by agents. The Russian photographer Edward Mandinian, who worked for the Free French Army in England, became a true friend when he lent him his studio in Ebury Street.

Meanwhile I was still going some evenings to the fire-watching post but as the incidents were fewer at this time, the work consisted mainly of checking with headquarters and making cups of tea when it was available.

The quarter's rent had long since been expended. We were sitting rather moodily rolling cigarettes from our 'butt' tin, when the cheerful ting of a taxi meter being stopped came from the road below us. We hung out of the windows to see Sophie, arms bulging with flowers, bottles and brown paper bags. She came bounding up the stairs looking blooming, extremely smart in new clothes. It was almost a year since we had seen her.

Yes, she had a new job, a good one at a large hotel in Park Lane, and the manager had taken a 'fancy' to her.

'I thought we'd have a party, just ourselves,' she said, as chickens, salad, salami, cheese, wine, whisky, gin and brandy were all disgorged from the large brown paper bags.

'But how did you get it all?'

'Arthur made me up a parcel. I nearly brought him too, but he's on duty. I'll bring him next time. Tonight, just us.'

We didn't know whether to eat (for we were permanently hungry) or drink first: I think we did both together, talking all the time. Peter's eyes had the lazy smile in them that always showed when he was happy or excited.

'Dear little Sophie, this is a change from the dried milk powder.'

She beamed with delight and filled up his wine glass.

'What a lovely flat. Is there room for me?'

Aunt Zenobia, phase two, was obviously over.

I suppose it was Gwladys who reminded me that I hadn't had an animal of my own for some time (for Jason had become my mother's dog), so I bought a brown standard poodle puppy, who to begin with was only tolerated by Peter because she was of French origin, always called by him a *caniche*, and also called, on account of her proclivities, *Merde*. Finally we settled on Mouche; she became the mother of almost all the brown poodles in Chelsea, and a much-loved animal.

The nearest we ever got to a holiday was to spend the evening on the terrace of The Doves pub at Hammersmith when Dylan, Caitlin and their small son were living in A. P. (now Sir Alan) Herbert's one-room studio. It was highly unsuitable for a family, so in early summer Caitlin reluctantly went back to a cottage they had rented at Talsarn in Cardiganshire. Once more Dylan made the endless journeys back and forth to London. He was writing a short novel about a man who lost an article of clothing each time he went through a new experience, ending up stark naked outside Paddington Station, the most high-class London station, as Dylan said. During that summer Caitlin became pregnant so he begged me to find them the impossible: a cheap furnished abode, for all they owned was a 'deck-chair with a hole in it, half a dozen books, a few toys and an old iron'. His great childhood friend, the musician Dan Jones (now Dr Daniel Jones the composer), had at some time lived in Wentworth Studios, Manresa Road, Chelsea; it was empty and seemed, by peering in through dirty windows, furnished. It became my job to find out who owned it (for Dan was away in the army) and to get the keys.

In early autumn they moved into the enormous square room with a partitioned-off kitchen, a bathroom built not later than the turn of the century and a glass skylight that leaked when it rained. The furniture may not have been entirely solid, the strips of carpet threadbare, but Caitlin soon made it into a real home: the large round table shining with polish, the Welsh dresser gleaming with assorted crockery. There were books everywhere (mostly Dan Jones's) along the walls on the floor, as well as in lurching book-cases; some large volumes, piled one on the other, made low tables. Dylan's drawings were *passe-partouted* and hung on the walls, along with reproductions of paintings that took Caitlin's fancy. Her Welsh-Irish stew, made mainly from vegetables, was permanently bubbling on the stove, a true *pot-au-feu*. There was always a ladleful for callers, a hunk of the grey wartime bread, and sometimes a glass of Guinness or pale ale. Indeed, it was difficult, even if one had just finished a meal, to resist the mouthwatering aroma.

Llewelyn had gone to stay with his grandmother, so Caitlin was able to accompany us in the evenings, for she was a conscientious mother and never left a young child alone. This may have accounted for a certain wildness sometimes when she did get out, for whilst we were enjoying ourselves she would be baby-sitting – and often understandably ready to throw the first thing to hand when we came back hours late and not entirely sober. Dylan would send me in first, hanging behind with a sickly smile on his face, an expression of mock astonishment which tended, if anything, to make Caitlin crosser. All in all she was very tolerant, far more so than I would have been under the same circumstances. For it was all work and worry, with very little play, to a vital and beautiful young woman in her twenties, who saw all her contemporaries enjoying themselves. Friends of later years can scarcely imagine the deprivations she underwent, both before and after this time; Dylan, the enchanting companion and friend, was far from the ideal husband.

Despite our concessions to the bourgeois life it was a summer of unease and restlessness. Towards the end of it Peter was called up in the fire service to a post in the East End of London, where some of his cockney colleagues called him 'Uncle'. This he seemed to like: what he liked more was that he worked for two days at the post, and then got two days off, which meant he could continue with his painting. The pay was a little over three pounds a week for both single and married men. The first week he grandly said he was going to make me an allowance, handing me a ten-shilling note. I can't remember getting any more, but he was able to pay for his fares, food at the post and some beer or cigarettes. Sophie had to fill in endless forms about her call-up. Having been *enceinte* at my call-up time, I was exempt.

Arthur continued to 'fancy' Sophie, and was most generous to all of us in the way of food or drink. He was a hard-working yet gentle man, who realized his good fortune at not being in the forces, and shared what he could with his friends. Sophie worked until almost midnight, and was therefore entitled to an evening meal. Arthur saw that it was a hefty one, enough for three in fact, so Sophie would eat sparingly and bring the rest home. She was really extremely brave; for many nights, quite unable to get any form of transport, she would run through Hyde Park (all the iron railings having been removed for scrap, to help the war effort) down Sloane Street, then the King's Road, in all a good two miles, carrying the food, and sometimes a small bottle, or a jar of soup withal. I got so that I couldn't sleep until she came back, for then she would jump into our bed, and the three of us, when Peter was home, would eat our midnight feast, dropping off like young animals when our bellies were full. Mouche would finish up the pieces if there were any left, for the food was of excellent quality. But if the meat was tough we would tease her, saying a rich armament-maker must have left it, and she would be indignant.

'They're not left-overs. I've got friendly with the chef, too!'

My alarm would go off at 7.30 a.m. and how reluctantly I crept out of the warm nest, leaving one, and sometimes two, snug figures.

We had a charming milkman who climbed the four flights of stairs with our milk; on Sundays he first put the kettle on, then gave Mouche a run and, when he came back, would have a cup of tea with us, sitting on the end of the bed. If Peter was there he would say:

'The guv'nor can make the tea while I'm out with the dog.' It was a lovely treat on the cold winter mornings.

More and more forms came for Sophie to fill up, all left unanswered.

'I think I'll join the Land Army. I like the country and animals.'

My friends Hugh and Nikki Price Jones, from whom I

had bought Mouche, had a rather smart farm in Kent, with several land-girls, as they were called. But I could never get Sophie even to telephone them. She was maddeningly stubborn, never believing she would ever be conscripted, for as she used to say: 'I can't see myself in the army.' It came as a nasty shock when she was peremptorily told to report to a barracks in Oswestry, North Wales, in three weeks' time. The barracks square on a winter's morning and the army huts were a long way from the warm hotel, Arthur, and Rossetti House.

'I'll soon be back on leave,' she said shakily as Arthur took her to the station in a taxi.

But the leaves were few and far between, and Sophie was never a good correspondent. The rent was paid for a month, but on about a pound a week army pay she couldn't keep it up. Out of sentiment, Arthur paid it until the quarter's end, which coincided with her first week's leave. Back came Sophie disguised as a lance corporal.

Towards the end of the week she lay mulishly on the divan saying over and over:

'I will not go back to that bloody place. I'm just not going, so there.'

'Won't they arrest you, or something awful like that? I wouldn't like to think of you in irons, or a cell. Do they have cells for women?'

'I expect so. It's the most ghastly life you could imagine with all those bitchy women. You simply can't imagine what it's like. School was a picnic compared to it. They're the scum of the earth in my regiment: one even whipped a piece of my equipment when I was in the lavatory. I lost an evening out because I hadn't got the blasted silly whistle.'

'Do you feel ill? Perhaps we could get you out on health reasons?'

'I feel unnaturally healthy: except I think I'll go mad.'

This put an idea in my head, so for two days I coached Sophie in mute, staring madness. She looked quite alarming when she was playing well. I got a doctor none of us knew to come and see her; a very sensitive-looking Indian.

'I don't think I can go through with it,' she said, clutching at me, 'not in front of you, I shall giggle.'

'All the better if you do,' I replied.

The doctor rang the bell and when he came in I explained the appalling apathy and sickness that had struck my friend, so unfortunate, just as she was due to report back to the army.

Sophie's huge saucer eyes looked truly frightened when she saw him, and after endless examinations and questions he gave her a certificate for an extra week at home. I led him quickly out lest he notice the joy in her face, but in the hall he said:

'It's a sad case; if she isn't better in a week, we'll have to commit her for further investigation.'

'I don't care. Anything's better than the army. I'll go and be investigated,' Sophie said as she leapt out of bed and started making up her face.

She did indeed go for one investigation, but when it came to the pinch, the army seemed better than a looney bin, so back she went, resolutely determined to find a way out. It was agreed that I would let one of her two rooms (keeping the other one for the joyful return) as a bedsitter to meet the rent.

'I wonder what sort of lodger will apply for the room,' I said to Peter. He twisted his nose with distaste as he said:

'I think I shall move upstairs when they come, and I prefer the word *locataire*.'

Chapter Fifteen

I took the first *locataire* who called within an hour of my putting a notice in the paper-shop window. He was a medical student, delighted to find a landlady about the same age as himself. He didn't upset our lives half as much as we did his, for in a few months he had married a partly West Indian girl-friend of mine and given up medicine. Peter was an avuncular, beaming best man.

In fact the place turned out to be almost a marriage bureau, for the next one was a strange and beautiful girl called Margery Morrison, who later married John Davenport, one-time poet, literary critic, an old and good friend of both Peter and Dylan. Then Mechtild sent round a shy, pale, dark-haired girl with a sweet smile, and the most unbecoming hair style I have even seen. Her long hair was screwed into a small bun which rested on the top of her head like a small chocolate cake. When I met her coming out of the bathroom with long waving tresses reaching her shoulders, I only recognized her by the sweet smile. She was so quiet that we never knew whether she was in or out: her name was Mary Smith.

We both missed Sophie bouncing in and out, with her schoolgirl midnight feasts and her unpredictable moods. The milkman missed her too, for he said it wasn't proper him sitting on the bed with just me in it. When Peter was off duty, we usually went to the Eight Bells in the evening, but as we had a little more money to spare we would sometimes go up to Soho with Dylan and Caitlin, who was now hugely pregnant. There, we would drink, mostly in pubs, or one-room clubs such as the Colony, Horseshoe or Mandrake, with young, as yet little-known, painters like John Minton, John Banting, Lucien Freud or Francis Bacon; Peter always thought Francis looked like me, and was delighted to find that we had both been brought up in the same part of

Ireland. Francis was always my favourite, a brilliant painter working under great difficulties, yet he was, and still is, totally without malice. His face, to the world, was one of gay equanimity; his troubles were not brought out for drinks.

On very slap-up occasions we would go to the back bar of the Café Royal where Jimmy the barman presided priest-like over a vaguely literary gathering. Dylan loved Peter's story of once seeing Chaliapin the great Russian singer there, towering over everyone, his deep, powerful, resonant voice ordering 'Kvass', then being promptly served with a glass of Bass. If we had even more money to spare we might go through to the huge dining room, resplendent with red velvet seats, glass chandeliers and marble-topped tables, to have a cheap meal. It was possible at one end of the room to order food of the snack variety; the other end catered for diners. We were always intrigued by one item permanently on the menu: *pie froid*. Was it *really* cold magpie? We so wanted to think it was that it was never ordered lest we be disappointed. On the back of a menu Peter drew us his impression of the sportsman who only hunted magpies for the Café Royal. Across the room we might see Augustus John with a girl, Brian Howard, Francis Rose the painter, Gerald Kersh the writer, looking wonderfully Assyrian, or any one of many friends. But more often it was the pubs: the Scotch House, the French and the Swiss, all crowded to overflowing, mostly with soldiers (some of them friends) from many parts of the world. Francis Butterfield, another painter friend of mine, told me of a hefty coloured soldier he saw hanging over the bar, staring at his reflection in the mirror opposite and saying:

'Ah don't want no more women; ah don't want no more liquor; ah jes wants maself.'

There were many times when I felt the same way!

One such evening in early March, Caitlin and I got separated from the others. The heat, noise and crush were worse than ever, and Caitlin became faint, her huge belly squashed by milling soldiers. I battled my way through the sweating bodies, my face rubbed by coarse khaki, my clothes slopped with beer, to find Peter. I had to shout loudly to make myself heard, and he gave me a few shillings for a taxi. There was no sign of Caitlin when I got back, but after more pushing and struggling I found her outside, leaning against the wall, the street heavily blacked-out, in a state of near collapse.

'Let's go to the Gargoyle' – a club owned by David Tennant – 'and have a brandy,' said Caitlin.

'I've only got just enough for a taxi if we can find one.'

'I've managed to wrench some housekeeping money . . .' She stopped. 'At least I *had* some housekeeping money . . .' She held up her open bag, empty of a purse. With my pocket torch we searched through it as best we could in the pitch-dark street.

'Oh, Cait, where could it be? I couldn't face that crowd again, and we'd never find it, there's no hope of even *seeing* the floor.'

She sighed, then in her clipped, quick voice she said:

'Easy come, easy go . . . I hope whoever finds it really needs it.'

A taxi drew up disgorging yet more soldiers, and after wheedling with the taxi driver, he reluctantly drove us back to Chelsea.

About a week later I met Dylan in the King's Road, outside the Sunlight Laundry. I was carrying a large wicker laundry basket, full of the *locataires*' dirty laundry.

'Cait has had a baby girl. We're going to call her Aeronwy.' His eyes rested on the basket.

'There's nothing much to put her in, when they come back from the hospital.'

On the pavement, we turned out the laundry and made a bundle of it. Dylan stayed outside with the basket. The gimlet-eyed manageress said:

'Where's the basket? There's five shillings deposit on it. You'll have to forfeit that.'

It was perhaps the cheapest and best bassinet ever purchased.

If anything Peter painted more during his fire service days than in the apprehensive days before he joined. The two days off were spent painting from early morning until it became too dark to continue: vivid pictures of flames, twisted girders, or charred wood; the horse's head set against melancholy or burning backgrounds, or crashed-aeroplane-like shapes. His painting was stimulated by the announcement of an exhibition of firemen's paintings, to be held at Burlington House. This was the first chance he had had to exhibit since the war started. (There were but few exhibitions, but I do remember with pleasure one given of Jankel Adler's pictures – Jankel Adler was then living in England; the sensuous, rich, thick swirls of paint, the strength and power of those large canvases, were like a feast to colour-starved wartime eyes.) It was an exciting time for both of us, selecting and then finding appropriate frames for the pictures. Finally he decided on three paintings, one from each phase of his development.

The standard of paintings in the exhibition was remarkably high, and I remember particularly a picture by Leonard Rosoman, the thought of which today strikes an emotion in me. The exhibition was given mention in the press, an unusual occurrence in the thin double-sheet newspapers of the time. Two days after the opening, a letter was forwarded from Burlington House for Peter, inquiring the price of the crumpled-paper-aeroplane painting. The writing paper was first quality, die-stamped, with an address in Admiral's Walk, Hampstead. As Admiral's Walk was commonly known as 'Millionaire's Row' our hopes ran high when Peter went out to call. Alas, it was a young girl, a student, who was unable to afford more than five pounds. Nevertheless it spurred Peter on, encouraging him enormously. It also paid for the frame, more canvas, and gave us a good dinner, as well as boosting his reputation at the fire station. Two of his colleagues, namely Syd and Reg, became his champions. Part of Peter's fire service training was to jump from the top of a high building into a blanket. He was not at all cowardly, but expressed the fear to me that the blanket would split under his weight.

'The others seem such small men compared to me,' he would say ruefully.

One evening Syd and Reg were at the front door, small, almost wizened men in their early forties. One was carrying a green parrot in a cage.

'Is Uncle in?'

I replied he was, asked them in, stupidly poking my finger at the parrot, who straight away gave it a feeble peck and then in a shrill voice said:

'Bugger it, I've done it again.'

Syd apologized for the language 'in front of a lady' and explained at great length that he'd been picking up his mum's parrot who'd been staying with his auntie in Chelsea while his mum was with his daughter who'd just had a baby.

Peter, hearing the voices, came down to see them. When they saw him, Syd and Reg became tongue-tied, so to put them at their ease he showed them round his studio, giving Reg a small painting for his 'gran' who was bed-ridden and apparently a 'picture-fancier'. I offered them a glass of beer when they came downstairs, by now quite relaxed and chirping like sparrows. The parrot gave an eldritch-like shriek when it saw them.

'We wus thinking, me and Reg,' said Syd, 'about your blanket jump. We've decided to change our days off, so that we're there to hold the blanket. You'd feel safer with us, wouldn't you, Uncle?'

They appeared even smaller standing in front of Peter than they did on their own. The gesture touched us both deeply and brought a lump to our throats. For many months, as their days off coincided with Peter's, they would make the journey to Chelsea, to drink with us in the Eight Bells. They were delightful chums.

Chums and friends were what I missed most with Sophie and Peter away. The two days he was on duty seemed like two weeks, the large flat very empty, for the *locataires* lived their own lives. But for the bounding poodle to greet me on my return I would have been very lonely. If the weather was fine I would take her for long walks in Battersea Park, sometimes calling into the Eight Bells for a glass of beer on my return; to begin with, it was strange sitting alone in our usual corner. Caitlin was feeding the baby, so seldom came out in the evenings. Acquaintances would ask me to join them, but I wanted my big kind man.

Although our relationship had never been a passionate one in the accepted sense, there was mutual affection and deep love between us. He was too indolent to be a sustained lover; what energy he had went into his work. Materially Peter gave me practically nothing: intellectually and spiritually he provided me with the qualities I lacked. By careful example he made me intellectually honest and truthful, giving me an appreciation of many things I might not have found for myself. He gave me much-needed security, not of the prosaic, monetary kind, but of understanding my purpose in life. He was, truly, my mentor and friend. He knew I was impulsively quick-tempered, so tried to avoid upsetting me. He seldom reproached me, and unless in a devilish mood, I did little to provoke him, for I could tell instantly, from the expression in his sad, dark eyes, if he was displeased. However, when in extreme poverty I cut off my long blonde hair and sold it to a wig-maker for five pounds, he demanded we go immediately to get it back. Part of it had already been used, the rest was bought back, and made into a kind of fly switch which was hung on the wall to remind me of my folly. In these days of wigs and hairpieces, it is once more being worn.

When I came home from a party in the early (or late) hours of the morning, he was sitting up in the monkish habit writing his journal (which he wrote in mirror-writing, like Leonardo da Vinci); he looked up, smiled and said:

'Goodness, I'm glad you're back. I was beginning to think you'd nipped off with someone.'

His faults were of omission: the maddening slowness and apathy when faced with something he did not, or would not, do. In the four years spent together, the greater part of my adult life thus far, we lived life ten times over: sharing the horrors of war, invasion, bombing, near starvation, and the bloodiness of botched birth. From this we kindled our own small fire at which we warmed our hearts.

Briefly I worked for the Free French army in London, but *mon colonel* was a zealous man, and a nine-hour day with only a half-day off a week, and one Sunday a month, strained even my francophilic feelings. I was glad when they transferred to Algiers, for then I was able to leave. As I became adjusted to the changing life I did see my old friends, sometimes unexpectedly.

The nights were often still peppered with gunshots and distant bombs, but the sound no longer wakened us. It was strange, small unaccustomed noises that penetrated sleep. I awoke to the whimpers, and then hesitant low growls turning to rumbles of the dog as I lifted my head from the pillow. A soft footfall: was it the *locataire*, or my sleep-bound imagination? Fumbling, I switched on the light; standing in the middle of the room was my cat-burglar friend, whom I shall call Nemo, in army uniform. The blackout curtain hanging over the open window flapped gently.

'Why ever didn't you ring the bell, Nemo? Do shut the window, or else the wardens will be here.'

'I wanted to keep my hand,' he smiled angelically, 'or, rather, my foot in. There's not much chance for practice these days.' He drew in his lithe, slim body. 'These four storeys, with a perfect drainpipe, were a challenge, my dear!'

The gaunt face was deeply tanned, and more handsome than I remembered it. From his hip pocket he took a flask.

'Let's have a good drink, and then go to a nightclub and have masses of bad drinks. I'll deliver you back in time for breakfast. In fact,' he delved into his tunic pockets, 'I've got some sausages, and,' he folded his hands over like a magician, 'two eggs.'

Off we went in a curious motor-car (I asked no questions) to the Nest, the dog as well, drank whisky of 'Four Nations', very bad nations from the taste, but we danced, and talked, and drank, and got home in good time for breakfast.

The word 'cat-burglar', in common with 'Raffles the Gentleman Burglar', has gone out of currency in these days of knives and guns. Burglars used to be like snakes; they were more frightened of you than you were of them, and only attacked in self-defence. In any event, Nemo had once proved his worth by restoring the indiscreet letters of a young woman I knew, who was being blackmailed.

There were many pleasant times, especially when Peter's days off coincided with a weekend. I had taken a part-time temporary job, so as to have more free time, as we now had two *locataires*, and the large flat had to be cleaned and otherwise organized. Some evenings were spent with the tiny exquisite Grete Wyndham, estranged wife of Richard Wyndham the painter, in her delicate doll's house, which suited her to perfection, with its lovely Chirico paintings, and always a large ginger cat, called Teddy: it was, or it seemed, half the size of Grete. It was there I met Constant Lambert's first wife, Flo, her Javanese features looking exotically beautiful, set off by a prim VAD uniform. Simon Harcourt Smith, the diplomatist, lived in Lawrence Street, with his amusing wife Rosamond, then encased in plaster up to her waist after a car accident. When I first met her, sitting perched on the end of her bed, she said:

'Well, shall we talk about people we know, or shall we talk bawdy?'

There were unpredictable, richly amusing evenings with John Davenport; dinner with Philip Toynbee, on leave from the army, with his first wife, Ann, at the White Tower; a luncheon we gave at Rossetti House for Edouard Mesens, the Belgian poet and surrealist leader, who was working for the Belgians in England. From him we learned welcome news: Giacometti was safely in Switzerland, and Max Ernst had married Peggy Guggenheim, and was in New York. There were many others, all Peter's friends. Caitlin and Dylan, with the baby in the wicker basket, came to share the piece of meat the size of a spectacle case one Sunday. Dylan was enthralled by a story concerning an elderly Welsh woman of his acquaintance who had gone mad.

'She was seen pouring the milk on the ground outside the front door' – a considerable actor's pause – 'and then trying to put the cat into the milk bottle!' He drew in his breath and then gave his characteristic snort-snigger.

But the old pattern had broken: events had to be arranged ahead according to days off. There were fewer spontaneous meetings, for we were both on the side of authority. We no longer made arrangements as one person, but as two. Inevitably, I did make new friends as the months ran on, some of whom shared no part of my life with Peter. *Mon colonel* was equally zealous on his half-day off; his long, lean, agile Norman body springing up the four flights with a bottle of wine, but I did not see myself as *une fille du regiment.* Subsequently I heard he had written several highly praised books. I met Bertram Wedgwood, the Casanova of that large and distinguished family, who had recently returned from occupied France and who, although in his sixties, spent most of his time trying to get back as an agent. Through him I met other members of the Wedgwood family. Also a strikingly outrageous Austrian girl, Lieselotte Sworn, recently married to a Staffordshire surgeon.

'But he *had* to marry me, darling. I vas staying at his house for the veekend, vhen they said enemy aliens couldn't move from vhere they vere. You can't live in sin in Stafford.' The marriage was dissolved more than twenty-five years later, by the death of her husband.

Gavin de Beer (later Sir Gavin de Beer), eminent biologist and writer, then a captain in the Grenadier Guards, with the bluest eyes I have ever seen, and his gentle-voiced wife, Cicely: to my subsequent immense embarrassment, I spent the first evening I met him explaining the functions of the liver in the body. How it came about I cannot imagine; we laughed about it later, but why, oh why, couldn't someone have told me! Yvonne Chudleigh would appear like a blast of strong sea air from Cornwall, tell me the latest gossip, then disappear into a waiting taxi with the elegant young naval officer she was shortly to marry; Jane Donn Byrne, daughter of the Irish novelist, a Rosalind-like figure in the trousered uniform of the fire service; Geoffrey Sansom, with whom I spent pleasant evenings, and a day at the zoo –

he was later reported missing, believed killed, after an air raid over Germany.

There were pub friends too: Felix Hope Nicholson wearing old, finely embroidered silk waistcoats, and his two good-looking sisters, Lauretta and Marie-Jacqueline; the Coopers, alike to look at, both lawyers. A charming elderly Irishman called Brading who came from Nenagh (near my family home) whose family owned property which housed the Garda station. His married sister who lived there collected the rent from it. When she died during the war, he wrote them a polite letter (which he showed me) concerning the transfer of the property to his name. Some months later they replied, saying they had always paid the rent to Mrs — and they couldn't consider handing anything over to a stranger. Robert Herring, editor of *Life and Letters*, who lived opposite the Eight Bells, added a touch of colour when he joined us from time to time, dressed in a pillar-box red, nineteenth-century army uniform.

Some months after Pearl Harbor a new uniform appeared on the streets, and in the pubs of London: the curious parti-coloured (mushroom-pink trousers, and olive jacket) uniform of the American army officer. To begin with it was a rare sight, seen only in the West End of London, and as such it provoked certain interest. It was some time before this uniform was seen generally, particularly in the borough of Chelsea. For specialists of military uniforms (such as Barbosa) there appeared in the Eight Bells a puzzling anomaly.

A tall, extremely slender young man with penetrating yet friendly brown eyes, a pleasing, ready smile revealing very white teeth and dark curly hair was dressed in the uniform of a British army officer, yet with badges both of rank and regiment unknown to us all. As we had long been told to look for German spies dressed as nuns (we would know them by their boots) and other like discrepancies, for a few days he and his companion, a tall, beautiful blonde with slanting eyes, were a subject for discussion, as they sat apart, talking quietly together. Standing next to them at the bar one evening, Peter heard the girl address him as Constantine.

'He must be a Russian officer,' said Peter authoritatively.

This remark carried a certain weight, and those regulars convinced we had a spy in our midst were silenced. When he looked around the pub, his cherubic smile was returned by the less fanatical clientele as their fears subsided. The ten-day wonder was over as they became 'regulars' themselves, sometimes in the company of a dramatically thin, black-haired girl, with eyes like a Byzantine empress, and a tall handsome blond man. They always left enormously long butts to their cigarettes, which Peter and I would carefully collect for our butt tin.

Several weeks later I was enjoying my drink and reading a book after walking the dog, when he came alone into the almost empty pub. I looked up and smiled as he walked to the bar, then bent down to attract the pub-owner's attention through the tiny glass aperture, to order his drink. I looked up again; surely the colour of his jacket and trousers were different? As he turned round, I saw he was dressed in an American olive army jacket, with unmistakably British khaki trousers. He leaned against the wall at the end of the bar, his long legs crossed at the ankles. An elderly man whom I hadn't seen before got up and went over to him, took his hand and pumped it up and down vigorously.

'You're the first Yankee soldier I've seen since 1918,' he said enthusiastically, 'you boys pulled us out of a tight corner in France then. Welcome back. I'd like to buy you a drink. What'll it be, whisky, gin?'

Towards the end of his speech, the old men's voice had acquired an accent he assumed to be American.

The young man gave a rather embarrassed smile. He tapped his toe on the ground as he said:

'Thank you so very much, I'll have a mild and bitter.' This was delivered in the purest tones of the accent known as Oxford English. The old man looked flabbergasted and not a little annoyed. He felt gypped, so sure was he the answer would be 'Scartch', delivered, with luck, in a Brooklyn accent. Two regulars exchanged significant glances.

The young man's name was Constantine FitzGibbon, and although American born, with an American mother, he had been brought up and educated in England, France and Germany. It is therefore not surprising that he spoke with an Oxford accent, having attended that scholastic settlement for some years. His curious succession of uniforms was explained by his transferring from the British army at a time when there were scarcely any American soldiers, and certainly not uniforms, in England. Later on when we became friends, Peter would tease Constantine by calling him the 'Middle-Western Max Beerbohm'. From now on I would occasionally join his party, at their request, if I was on my own. The Byzantine empress became a lifelong friend of mine; she was the actress Diana Graves, niece of Robert Graves the poet. Her father, an immensely well-groomed man, when adviser to the Tangier government, was known by his colleagues as 'Graves Superieur'. The handsome blond man was her husband, the actor Michael Gough. Sometimes they were joined by an extremely pretty girl, her superb figure set off by an immaculate uniform of the ATA. Her face and elegant figure seemed familiar to me as she walked across the pub, with the assurance that very attractive woman have, to greet Peter. She was one of the 'beauties' of those far-off Paris days, and Constantine's sister, Mimi.

This incidental meeting hastened our friendship, for in those alarming times of departure 'to destinations unknown', sometimes with no return, even the most unsentimental of us tended to cling to the friends and customs of the peaceful past. Perhaps quite erroneously, if you had known someone 'before', they had a verity not easily acquired by wartime acquaintances.

For some time Peter and I had been, almost imperceptibly to ourselves, growing apart. Some days of his off-duty time we didn't see each other at all; instead of being home to greet me in the evening, there would be a note saying he had gone to dine, with Isabel, Anna, Joan, Donald or one of a dozen other friends. This happened very gradually; I realized it only when I found myself making appointments for the days I knew he would be at home. There was no change in our attitude or feelings to each other, but the tough outer edge of the fibre that had bound us together for nearly five years was beginning, very gently, to fray; the kissing time was almost over. Yet he was to me, still, as Charles Lamb wrote of Thomas Fuller, my 'dear, fine, silly, old angel' and always would be.

It is difficult to know the precise moment when one becomes attracted to someone else. It is certainly some time before one is conscious of it and even then it is often not immediately realized or, if it is, pushed by safety-valve impulses into the back of the mind. Often if opportunity, fate, call it what you like, does not arise to nurture the attraction, it will lie fallow, eventually wither and die.

Constantine and the tall beautiful blonde with slanting eyes quarrelled and parted. Constantine spent more time in the Eight Bells, both with friends and alone. How or why it happened I shall never know yet, in the course of an evening spent alone together, we found twelve hours later that we were passionately, irrevocably in love.

I told Peter of my feelings the next day. He hunched his shoulders, the eyes clouded slightly, as he said:

'I'm not really surprised, Pussy, I always thought he was just the chap for you. Promise me one thing: if we meet together, don't call both of us darling; behave as if we had just met.' He caressed my ear, and went to his studio.

When he was on duty I packed my personal belongings: there was a letter addressed to me propped in front of my carriage clock on the mantelpiece. I avoided opening it until I was finished. The two suitcases were heavy; I took the first one downstairs to the hall; on the way back I heard the phone ringing. It was Sophie.

'I came home on leave yesterday. Peter says you've gone off with an American. You haven't, have you? What are you up to?' We arranged to meet later in the day.

The front door was blocked by a tall figure in a dark overcoat, although the August day was warm. It was Donald Maclean. His manner was stern, his immense height overwhelming.

'I've come to talk to you about Peter. You can't seriously consider leaving him after all these years. He loves you, and needs you.'

I was almost in tears as I put my hand on his arm.

'Let's go and have a drink, Donald. I want desperately to talk to you.'

The sun was strong, casting long black shadows as we walked along Christchurch Gardens to an unfamiliar pub called The Surprise. The high ceiling inside, the open double doors, made it unusually bright, and I wished I had brought my dark glasses. As I talked, and he understood my inner turmoil, he became less forbidding, but still I couldn't convince him that what I was doing was right for both Peter and myself. He saw it only as self-justification. Finally I took Peter's crumpled letter from my handbag and handed it to him. He unfolded the long sheets torn from a sketching block, written in Peter's distinctive left-handed writing, and read:

> Friday Night.
>
> My dear Pussy,
>
> Unless I write now impromptu, if one can use the word of so prompted an action, I am sure I shall never do so; and I wish you to go away knowing that I know how much I am grateful to you, how much I owe you. Of myself, of course I speak: when I came back here to England I think I was as much in a state of collapse as France was: the war, other things, had entirely upset me and I was completely adrift and incapable of action; you rescued me and put me on my feet, made it possible for me to do the one thing I want to do but which without you would have been so much more difficult; you made it practically possible for me to paint and gave me the mental armistice from the war without which I would not have been able to continue; and I shall always be grateful to you.

I'm not in love with you and except for a brief spell (not when I first met you; much later) didn't see how I could be – I like dirty, black-haired women – but I do love you very much, and it would make me happy that you should be so. I've tried to love you – I would so much have liked to, I admire you so much, you have all that I lack: but I can't and you know I can't. I've been 'faithful' to you longer by a dozen times or so (not wholly by laziness, but because I wanted to be) than ever to anyone else; but it wasn't possible and I'm very glad indeed that you've found someone else, it seemed such a terrible shame that you should be wasted on an unresponsive person. Dear Pussy, I hope you'll be luckier this time, you do deserve it.

Love,

Peter.

P.S. (i) Can't I have 'Mouche'?

(ii) Don't keep saying 'I can't tell you . . .'

(iii) Can't I have 'Pinkie'? [the tall, beautiful blonde with the slanting eyes]

(iv) Will you give me the address of the shop at which you get the coffee?

(v) I like Constantine and rely on you to persuade him to behave as if I met you this evening with him.

(vi) Would you write and have printed a short circular which I can send or hand out to such people as Pendock, Mr Brading, Cooper's, Maybee's, answering in a nutshell, such questions as 'How is, where is T—'?

(vii) Don't drink very much. Have some children, and be as good to everyone as you were to me.

Dear Pussy,

adieu

Peter.

The lock of golden-brown hair fell over his forehead, the steady hazel eyes looked at me, as Donald carefully folded the letter, put it into my hand and closed his large hands around mine.

'Forgive me for interfering,' he said, 'it's almost impossible to understand why people do things unless you know the whole story.'

PART TWO
CONSTANTINE'S BOOK

(1943 to 1946)

Chapter One

'I am,' he said, 'the marrying sort; some men are, you know. Thanks to Mr A. P. Herbert,' he emphasized the word *Mr*, 'I can't marry you until at least next March.'

I watched his reflection in the large Empire looking-glass as I wondered how the inoffensive-looking, mild-eyed man we saw in the local pub could possibly stop Constantine from marrying. It passed through my mind briefly that he might have a persecution mania of which I had no experience. The tick of my clock seemed unnaturally loud for such a delicate instrument and appeared twice as fast as I remembered it.

'You do want to marry me, don't you?'

I replied with complete honesty that I hadn't thought about it. Due to my upbringing I considered marriage was for life and shouldn't be entered into hastily. The penetrating eyes fixed on me, then he smiled.

'Quite right too. Let's have another glass of your grandmother's delicious elder-flower wine. Put some gin in it, and make it good and strong.' The wine, like floral-tasting pee was very strong on its own; nevertheless I complied with his wishes.

'What's A. P. Herbert got to do with our getting married?'

'He put through some ridiculous legislation saying you had to be married for three years before you can get a divorce. My three years doesn't expire until March. Damn fool,' he said, as though it had been especially designed to inconvenience him alone.

It was the late summer of 1943 and Constantine and I were living in a small charmingly furnished house in Godfrey Street, Chelsea. On one side there was the gaping void of a bombed house and on the other side our neighbour was Stephane Grappelli, whose hours of dexterous practice filtered through the walls and gave our house a marvellously weird sort of enchantment. This only took place during the daytime as he was playing in Piccadilly with the Hot Club de France in the evenings, at Hatchetts I think. He was very friendly, and when we expressed our enjoyment he would leave his door open for us to hear better on warm summer days.

My life had changed considerably: there were always people calling, the ping of the arriving taxi; the phone ringing constantly, the sweet smell of American cigarettes and impromptu parties. As well as going to pubs we went to very different places like the rather grand American Club in Piccadilly, the Ritz and the Berkeley. The five-shilling limit on meals meant that almost everywhere was accessible. I had given up my job and concentrated on reading all Constantine's books as I had read Peter's, listening to music and making as comfortable a home as I could. Even Mouche became domestic and gave birth to six splendid poodle puppies.

There was, too, the difference of the life passionate as against the life affectionate. Constantine's paradoxical nature, which was in turn bohemian, puritan, yet sybaritic, inspired arguments, and in a way competition, which had never happened to me before. Yet there was always the sweetness of reconciliation: the long, lusty connubial Sunday mornings in the downy double bed; the noise of gunfire and bombs drowned by the gushing rushing tumultuous lovemaking.

Every day seemed to produce some new experience or excitement: I was living with a man who wanted to, and was convinced, he could, do everything. My domesticity became ever-increasing. The search for food took more and more time, for with the many callers, some who stayed for hours, even days, meals had to be provided. I would make huge pots of onion soup, and when the horseflesh shop opened in Chelsea Manor Street not only the dogs profited, but also ourselves, for I had no scruples about making enormous horse-liver pâtés and jellied tongues. Would everyone's enjoyment have been so great had they known, I wonder? I even made a rook pie one day, which was eagerly devoured.

On my shopping expeditions I often met Peter doing his shopping while Mary was at work, and sometimes we would have a drink together. It was during one of these meetings that he said hesitantly to me:

'How do you get married?'

'Why ? Are you thinking of it?' I asked.

He mumbled something about Mary and then stopped. I explained that you had to get a licence, or go to a clergyman, whichever you wished.

'How much does it cost?' he asked.

I didn't really know but said that I would find out for him, and we arranged to meet in a pub the next day.

Over the months I had thought of him often and of how he would survive on his own, so I was exceedingly happy about Mary. The next day when we met I pushed an envelope into his hand saying:

'Take this as a wedding present.'

It was the details and money for the licence. He smiled the sweet lazy smile of his and patted my knee.

'Dear Pussy, what would we all do without you?'

He had hardly finished speaking when the door opened and a beaming Donald Maclean came in, his face dropping slightly when he saw me.

'It's all right, Donald,' I said, 'we were just discussing Peter and Mary's wedding.'

He immediately relaxed and bought some drinks.

'Here's to it, isn't it marvellous news? All the world loves a wedding.'

'No, Donald: all the world loves a lover.'

He made a slight *moue* and it is that expression I remember, for it was the last time I ever saw him.

Chapter Two

Constantine had three sisters, all older than he was, and all different both in looks and personality. I think he felt closest to Mimi the youngest one for they had seen more of each other as children. Mimi was exquisitely pretty and a temptress. Whenever she appeared something unexpected, and frequently odd, happened. This you knew in advance, and if you went on any expedition with her you gave yourself up, wholeheartedly, to whatever took place. Mimi was married to Claude Mounsey, who was in the Navy, and at this time she lived just a few minutes' walk away in Markham Street.

It was on a Sunday in March that Mimi arrived at Godfrey Street with Armor Archbold, her 'young man' of years ago, and a delicate, good-looking young woman: 'Flea' she seemed to be called. I don't think Constantine had seen Armor since the palmy days in the south of France before the war when he was about seventeen. Armor was now in the American Air Force, and it was a reunion *par excellence*.

After an extremely boozy lunch, Mimi decided she wanted to go swimming. This was the fifth year of a tedious war and the end of a long winter. But where to go to satisfy this curious desire? Flea Selsdon in a very quiet voice suggested her club. By this time we all wanted to swim very much indeed. The club was the Lansdowne in Berkeley Square, and we were bowed in. The swimming pool of course was closed for the winter, the lights out, and the water cold. Mimi, however, never daunted, said she wished to look at the swimming pool. This curious wish was granted, and we were led down to the pool, which was in complete darkness. A dim light was switched on, and with a look of complete incomprehension on the porter's face, there we were left.

It was a long pool, dark and cold: Armor, used to Miami and other warm watering-places, shivered. We of sterner stuff decided to look around. Mimi, Flea and I found a small room rather like in a girl's school with standing coat-rails and, on the numbered hooks, a great selection of bathing costumes. We looked them over, took our choice and quickly undressed to put them on. We couldn't find any men's costumes, so we took the most conservative of the ladies', for Armor and Constantine. On the way back to the swimming pool through a very dark corridor we encountered a very small old lady. I was ahead of the others and she stopped me. Thinking she wanted some directions I was about to say that I was a stranger there, when Mimi and Flea caught up with us. The old lady took my hand and, leaning forward, said in a very sonorous voice: 'It's the Ides of March. Never do anything unusual on the Ides of March!' We thanked her and hurried along. Of course we laughed about it, but it was weird; what was she doing down there, and why did she feel so anxious to impart to us her doleful message?

We had our swim, shivered, and while we were dressing it was discovered that Flea had forgotten to take off her earrings, rubies and diamonds, as I remember, and had lost one of them. Mimi and I put back the wet bathing clothes and dived into the pool to see if the earring was on the bottom. Perhaps Constantine did too, I can't remember. It was never found, so we dressed, and in a more subdued frame of mind went to have some warming drinks. Too many, no doubt, as later that night we were involved in a fight through someone making insulting remarks about American soldiers – a common occurrence in those days, and one which never failed to make us angry. By that I mean Mimi and me.

Two days later, on 21 March 1944, after a tremendous official wrangle with the army authorities, Constantine and I got married. The difficulty was that his divorce hadn't come through in time for him to give the three months' notice of marriage. One dialogue went as follows:

'It says here, captain, that you married Margaret Aye Moung in 1939, and now you want to marry Theodora Rosling. Can you explain this?'

'Haven't you ever heard of bigamy?'

Not the way to deal with humourless officials. It was eventually due to General Bradley that permission came through on the very day, but that is Constantine's story.

It was a pretty busy Ides of March that year.

Dylan Thomas and Teddy Rose were to have been our best men or witnesses or whatever they are called. Also Nikki Price-Jones had bought the wedding ring. (Sophie by this time had been conscripted into the ATS.) Rings were extremely difficult to get then, at least the kind I wanted was, and Nikki had been deputed or had volunteered to get one. She arrived at Godfrey Street about ten o'clock in the morning. The wedding was fixed for eleven o'clock at the Chelsea Registrar's Office where Constantine had been married to Margaret a few years before. No permission from the army had been granted by the time Nikki arrived, and frantic phone calls came from Constantine to go ahead no matter what. At 10.30 Teddy came, still no groom; at 10.45 Constantine arrived in a taxi waving a piece of paper and carrying two floral sprays. The one for me was quite the wrong colour, a deep red, to go with my cinnamon coat, so Nikki had to have that one, and I pinned a somewhat inferior but nevertheless more fittingly coloured one to my lapel. We got into the taxi and decided that before getting married we would have a drink at the Six Bells, which was opposite the registrar's office.

'Sorry, no spirits.' With what delight that used to be uttered. I had a glass of port and the others a half-pint of cold bitter. Mr Algernon Whiting was the registrar: a Victorian looking gentleman, and well named.

'Good morning, Mr FitzGibbon, it is indeed a pleasure to see you again.' ('My boys are doing well.')

This put us in a very giggly frame of mind. My mother hadn't yet appeared and neither had Dylan, but that was understandable as he was coming from Bosham in Sussex and trains were often a day late if there had been air raids *en route*.

Just as the simple ceremony was ending, my mother

appeared in the doorway with her hat on back to front. She really did look very comical and we all burst out laughing.

'I hope you realize that this ceremony is binding?' said Mr Whiting, looking over the top of his spectacles.

We had arranged to have a reception in the Rivoli Bar of the Ritz Hotel. On no account would the Ritz allow the two large poodles, Mouche and her son, to share our nuptial celebrations, so they were left disconsolately at home. It was a pleasant party; you simply ordered what you wanted to drink, and my aunt, very handsomely, was going to pay the bill afterwards. What could have been better? Quite a lot of people who usually drank there at that time of the morning joined in our party and at least one old friend of Constantine's, Halsey Colchester, was among them. Generally, most of the guests drank Pimm's of one form or another. Constantine's father, who liked his drinks very strong, had a double Drambuie put into his. Two of these were inadvertently drunk by young Janie Donn Bryne, who behaved very oddly when she got back to her fire service post in Westminster.

Teddy had to go back to the army, but another American friend called Ferdinand Helm had taken his place by the time it came for luncheon. Constantine's family had all, curiously enough, gone off to see Tallulah Bankhead in *Lifeboat*, and so my family and Ferdie, Nikki and I went in to eat. But where was Constantine? A rapid search of all possible places proved fruitless. Well we'd better start – oysters, a foolish choice after all that whisky Pimms, but there you are. After at least twenty minutes, Constantine appeared.

'But where have you been?'

'To the bank to cash your aunt's cheque so that I could pay for the lunch.'

More wine and more oysters were ordered. A very punctilious flunkey then appeared, bent low over my new husband's shoulder, and in solemn tones announced: 'There is a personage in the bar, sir, who *says* he is a member of your party.'

We both went to see who it was, and there perched on a

bar stool, wrapped so it appeared in two or three very long woollen scarves, sat Dylan. I still think of him as the best man no matter what.

As there was only two days leave going, the honeymoon was spent in some rum dives, and usually with at least two other people if not more. After the wedding breakfast we did a round of those afternoon drinking clubs that mushroomed during the war. Pluto's, Maisie's, Eileen's and so on. It was in the latter than an incident took place which to this day I don't remember, but Dylan, Ferdie and Nikki all swore it happened.

I suppose that by this time I was 'over-excited' as my mother tactfully put it, but it appears that Constantine and I had an altercation and I threw my drink at him. He ducked and it landed smack on the brand-new hat of a tart sitting at the next table. According to all reports she behaved splendidly and on finding that it was our wedding day bought us a bottle of champagne. Well-intentioned though it was, it didn't mix with the oysters and everything else. Not that I'm blaming her for anything that happened later.

Sometime in the late afternoon we got back to Godfrey Street; to a house full of dog shit and biscuits as Dylan put it. There we found a case of Madeira sent by my grandmother. Even we couldn't broach it just then. At Nikki's persuasion I had a lie down. As I went up the stairs I heard Dylan declaring from Joyce's *Ulysses* , in that wonderful voice: 'The son unborn mars beauty: born, he brings pain, divides affection, increases care,' etc. Nikki, not realizing it was a quote, thought he was being prophetic.

Very much later, it seemed to me, I woke up to darkness. The faithful Nikki was still there, having fed the dogs and washed up endless dirty glasses. She had to catch a train to Kent. I inquired where everyone was. They had just left to go to the King's Head and Eight Bells, on Chelsea Embankment; the dog had gone too, she loved pubs and often went to them on her own. I got a taxi for Nikki and then made my way towards the river.

I had got as far as the top of Upper Cheyne Row when I

heard the sound of many voices singing to a guitar accompaniment. I hurried on in the blacked-out streets, and a little further down a wet dog's nose was put into my hand. It was Mouche, the poodle, begging me to join the fun. Although such a party might be a common occurrence today, in wartime London it was not.

Constantine, Dylan and Ferdie had made at least one stop before the Eight Bells. There they had encountered an elderly gentleman named Bill Gee with his guitar. He was a delightful character, and after an evening spent together we all went back to Godfrey Street. Bill Gee's trousers may well have been split from end to end, but as an entertainer he was superb. He told us that he lived with his eldest son. Dylan, the family man, asked him with an almost smile-in-the-voice tone one uses about children, how old his son was. 'Fifty-seven.' At one point during the long night Dylan said to me: 'You are lucky, you have jesters, musicians and tumblers at your wedding. I didn't have any.'

Now Dylan was very frightened of air raids, and announced this during the night. At about four o'clock when we went to bed Dylan was tucked up on the sofa, and Bill Gee still in the armchair. When the sirens went, Bill Gee woke up and said: 'You don't have to be frightened, your old friend Bill Gee is here.' Dylan said that was the one air raid he *might* have slept through.

At eight o'clock in the morning I heard Bill Gee leave the house, strumming 'Daisy, Daisy, give me your answer do'. It was the only time I ever saw him except on Victory night the following year when there he was standing next to me at the bar of the Black Lion in Paulton's Square.

When I came downstairs the day after my wedding I found three rather green faces. The case of Madeira had been broached and wasn't the answer at all. Nobody either looked or felt very well. We went off to Fred's bar at the Royal Court Hotel in Sloane Square to have something like a gin fizz, or a Tom Collins, that didn't taste like drink. Robert Newton, the actor, with a face the colour of old mahogany, was already there having just ordered one of them. I sat on the bar stool next to him, Dylan on the other side of me. I looked from face to face. Dark mahogany on one side, and unripe melon on the other. 'There's men for you,' I thought. Annie Newton, Bob's wife, came in and Constantine said: 'Oh Annie, Theo and I have just got married.' Annie looked around at all the faces and replied: 'What gluttons for punishment we all are!'

Nevertheless that marriage lasted for nearly seventeen years.

Chapter Three

The next three or four months were perhaps the most idyllic I have ever spent. Constantine was the first 'young man' I had ever liked, he was twenty-four at the time, and we loved and laughed, and talked, and drank; but for the war everything would have been perfect. He used to say: 'Won't it be wonderful when the war's over, and we've nothing to worry about except money?'

I, who had determined not to marry until I was thirty, was enchanted by my new domesticity. The 'snail with the house on her back' had a house at last. For the first time there was money, although we were always broke by the end of the month. Shopping for the hard-to-find food could be done during the day, instead of in a rushed lunch-hour or on Saturday afternoons. I enjoyed finding out about food and how to cook it; in fact I enjoyed everything.

Most of all I loved listening to Constantine talk. His conversation was as bright and vivid as the sight of a kingfisher. Our friends at that time numbered some of the most interesting minds of our generation and, disliking compulsory education, I would say that any knowledge I have gained has been through listening to the conversation of intelligent men and women. I had read all Peter's books, and now I read most of Constantine's. Constantine's mind was like an Aladdin's cave to me. We used to love to argue, and often I would take a side that I didn't really believe in simply to enjoy the argument. Not for nothing had I been dubbed 'the intellectual's moll' by Peter.

What was Constantine like then? Very tall and slender, curly hair, and quick brown laughing eyes, with a natural, easy smile, would be the immediate impression. Charming, immensely full of life. Full of everything: love, ideas and a spontaneous gaiety which I have never found since.

It was all new and wonderful. He was quite unlike anyone I had ever known.

He seemed so very mature that I never realized how hurt he had been by the failure of his first marriage. It wasn't entirely preoccupation with myself, as even now Constantine in periods of deep misery and unhappiness can, and will, exude the same gaiety if his mind is entranced. I simply didn't believe in his jealousy; I thought it was play-acting. Not that I did anything at that time to cause his jealousy, but it was there even without any cause. Perhaps the most alarming side-issue of jealousy is that it is contagious or infectious. I, who had never known it, was to become contaminated, and that was to lead to sorrow.

It was a warm early summer, and we would wander in the evenings through the pleasant Chelsea streets to one pub or another, whichever had the supply of beer. Constantine, although it was strictly prohibited, used to change from his army uniform to his prewar faded corduroys, and I would take off my shoes and walk barefoot beside him. There was a little wall about two feet high outside the Godfrey Street house, and this we would sometimes sit on. An American woman who lived in the same street talked to us there one evening. 'What war work are you going to do?' she asked me. Constantine answered for me: 'She's going to look after me, and have twelve sons, all named after Roman emperors.'

It didn't happen quite that way. But I did want to look after him, and I would have been quite happy to have the twelve sons, although I feel the one called Heliogabalus would have had a halter round his neck. We were, as Constantine's mother would say, 'on the crest'.

I have always felt, and still do, that women lost an awful lot by emancipation. True, they gained certain privileges, but by and large to be a woman in the correct sense of the word had been dissipated. I would no doubt have been a suffragist, but never a suffragette for instance. Had I been of an age in 1916 in Ireland I would certainly have been in the Cumannna m'Ban, and I hope the College of Surgeons with the Countess de Markiewizc. And in fact, Irish women, when all their men were in prison, carried on the revolution, and afterwards they went back, looked after their men, and in many cases had twelve sons, all named after saints. It is not an affectation when I say that I have never understood the English, nor they me. That is not to say that I haven't a few very good English friends – but I would never, for instance, have married an Englishman. Constantine *sounded* English, that is he had an educated English voice, but he was anything but English in his thought and behaviour. Indeed, how could he be? His mother was American, and his father half Irish and half Scottish; he was born in Massachusetts in America, and had served in the British army before transferring himself to the American forces.

One of the books he gave me to read was George Santayana's *The Last Puritan*. I thought then and still do, that the main character is remarkably like Constantine.

Quite a lot of people during the war got married because of the fear that one or other of them (this was a civilians' war, as well as the soldiers') might be killed and never see each other again; also for economic reasons. The army allowance for wives was, I don't care what anybody says, an incentive. The curious thing about our marriage was that when it actually happened we were much poorer. It came about like this. Constantine had already been married: when he married me his income was cut by some twenty pounds a month, *because* he was living with his wife *under the same roof*.

Dylan and Caitlin came back to the Manresa Road studio for a few months, unable to put up with the 'damned banned area' of Bosham as Dylan put it. The German raids on London were preferable. It was then that the sustained friendship I had found with Caitlin in the autumn flourished still more. They had the baby, Aeronwy, with them, and also the poodle puppy Dombey that they had in fact bought from us for a nominal figure. I spent one whole day clipping and bathing the puppy, and when Caitlin came to collect him she was convinced it was another dog, and wanted Dombey back.

Up until the time I had met Caitlin my clothes were very similar to the ones I usually wear today. Coloured woollen stockings (nylons were new then, and unobtainable anyway), a straight skirt, and either a blouse or a sweater. This was my winter garb; in summer it would be a cotton dress usually gathered in at the waist as the dresses were then. Oh! and the snood. This was a wonderful invention for wartime England, when there were many disturbed nights, and no time to go to hairdressers (not that I ever did); they were made of a coarse fishnet, like a bag, and threaded with elastic. You popped all the back of your hair into them and there you were. It was a mark of defiance then for young women to have shoulder-length hair, as it meant that you weren't in the forces, and therefore, not conforming. Until they became over-popular, they were both attractive and useful.

Caitlin's clothes, however, followed no fashion but made one. She knew a little woman who collected clothes made from beautiful velvets, Indian silk, damasks, nankeen, georgette, chiffon, ninon; a stream of beautiful names for forgotten materials. I never found out where this paragon lived, but occasionally Caitlin would give me one or another of these dresses which I particularly admired. I remember especially a midnight-blue velvet frock with a heart-shaped neckline which I wore when I got to New York in 1946 and which was admired by everyone. To this day I still have an enormously long, tattered raw silk, cream scarf, which I used to wear as a blouse, draped sari-fashion, and one little cushion is covered by a rose-pink velvet from one of the 'creations'.

Although we were both Irish, both blonde and from neighbouring counties in Ireland, we couldn't have been more different to look at. In fact it is a mystery how I could jam myself into Caitlin's clothes; I was a good two inches taller, bigger boned, and what used to be called 'classical-looking'. Nevertheless I did, to the amazement of both Constantine and, I think, Dylan. Once, Desmond Ryan's wife, Isabel, asked me if I was in fancy dress. I was delighted.

But if I was living the plush life it can have been far from that for Caitlin. How she managed I shall never know; there was little money, but always that delicious pot of Irish-Welsh stew on the stove, enough to feed ten people, and the studio was home.

We were all very quick-tempered in those days, it was a savage time, and I don't think Caitlin was any more so than the rest of us. We sincerely believed that to keep things to ourselves was wrong, and that marriage meant sharing everything. Perhaps I would behave differently now, but I doubt it. Although Caitlin could be fierce, she was no fiercer than I was with far less to be fierce about. I loved going round to their studio and noticing all the things that she had done, most of them no doubt missed by our menfolk. She had even planted the broken-down window-boxes with flowers.

Generally we would meet in the evenings for a few glasses of beer or Guinness. Spirits were never on sale in a pub unless you were a regular customer, then you might be given one; only in the hotels and flossier bars. In fact in a pub where you weren't known you had to bring your own glass! Our evening walks got longer and longer, but it was no doubt good for us. Whenever we gave a party it was my grandmother who supplied the booze; she was 'registered' with all the shops she had dealt with pre-war, and was allowed *one* bottle per month. Being the sane old granny who had 'lent the quid' a few years earlier, she always dibbed up, and we had our party. Occasionally Constantine got a bottle from the *PX*.

The Thomases and many other people would come to our house in Godfrey Street; Peter Rose Pulham and Mary, now married, John Davenport, Philip Lindsay, Vernon Watkins and quite a few American dons in the army. Generally, though, we spent part of the evening in a pub, and would then go back and eat in whoever's house was nearest, read poems aloud, play records, dance, or just talk. Dylan and I would often go alone to the Classic Cinema on the corner of Markham Street to see any old film which took our fancy. Once we were asked to leave as we sobbed so loudly.

One evening we were at Caitlin and Dylan's studio. The baby was being fretful, and although the stew was richly going strong, I had got some eggs from the country and we decided to have an enormous omelette as well. It is difficult to realize now that we were *always* hungry. There simply wasn't enough to eat. I whipped the eggs and looked round for something to fill the omelette with. Our ration that winter had been one pound of onions per person. I opened several cupboards and drawers, and in one I found a whole heap of shallots. Knowing that Caitlin and Dylan had been in Sussex, I thought they must have brought them up with them. I peeled, sliced and cooked them, made a magnificent dish and proudly bore it in. We all fell on it, and then seconds later started to feel not only odd, but sick. Caitlin questioned me as to where I had found the shallots: 'In that drawer.' Her reply was terse and to the point. 'You've taken my bloody tulip bulbs for the window-boxes.'

Never, never, no matter how hungry you are, eat a tulip-bulb omelette.

The studio was difficult for Dylan to work in, being only one large room partitioned off, so he would come round to Godfrey Street each morning, as bright and fresh as a home-baked bun, and work in our very small spare room. He wrote a poem there for our wedding anniversary differing from the finished poem in his *Collected Works*. We seldom ever drank at lunchtime; only on a special occasion.

We all seemed much older, we were at least twenty-five, than the footless days in King's Mansions, Oakley Street and Rossetti House. Somehow we had been able to make a pattern, no matter how small, of our way of living.

During all this time the air raids went on, but with less intensity than before. They didn't alarm me unduly unless they were very near. What did cause me to shiver was our mobile anti-aircraft guns, one of which was sited very close to Godfrey Street. The whole house would tremble as the noise reverberated through. Sometimes we would go outside, and see the German plane caught in the searchlights. Then to hear the guns was comforting, and not frightening.

One night they were particularly noisy and Constantine went out to see what was happening; perhaps the aeroplane would be shot down. I was reading and stayed in the sitting room. A little while later I could hear Constantine talking to someone, then I realized it was to the dog who had no doubt followed him out.

'Come on in, oh, do come in, Mouche, I want to shut the door.' All this in the darkened corridor on account of the blackout.

He came into the room; I looked up, and placidly standing beside him was the most enormous St Bernard dog I have ever seen. There was a growl from behind our sofa, and Constantine looked down. I have never seen such a look of surprise on anyone's face. We were all, including Mouche, too dumbfounded to speak. Quite quietly the enormous creature turned round and, slowly and majestically, walked out of the room and out of our lives. We quickly went out into the street. No sign of any dog, large or small, and never did we see a St Bernard again in the vicinity.

There was a knock on the door some time afterwards, and there stood Sophie beaming and looking very healthy. She never wrote letters, and always just appeared when on leave. She came in and we had a drink.

'I've deserted,' she said. 'I simply couldn't stand all those bloody women a minute longer.' She was in civilian clothes but with no luggage.

'But how . . .?' I asked.

'It was simple. I traded in my watch for a ticket to the station-master, said I had lost my ticket.' After a second she added, 'I gave your name and address. Don't tell Con.'

We had just started to talk when a blue-coated figure passed the window. (Chelsea Police Station, where Peter and I had brought the German airman to a few years before, was just around the corner.)

'Quick, upstairs.'

Sure enough there was a heavy official knock at the door. The police were looking for Lance Corporal Warren.

'But isn't she in Wales?'

'No. She's deserted.'

'How did you get my name and address?'

'The person in question falsely gave it as her own, to the station-master at Oswestry.'

'Oh dear, I'm afraid I know nothing about it, officer,' (he was a constable) 'but of course if I hear anything . . .'

'Sorry to trouble you, madam.' Here he hesitated and looked across the room. There were the two glasses we had been drinking from, one still half full. He looked at me again, squarely in the eyes. I opened my large blue eyes and looked squarely back.

'You will pass on any information, no matter how small, won't you?'

'Certainly, officer, but I'm sure there must be a good reason for this misdemeanour. You must excuse me – I have a friend staying here, she's just dressing, and then we are going out.'

Out went the law, and the sound of giggles came from upstairs.

'I heard every word he said. You were wonderful, you sounded so concerned for him.'

Sophie stayed for several weeks. We didn't tell Con to begin with, but she had no clothes, no money, and worst of all no ration book. To spread our rations around she and I would eat out at lunchtime. If Constantine thought it odd that she always dressed in my clothes, he didn't mention it. Nor did he mention the fact that whenever the policemen returning to the station passed us by, Sophie would hide behind the two of us. But after a few weeks he did say:

'What a long leave you've got, Sophie.'

It had to come out. He was quite horrified, and rightly pointed out that as an officer in a foreign army in a foreign country awful things could happen to him for 'harbouring' a deserter. Sophie couldn't stay with us any longer. We thought and thought. Finally, armed with several doctor's certificates, she went sadly back. I did have one postcard from her saying she was sick of peeling potatoes, but very shortly afterwards she got out on 'compassionate grounds', but that is Sophie's story.

CHAPTER FOUR

Second Front Now was scrawled on all the walls, and although I didn't know it, it was shortly to take place. Constantine, as an Order of Battle man, worked late, and came home sometimes full of tension. One night in June he was reluctant to go to bed, and we stayed up talking until dawn. At six o'clock in the morning he switched on the wireless and we heard that a landing had been made on the coast of France. Our relief was tremendous, but for many days afterwards we waited for more news than was given us. Anxious hours and days were spent until it seemed that it had been successful.

Then I knew that Constantine would soon have to follow his generals to France. He wanted me to go down and stay with his mother in Berkshire. My family, including my grandmother, was still in London; my mother was working hard all day with the bewildered and mutilated people of the East End of London, and at an air-raid post at night, so I was reluctant to leave.

One sunny evening in midsummer, he went, dressed in battle-dress, with what looked like a new wooden gun over his shoulder. I'm assured it wasn't, but was the latest American model. The taxi was called, and as he drove off I saw his bunch of keys lying on the hall table. I ran after the taxi. No good. Wherever he went, he didn't have his keys with him.

At Constantine's insistence, I did eventually let the house and go down to Berkshire with the two dogs. I hadn't been at all well. No doubt due to the bombing at King's Mansions, I had miscarried, and needed a minor operation.

Church House, Hurley, had originally been a long row of alms-houses, built about the time of James II, and made into a long grey house about the beginning of this century. From the outside, the rather derogatory word 'picturesque' could be applied to it. Inside, the large rooms were dark, bitterly cold, even in summer and, to tell the truth, depressing. The garden was pretty whenever it was warm enough to sit in it and the Thames snaked along the end of it, periodically flooding over, reducing the ground floor of the house to dank silt. I believe that the previous occupants of the house had been a Protestant clergyman and his family, who no doubt lived on too small a salary, as all the old large fire-places had been removed, and in their places 'all-night burning stoves' had been installed. Now these stoves are excellent if a steady, small heat is needed, but they are not the thing for a forty-foot-long drawing room which never, ever had a glimpse of the sun in it. Also, as fuel was difficult to come by, the doors, which when open gave out a welcoming glow, were usually kept closed to conserve the heat. In front of this useless contraption stood a highly polished brass stand called, I think, a footman.

It was on this that Mimi was always crouched whenever she was at Church House. Even if the doors were open, when Mimi (who was a tall girl) was sitting on the footman in front of this stove, it was impossible to see any fire at all. The family joke was to say: 'Is the fire in, Mimi?' To which she always replied: 'Oh, yes.' We, in the hinterland, put on yet another woolly.

The whole house was impractical. Although there was electric light, the cooking was done, for a minimum of eight people, on an enormous paraffin stove which belched out huge black clouds of smoke on a bad day. Only May, the cook, really understood its temperament.

But if this description of Church House makes it seem grim, the occupants were as colourful a group of people as could be found anywhere.

The atmosphere of the house was dominated by Georgette, Constantine's mother. This is not to say she was dominating, because she was not; nevertheless, an extremely strong and fascinating character. At that time I had met her only a few times and, as good-looking women of all ages all the world over do, we examined each other thoroughly, before committing ourselves to affection, dislike, indifference or whatever other emotion should arise. In fact, we needn't have bothered, as from almost the first day of my arrival until her death, through all the vicissitudes of remarriage, we have shared a great affection for each other. She was then a tall beautiful woman, with golden hair and golden eyes (like a marmalade cat, as Francis used to say), a gentle, soft smile, and one of the most musical laughs I have ever heard. It makes you want to laugh to hear it. She had the manners of, and was, a 'grande dame'. The hardships and unhappiness she experienced only made her more humane in her relationships with other people. A magnificent woman, in all senses of the word, and one whose advice and friendship I valued for many many years.

She was marvellously paradoxical: the housekeeping varied between lavishness and penury accordingly. Mimi defiantly maintained she had once been given grass to eat, dressed with liquid paraffin. As meat was severely rationed I brought back some chickens from a shopping expedition, and was thought wonderfully practical, but I might just as well have been thought hopelessly extravagant. Once coming back exhausted from a cross-country bus trip she told me that the best way to overcome tiredness was to have a hot bath, then lie with one's feet higher than one's head and have two Pernod frappées. A bit difficult in wartime, but I found it successful later on.

Francis, Constantine's father, was staying at Church House during the summer I was there. He was a rotund, merry man, who told very funny stories at which he chuckled himself as he was telling them. His moods never seemed to change: as long as he had enough food, drink and company he seemed content, although he sometimes grumbled about his false teeth which didn't fit properly. It appears that in his brief spell in prison they had taken out all his teeth and given him ill-fitting dentures. This annoyed him, because he said they made him lisp when telling his stories. Before that he had had a perfect delivery. He would, of course, have liked to be immensely rich and give grand dinners and so on, but he never harped on it, and took life very inconsequentially. Whenever he got a cheque he would take me to

Maidenhead, or another nearby town, and blow it on as good a lunch as we could find, endless liqueurs, with taxis all the way. Drink had little or no effect on him; but sometimes the stories got funnier. We were always late home, and he used to say: 'Let's wait until G. has gone to the Old Bell for her drink. She can be a bit sticky before she has her drink.' Often we waited far too long, but Francis would chuckle away no matter how 'sticky' Georgette was. He told me about his time in the French Foreign Legion and the British navy. His comment on the conversational standard in the latter was terse: 'Positive statement, flat denial and personal abuse.'

We would go for long walks along the river-bank, and sometimes be given a basket to pick mushrooms.

'But there aren't any,' Francis used to say, as I jumped over a hedge into a cow-pat. 'Let's go to the Dewdrop Inn or the Black Boy instead.'

We did, and got back late for dinner every time. Very soon we weren't asked to pick mushrooms. He was very boyish. On one of our walks with the two dogs, a sportsman was shooting on the opposite bank of the river. His quarry fell at our feet. Quickly Francis picked up the mallard, and we ran home with it, the sportsman shaking his fist at us from the other side. For the next few days we didn't take that walk, but we were always on the lookout for the fruits of the field. We also tapped the ARP brandy kept in the first-aid box, and very soon it wasn't kept there any more.

It was impossible to be cross with Francis, as Georgette knew so well. She told me that she had never seen him in a bad temper, which surely is unusual in many years of marriage. 'Not even', she said, 'when I was swatting flies in bed one morning, and by accident brought the fly-swatter down on his stomach.' Such a rough awakening did not provoke a word of anger, merely one of those infectious chuckles.

Constantine's eldest sister, Geraldine, was also staying at Church House. She was a beautiful woman, capable of making an extremely pertinent remark from time to time, but in those days preoccupied with looking after her baby daughter. The baby was being brought up as a vegetarian, as commodities like nut butter were ration-free, and she thrived on it. However, when teething time came and tears were frequent, I gave the baby a juicy chop bone to chew on. The tears cleared, and the little sore gums chomped on the bone. Unfortunately, Geraldine came in in the middle, snatched it from the baby's hand, and said indignantly to me: 'She's not a puppy, Theodora!' Francis loved that little *contretemps*.

I was at last notified that there was a bed for me at the Chelsea hospital where I was to have my operation. Constantine wrote from 'somewhere in France' that I was on no account to attempt the journey back from the hospital by the crowded train, but that I should hire a car and driver from Harrods. Constantine had great faith in Harrods.

CHAPTER FIVE

Mimi came to see me in hospital, and when I told her the plan she said it was ridiculous to pay for a man to drive me to Hurley. She would find someone only too pleased to do it. It seemed a good idea. A certain naval commander was produced (Claud, Mimi's husband, was in the Navy, and it all sounded terribly correct), and everything arranged with naval precision. The commander would pick me up at the hospital, bring me to see Mimi and Claud, and then transport me in the greatest luxury to my destination. So it happened. I met Mimi and Claud at a pub in Smith Street, Chelsea, and also a large chow dog that Mimi had found somewhere.

It was a great relief to be out of that clinical atmosphere, and I felt better than I had done for months. I was gay again. Several drinks later Mimi suggested that we drive to Norfolk where they were going to stay in a beautiful old house with Rosemary Langton, whose husband was David Langton, the actor, then away in the army. As an added attraction I was told that Peter and Mary Rose Pulham had a cottage nearby. Peter had gone back to as near to Pulham as he could.

'But what about the petrol?' I inquired. Oh that was all right, Claud's uncle was a rich farmer in Norfolk and everyone knew that farmers had a lot of petrol for their tractors which they didn't use. I still wasn't quite convinced; but they were all, including the naval commander, convincing. I had to telephone my mother-in-law, Georgette, and tell her of the change of plan. It would only take a few hours, in fact it was almost on the way to Berkshire, and I could ring from Norfolk. I looked at the naval commander, now on his fourth pink gin (he was obviously a regular regular). Yes, he was willing; he was only the driver.

An enormous amount of Mimi and Claud's luggage had to be collected and, finally wedged in the back of the car with some of it, Mimi, the chow and I set off.

The journey took much longer than I expected; indeed it was much farther away than I had thought. We arrived at dusk. Rosemary had no telephone; the chow was a present for her and took an instant dislike to her, her children and the country generally; there was no proper bed for the naval commander, not enough food to go round and nothing to drink except a bottle of whisky my grandmother had given me to bring to my mother-in-law. That went first. Then I was anxious to telephone, so the naval commander took me to the nearest pub some three miles away. There was no line to Berkshire unless it was a 'priority' call. One only got these if one was in the forces or some civilian force such as the ARP.

There was a wasp's nest just outside the bedroom window; in the morning hundreds of the stripey creatures were circling around my face and head, dive-bombing with remarkable accuracy. I got a sting on the lip, and from then on kept under the clothes. The noise was appalling.

At breakfast, speaking thickly through my swollen lip, I started on about the telephone, the uncle and the petrol. Nobody paid any attention to me except Mimi, who said quite firmly that 'Mummie would understand,' and there was no hurry. Whereupon they went off to do the shopping, find the uncle, and I, on the grounds that I was just out of hospital, was left to mind the children. Hours later they came back, with very little shopping and no news about the uncle. They were all very gay, enjoying the weekend in the country. I got the naval commander to drive me again to the pub to telephone, unsuccessfully.

I found a bicycle in a shed, and that evening set off for the pub. Still no line to Berkshire unless I had 'priority'.

By the next morning I was very disconsolate. I saw no way of getting to Berkshire, and the naval commander whom I had hired showed even less interest in my plight than the others. I must have been an awful nuisance; also I wasn't feeling all that good. The elation at being out of hospital had passed; the bicycle ride of six miles had done me no good at all, and the wasp sting was painful. Force would do no good, so I started to cajole.

'Let's go over and see Peter and Mary,' I said. I felt Peter would understand and somehow be an ally, and after all Mary had worked at the American Embassy, or something like it, and – who knew – perhaps she had this divine right called 'priority'.

They lived in what appeared to be a tower; it was very picturesque and very primitive. They were delighted to see us all, quarts of beer were produced, and it was obvious that they were both a bit homesick for people, talk and excitement. Peter and Mary thought it very comical that I was in Norfolk and not Berkshire, and when I attempted to explain my predicament, Peter airily waved his hand, took a deep drink and said:

'Don't worry, Theo, you're so practical, of course you'll think of something. I *never* could.'

Mary had no 'priority'.

Much later that day we went to see the uncle. We were not all allowed to call, only Claude. The rest of the party were deposited in a seedy country hotel nearby. We made for the bar. Some hours later on Claude appeared, but no uncle. I heard him say to Mimi:

'He'll be along when she's gone out. It won't be long.'

I had already initiated the call to Berkshire, and there was some hope that it would come through in an unspecified number of hours. I felt more cheerful and enjoyed my drink. The alcohol was doing my wasp-sting a lot of good.

The door was flung open, and a good-looking dapper little man with huge brown eyes came in walking at a crouch, rather like Groucho Marx.

'Where's the car?' he said. 'We've got to get going. She'll be back soon.'

Mimi, Claude and the naval commander sprang to their feet, and I was hustled out despite protesting cries about the phone call.

'Uncle Roly will arrange all that,' said Mimi with remarkable confidence.

As soon as were were out of the village, Uncle Roly snapped into action. He gave directions, and the naval commander appeared to love taking them. Right, left, left fork, hairpin bend, and off we sped. Uncle Roly was clearly a man of action.

'*Stop*, we're here now,' and the hired limousine whined to a stop. A huge notice greeted us: *The Devil's Punchbowl. All Welcome.*

It was what looked like a large private house with a long avenue. We drove up, and a mild-faced brown-haired woman greeted Uncle Roly as though she were his long-lost housekeeper. I immediately felt that the brown-haired lady would be an ally. But once inside, the picture changed rapidly. All the downstairs rooms of this large house had, it appeared, been turned over to make a bar, restaurant, games room and so on for the American base nearby. It was packed. We made for the bar, and there the brown-haired lady left us, smiling kindly and saying: 'I know you'll be happy here.'

Uncle Roly was delightful company, and gave one a sense of well-being. Several American officers started a crap game on the floor, and it wasn't long before Mimi joined them.

'Come seven, come snake eyes,' was repeated over and over again. I took a throw, lost and retired. I didn't follow the game, so felt best out of it. There was no sign of the naval commander, and Claude and his uncle had a lot to talk about. I wandered about the house. Everywhere were soldiers, playing records, eating or just lounging about. I asked for the telephone, and put through my call once more. I would have to wait.

Coming back to the bar I found Uncle Roly alone. I asked him what the petrol situation was like in the country. He said he had no idea as he hadn't got a car. I thought this odd for a farmer, but maybe he had an efficient steward.

I was summoned to the phone: there was a three-hour delay. It was now about 6 p.m. and I was getting hungry. I pushed open a door, went down a long corridor and at the end heard kitchen-like sounds. There was the naval commander sitting down at the table finishing what must have been quite a substantial meal. The brown-haired lady was fussing over him. I told him about the phone call, and asked him to broach the subject of petrol to Uncle Roly. At this the brown-haired lady uttered an eldritch scream and then sat down in gales of laughter.

'Roly get you petrol?' she said, 'Roly *always* has to have people get things for him.' She said this with pride.

This was when I had what Mimi subsequently termed my first attack of hysteria. I was soothed and calmed by the brown-haired lady, given a cup of tea, and a promise by the naval commander that he would ask the Americans if there was a chance of any petrol.

'What a charming, efficient man,' said the brown-haired lady. 'I could do with someone like that here.' Then I told her my predicament about the telephone call, and was told it was always difficult to get cross-country calls, but London wasn't too bad. This gave me an idea; I would telephone my mother and get her to pass on a message. There was however no reply from my mother's number; she was obviously still at the first-aid post where she worked.

I was still rather shaken by the temperament I had displayed, and so forthwith explained the situation to Uncle Roly.

'Berkshire,' he drawled over the word, 'a lovely county, haven't been there for years. Wouldn't mind a trip there myself. Mmm, might consider it.'

'Petrol,' I said weakly.

'Oh, these American chaps are riddled with it, don't know what to do with it all. They'd give a pretty girl like you any amount.'

'But surely, not for me to drive away,' I replied.

'Shouldn't be surprised; whatever you might say about these chaps, they're damnably generous.'

It was now nine o'clock, time for the call to come

through, and far too late to set out for Berkshire even if we had got any petrol.

I asked Uncle Roly when he was going home.

'Never, I hope,' he said. 'It's damned nice to have a weekend out. Mmm. Berkshire.'

The naval commander was still in the kitchen, this time cutting a large pile of sandwiches. I ravenously took one.

'I've got a job,' he said.

'Yes, you have.'

'No, I mean a real job. Mrs H. has hired me to be the manager.'

'But what about getting me to Berkshire?'

'Oh, I'll get that fixed up, and get back here as soon as possible.'

A ray of hope.

'But the car has to be taken back to Harrods,' I said, 'and what about the deposit?'

'That's gone now,' the naval commander answered cheerfully. 'And I expect you'll have to pay a good bit more for all these extra days. I'm on the track of some petrol.'

'Can Mrs H. put us all up here tonight?'

She had apparently 'fixed up' Mimi and Claude, and the naval commander had permanent and splendid quarters. No provision seemed to have been made for Uncle Roly or me. I wandered out into the large overgrown but beautiful garden. There was a dilapidated swing. I sat on it. A lonely-looking American soldier approached me. I thought of Constantine, and not for the first time wished, oh, how I wished, that he was here. We talked, and I told him about the petrol, and Berkshire.

'I wish you would stay here, nice girl,' he said, and kissed me gently on the cheek. I felt like crying and hurling myself into his arms, and being comforted.

'I'm in the office, and don't have nothing to do with the petrol, but you might try the loot. But later, please.' He pressed my arm.

I said I had to find my sister-in-law, and hurried away lest I broke down.

In the lounge, Uncle Roly was asleep on the large sofa. He was curled up, and looked even more like Groucho Marx than ever. He opened one eye and patted the sofa. 'Jump up,' he said as though speaking to a pet dog.

I went to the naval commander's quarters and found him sitting in a large armchair, relishing a glass of whisky. I said that I had nowhere to sleep and couldn't find anyone to ask. He said he expected they were all in bed. 'Try the lounge.'

I had, but Uncle Roly was sleeping there.

The rip-roaring weekend had been too much for me. I wept. Phone calls, petrol, beds, Berkshire, all tumbled out amidst sobs. Then the naval commander did a very sweet thing. He patted my head and shoulders and said:

'You can shake down in my bed. I shall be quite happy in this chair.'

I was led into the other room and left. I took off my skirt and blouse, climbed into a bed of down and slept well for the first time since I had left Berkshire two weeks earlier.

The naval commander awakened me with a cup of tea and everything was shipshape. He was dead on the button in his new job.

'Breakfast in the dining room, and I've laid on some petrol. Got to get cracking. Mrs H. wants me back first thing tomorrow morning.'

Uncle Roly was at breakfast looking as spry as when he had first stepped into the dreary little hotel bar.

'Berkshire, mmm, and then London.'

He said this with the glee of a child at Christmas.

I found I had no money left, but the brown-haired lady cashed me a cheque. She said she hoped I would come again, she had enjoyed having me. I smiled wanly.

We had to go back to Rosemary's to get our luggage. Most of it seemed to belong to the naval commander, no doubt used to having all his belongings in one place. We told Rosemary where Mimi and Claude were and she said if she could find a babysitter she'd join them; it sounded fun. Perhaps Peter and Mary might come over?

The car was started and a dreadful noise like a big-end

going deafened us. 'Good God,' said the commander, 'it was shipshape when we drove over.' My heart thumped; another hold-up. However, after investigation it was found that Simon, the older boy, had inserted a piece of metal in the rear wheel. After what seemed like hours it was extricated and we were ready.

Uncle Roly and I sat in the back, the naval commander with his luggage in the front. It was a hot August day. Many adventures overtook us on the journey, but it was nevertheless enjoyable. I found out a lot about Uncle Roly that I hadn't known before. He had apparently no money, and wasn't allowed to have any lest he should disappear just the way he was doing. He was as intent on London as any 'Tommy' in France in the First World War. But what was he going to live on in London? I inquired. He patted his breast pocket and smiled:

'I didn't forget to bring it,' he said, 'even though I was rushed.'

'But what?'

From his breast pocket he produced an enormous gold cigarette case. He patted it.

'She'll see me through,' he said, patting it again and putting it back.

As we got nearer and nearer to Hurley I began to feel sensations of panic. What could I say without involving Mimi and Claude? This was the fourth day I had been 'missing'. Straight from the hospital, too ill to come down by train, and then to turn up with two strange men, and one tipsy?

'I don't think I'd better ask you in, as I'm so late.'

'Pity,' said Uncle Roly. 'I would have liked to have met me nephew's in-laws.' He was by this time lying along the back of the car, and I had to sit forward.

'Another time,' I said, 'when we're not quite so rushed. The commander has to get to London.'

I crept in hoping to get to my room and, I suppose, pretend I had been there for hours. But the dogs spotted me and were delighted to see me. I'd never been so pleased in my life to see them.

'Your mother has been very worried about your disappearance,' said Georgette, my mother-in-law. Francis appeared, beaming all over his face. He loved situations like this.

I explained about the telephone calls, Rosemary, Norfolk, petrol, carefully avoiding what I thought might look like a betrayal of Mimi.

'Oh, you were with Mimi,' said Georgette. 'I quite understand.' She did too, and it was never mentioned again. Mimi had been quite right.

Chapter Six

The quiet country summer of 1944 passed slowly like the smile on a ploughboy's face. I went for walks with Francis; with my baby niece-in-law; we played games in the evening; I read, and wrote long letters to Constantine. Sometimes Mimi would come down for a few days. Quite a few evenings we would all have drinks in the Old Bell at Hurley, which was almost next door. A rich Russian gentleman who was staying there offered me a large diamond which he took out of his jacket pocket for my young dog. His offer was refused with great politeness although Francis said I should have taken it. Occasionally I went to London for a few days, and it seemed as though I had never lived there. I had become that most unlikely, for me, person: a grass war-widow.

One sad incident happened in Hurley. I was good at reading the Tarot cards, and sometimes I would read them for my sister-in-law or guests in the house. A strange little dark woman appeared one day, and that evening I read the pack for her. I never told her or anyone else what I saw that evening in those cards, but try as I would it always came out to her dying by her own hand. When she did so, about a month later, everyone else was most shocked and surprised. Had I told her, would it have hastened that event or stopped it? That I shall never know, but I have never read the Tarot since that evening, no matter how insistent people may be.

We also had several evenings of table-turning. It takes a war for people to want to know their future immediately. Usually, in fact I would say always, the table would give deliciously absurd answers, and we would all vote it the best parlour-game of all. But after one session, when it had been particularly nonsensical, Georgette said to it: 'Would you like to dance?' The most extraordinary thing was that it did: four people still with their fingers meeting on the delicate top of the three-legged table, were danced about the room, and truly, out of the door and up two stairs, after which it and all of us collapsed with laughter. However, after one of those table-turning evenings I went to bed, the two large dogs lying on their mats in the room. At some time during the night I was woken up by a strong, but so strong, smell of garlic. Now this was all the more unusual because in wartime England no garlic ever passed the portals of Church House, Hurley. Would that it had sometimes. As Rosemary used to say:

'We rise from our meals stiff with starch.'

I turned on the bedside lamp. Both the dogs were bristling and snarling about something, and anyone who knows standard poodles knows they never bristle or snarl. They paced about the edge of the room and were loth to come to my bedside. It was really terrifying. Eventually I got out of bed, and we all went for a walk around the garden. When I came back the overpowering smell had completely gone, and we settled down for the rest of the night. The next day I changed rooms with Francis, and we all of us slept soundly thereafter. But I don't remember any more table-turning after that.

As I have already said, my birthday has played an important part in my life. It has to be looked forward to, planned to a certain extent and enjoyed. Usually I am disappointed, and sometimes it has ended in tears. As a child I tried hard to get my feast day counted as an extra birthday, but it never really worked. Had it done so, it would have been perfect. For my feast day is in May, and my birthday in October. But the fivers never turned up in May; only chocolates, or some quite unsuitable piece of wearing apparel. It was dropped on both sides for the fraud it was.

This October I did not know what would happen. Parties were difficult to organize on account of the scarcity of drink, and my grandmother, the only true source of liquor, was still in London. I had decided that we would all have a few extra drinks at the Old Bell, and that would be that.

On the morning of Trafalgar Day, the telegraph boy from the post office next door arrived with a telegram for me:

'Expect me today. Will ring from London. All love, Constantine.'

But where had it been sent from? We all peered at it, but nothing but numbers filled the top of the form from next door. Could it be a misplaced joke? Georgette, whose first reaction to anything unexpected has always been a quick burst of annoyance, said:

'Oh, it's just like Connie to do something unexpected like this.'

All day we speculated and waited for the phone call. I was dressed and re-dressed in various clothes, and finally by six o'clock I was quite dejected. In desperation we all went to the Old Bell. May, the cook, came puffing in just as we were on the first drink.

'Phone . . . quick . . .'

Dressed in a borrowed suit I took the old overstuffed taxi to Maidenhead Station. The October mists swirled about us as in a bad Hollywood film. Trains came and went, but no London train. I was cold and the suit too tight. At last with a roar and a gasp it was there, and with it the 'dark slender boy'.

It appeared that his colonel had lost him in a poker game to the Sixth Army. Therefore Constantine thought the colonel owed him something, so asked him quite seriously if he could fly from Luxembourg, where they were then, to London for his wife's birthday. The colonel, whom I met much later on, told me he was so astonished that he said yes, and even lent him his personal plane and pilot to fly to Paris. However, that was only halfway. The rest of the story is Constantine's. But arrive he did, on my birthday, from the battleground of Europe in 1944.

My brief grass-widowhood was over.

Constantine had decided that the American Sixth Army

was not for him. He would get himself attached to the British army, we would live again in London, and that was that. Such was his personality that one never for an instant doubted that it would happen, and it did, within the space of exactly one week.

Yes, the quiet country summer was certainly over.

Chapter Seven

House-hunting is always a depressing occupation, and in wartime London it was even worse, many of the 'desirable residences' still being thick with the dust of bomb-blast. Then I remembered a pretty studio house, set back in a small cul-de-sac off Upper Cheyne Row, from the days of house-hunting with Peter after leaving Oakley Street. It was indeed desirable, but we could never find either who owned it or the agent. I went to see if it still existed. While strolling around the front garden the door opened and out came a friend, Mary Tolstoi, who was married to a grandson of the writer.

'How nice to see you,' she said. 'Have you come to call? I do hope so.' I didn't like to give my actual purpose, but followed her in. It was a late autumn afternoon and a glowing fire was burning in the comfortable sitting room.

'Let's have some tea and make toast over the fire.'

A delightful idea, and during the course of it I told her how I had found the house empty a few years ago, but could never find its owners. I was so completely at home there, I felt it really should have been mine. But I didn't say so. Anyway it would probably have been far too expensive for us then, and this I did say.

'Oh no, it's only fifty pounds a year,' she replied. 'I got it from the agents at Harrods.'

That was the last place I would have gone to look for a house or flat, which made it seem more elusive and less 'mine'.

'But why so cheap? It's quite large and so very liveable-in.'

'Quite simple,' Mary answered. 'It's haunted, you see. But they're enchanting ghosts, so friendly and happy. Maybe if we're lucky they might be here today: a little later is their usual time. But it doesn't happen every day.'

Well used to Celtic tales, I didn't for one moment doubt what she was saying and more or less dismissed it from my mind. We went on talking until darkness fell, which was fairly early at this time of year. A very delicate chiming clock sounded, which reminded me I should be going. I looked up to the mantelshelf but there was no clock there and I looked round the room.

'Sh-sh,' she whispered, 'they will come any moment now. That's not my clock, for mine doesn't chime.'

I sat staring at the clockless shelf above the fire; then there was the sound of people chatting and skirts rustling. Once a small dog gave a yapping bark. The noise got louder as though a small party of people were going upstairs in the next room. There was light laughter and the happy buzz of conversation. They were obviously looking forward to a pleasant evening. Gradually it faded away as they reached wherever they were going. The whole thing took only a few minutes but seemed an age.

'Mary, it's extraordinary, but what's the other side of this wall?'

We went out and I saw there was nothing, just a small path to the back of the house. It was a charming experience. Mary had been right: they were delightful and happy and induced that feeling in their listeners. I often wondered how their presence would have affected my life with Peter.

Eventually we took half a house in Paulton's Square, Chelsea, belonging to Maurice and Bridget Richardson. Bridget's mother, Mrs Tisdall, had the top half. She was a pencil-thin outspoken elderly woman who lived with a companion as she had lost the use of one eye. When I commiserated with her, she said briskly:

'It's quite all right. I've seen all I want to see.'

We had no furniture, and it was impossible to buy any except on 'points' allocated to brides; horrible 'utility' furniture it was called. This did not deter us in the least. Our respective families combed their attics, spare rooms and woodsheds and soon we had a lot of certain things but none of vital commodities like beds. It was then that I remembered that all my furniture from Rossetti House, which was too big or not needed in Godfrey Street, I had lent to Sophie, now enjoying an uneasy domesticity in Oakley Street. One should never lend furniture to anyone. Once it has become part of another person's home and personality it never becomes yours again, and causes the most bitter resentment when you remove it. Some of it I never took, but I did swap a rather small single bed for my old double divan. We had a home of sorts again, but it was never even remotely as pleasant as Godfrey Street had been. Even when, later on, Mrs Tisdall went away for some months and we had the whole house, it wasn't our atmosphere, and being sensitive individuals it reacted on us. The idyll was over.

Nevertheless I made it as much like me as I could. We had five Orpington hens and two Khaki Campbell ducks in the garden, and later on eight poodle puppies. One of the ducks flew off and Constantine reported it to the police. Two days later they rang: it had been located twelve doors up. We went to get it, were led through the hall and went to go out into the garden.

'Oh no, it's in here,' said the woman, opening the door of a book-lined dining room. And sure enough there was my duck sitting in a leather armchair. It never took to Paulton's Square any more than we did, but went on laying its daily egg with the others. As the egg ration then was one per month per person, I was the most popular girl around. That is, egg-wise.

One morning in bed I asked Constantine what he would do when the war was over. 'Be a writer, of course,' he said. He might just as well have said a balloonist, as it didn't seem then that the war would ever end. A glassed-in verandah was converted into a writing room, and some evenings he would go there and write surrealistic short stories. 'Old Uncle Onion-head' was my favourite, and many of them have since been published.

This was when my grandmother gave me the bicycle, and I used to go around on it at Constantine's behest to find out which pubs had their beer delivered and when. But generally our local was the Crossed Keys in Lawrence Street, with new owners since the Chelsea Old Church bombing, and the most gorgeous queen of all the barmaids called Dorothy. She was like a young dark-haired English Mae West, if such a person can be imagined. She flirted, yet kept all the gentlemen in their place. She was also quick, efficient and kindly. Owing to a misunderstanding, which took us years to find out about, we had been barred from the King's Head and Eight Bells. The ban was so stringent that when an Irish girl who had never been to London before took my dog Mouche in there one night, she was also refused a drink. Sometimes we went across the road to the Black Lion in Paulton's Square, but to begin with it was crowded with people we didn't know, and there was nowhere to sit.

If it seems that undue importance is being attached to pubs it must be explained that they were the only places in wartime London where one could entertain and be entertained cheaply, and find the companionship badly needed during the war. For people of our age with no solid, regular accounts behind us, it was difficult to come by even a bottle of sherry. Food was very scarce indeed, and food for the occasional dinner party had to be hunted for and often took many hours and much traipsing about. Many middle-aged people used to drinking at home found their only source of supply was the pubs. Bombs dropping on London could not be so easily heard when one was in them, and the company lessened apprehension. I loved pubs, they were new to me and I liked being able to find friends I wanted to see in a certain place at a certain time. Dylan had previously pointed out to me that the link between host and guest was a tenuous one, but that it never arose if one met in a pub.

The Irish country pubs I had known were not at all the same. In them all women were put into a small place resembling a railway carriage, and known quite erroneously as a 'snug'. Not that I'm saying anything against the snug for certain occasions.

Chapter Eight

Intermittent bombs were dropped throughout this time, but after D-Day, 6 June 1944, a new horror arrived. These were the pilotless flying bombs, called V1s and known almost affectionately as 'doodlebugs'. They arrived almost as soon as the siren sounded. A characteristic drone announced them. Then silence before the indiscriminate bomb fell. They nearly all fell on London, and over six thousand people were killed. Before they stopped at the end of August over one and a half million people had left London.

Among them, Dylan, Caitlin and the baby left their flimsy studio home and went back to Wales. Early in August, Constantine had gone to France with the Americans. In September, Duncan Sandys, then in the Ministry of Defence, announced to our great relief: 'The battle for London is over.' However, he was almost immediately proved wrong, for the next day the first rockets (V2s) reached London. These were even more terrifying: there was no warning siren; it was useless taking shelter for it was all over so quickly. Over a thousand fell on London and killed nearly three thousand people. They were to continue, in desultory fashion, for over six months. It was a curious time and life became a valuable stroke of fortune, for we had no idea when death would fiendishly fall from the skies. Sometimes it seemed the war would go on all our lives, increasing in devilish intensity. Equally unnerving was the sinister thunderous noise of the death-laden flying fortresses passing overhead on their way to cities such as Dresden for intensive morale-breaking raids, when some eighty thousand people are thought to have been killed.

I was beginning to feel bereft without Constantine and I also missed Caitlin, for not only had the studio-shack always been welcoming, but we would often meet in the King's Road when shopping, Caitlin and the baby Aeronwy colourfully dressed, the pram piled high with the rations, always a few bottles of Guinness or pale ale peeping out. The studio in Manresa Road was let to a painter friend of ours called Francis Butterfield. Despite the lack of any proper home, Dylan was writing a lot in Wales. It was during this year and the next he was to write his poems *Refusal to Mourn*, *This Side of Truth*, *A Winter's Tale* and *In my Craft or Sullen Art* as well as others which were to make him famous.

He had also written many BBC radio talks, later to be collected and published as *Quite Early One Morning*. They were relayed on the Welsh Service, which was not easy to get in London, but the quality of both his voice and the prose made many want to hear them. That kind and charming man Donald Taylor, whose company was Strand Films, had commissioned Dylan to write several short film scripts which necessitated frequent trips to London. Caitlin of course was usually left in Wales. Many times it would be to our flat in Paulton's Square that Dylan would come, always neat and spruce on arrival. He was an odd guest, for not only did he appear unexpectedly, but after two or three days he would disappear and we would assume he had gone back to Wales. However, sometimes he would turn up again, but always dressed in different clothes. This was an inherent and curious part of Dylan: he would slough his own clothes like a snake with his skin, and dress himself in whatever of his host's took his fancy. This proved difficult with Constantine, not only on account of the vast difference in height, but also because Constantine had few civilian clothes. Nevertheless, socks, ties and some shirts were there for the taking.

Sometimes he came with friends and it was through Dylan we met Vernon Watkins, another Welsh poet, at this time in the air force. They made an ill-assorted couple, Vernon being a very thin, ascetic-looking El Greco-like figure. Vernon had previously worked in a bank and Dylan told me he was extremely absent-minded, thinking mainly of his poems. One day he was counting out a pile of notes, as tellers seem so often to be doing, when he looked up and saw a customer awaiting him. Without further ado he pushed the pile of notes through to him. Luckily it was someone who knew him and just as quickly pushed them back. I think it was a surprise to all of us when he married the practical and robust Gwen and had several children.

It was at Paulton's Square that Dylan first told us about the radio play he was writing. It was about a Welsh village, peopled with what he called 'a good cross-section of Welsh characters'. He was going to call the village Buggerall, which of course he did, backwards, in *Under Milk Wood*. When we had talked for hours and Constantine had come home, we would go over to the Black Lion, our nearest pub, on the corner of Old Church Street and Paulton Street. Sometimes we would go further afield to the Crossed Keys, especially in summer, as it had a small garden.

Dolly Donn Byrne, widow of the Irish writer Donn Byrne, was in the local pub, the Black Lion, most evenings. She lived with her daughter Janie (who was to die so tragically just after the war) at number 9 Paulton's Square. Her other daughter and two sons were in the forces. The house was shared with Kathleen Raine the poet. Dolly had one of those india-rubber Irish faces that changed as quickly as the light on an Irish hillside. She was very talkative and very kind. Many the night a hungry writer was given a meal at Roma's café just opposite the pub. I think that *Wings of the Mornings* had just been made into a film, from her husband's novel, with Annabella starring in it, but there was always a drink, endless cigarettes (and better ones than the usually available, dreadful Clipper brand) and stories from Dolly.

However, it can't have been 'fairy gold' film money that made her so generous. She had four children and had taken a job way out of London at Lutterworth Press, at which she worked extremely hard. When talking about Donn Byrne she would say:

'Some Irish people have lost their country houses gambling. My husband made his that way.'

And it was quite true. In the twenties Donn Byrne had made a small fortune at Monte Carlo and brought a beautiful house on the Old Head of Kinsale, County Cork. I believe he had driven his car over a cliff there and died, but this she never talked about. Dolly could make you cross but, like so many Irish women I had known in my youth, you couldn't help but love her. Dolly was a good woman and a good friend.

Kathleen Raine was then married to the poet Charles Madge. She used to give Sunday-evening poetry readings, to which we were sometimes asked. She was a pretty brown-haired woman with a slight lisp and a quick smile. At her house, poets like George Barker, Dylan Thomas, Bernard Gutteridge, Bernard Spencer, Bill Empson, Pierre Emanuelle and many others met and read their poems. Constantine was never asked to read, much to his chagrin, so we didn't go there all that often. We had our own poetry readings at home; indeed I remember once Constantine being quite sharp with Janie Donn Byrne because she wasn't reading her poem with enough expression.

Many evenings until early in the mornings we would play 'Russian plays' and this on lime juice and soda. The game consisted of improvised Chekov-style dramas in which I was always Natasha, Dylan my mother (stuffed with cushions and heavily made-up), Constantine was Sergei with his jacket on back to front and my fur hat on, and sometimes an overworked and exhausted journalist called John Thompson who had the flat on the top floor was roped in when he came home late, to play a very subsidiary role. It was all very satisfying, stimulated our imagination and used up our energy.

But it wasn't all Russian plays. One Sunday night we had a poker party instigated by Dolly and Constantine. Dylan, Janie and myself were only stringers, and apparently talked too much for the experts. Sometime around midnight a tremendous thunderstorm started and Dylan, overacting, said it was because we were card-playing on Sunday. He worked this up to such an extent that Constantine almost believed it and became unduly emotional. The poker party was quickly disbanded, and Dolly and Janie slunk out. Dylan and I were left to face the wrath of whatever God Constantine was then invoking. It had become quite out of hand, and I was alarmed. In the middle of one of Constantine's harangues, out of the corner of my eye I saw Dylan get down on all fours and begin to creep out of the room. The excellence of the idea imprinted itself quickly on my mind, because instantly I was down on all fours, and out of the room, in the hallway with Dylan. We stayed on the ground, whispering together and we could still hear Constantine in the sitting room continuing to give vent to his anger. He must after a minute or two have realized that we were no longer there because we could hear him saying:

'Well, where the devil are they?'

It might read curiously in print, but it caused Dylan and me, still on all fours and huddled in a corner of the hall, the greatest amusement, as indeed it did Constantine when he realized what had happened and how comical the whole situation was.

The winter of 1944 was unnecessarily spiteful. There was snow and hard frost for about a month, and the roads were so bad that no horse-drawn coal lorry was able to deliver the coal. This was when the little spiv boys would turn up with the logs, but if you weren't there to watch when they were putting them down the coal-shute you found you had about a dozen logs, instead of a hundred.

Unless you were in one of the women's forces, trousers were not usual for women to wear and difficult to buy without coupons, so I wore my jodhpurs and hunting jacket during the days of this hard spell. Bertram Wedgwood, who was well over seventy (he eventually got into the Red Cross and was one of the first into Belsen camp), and I hired a hand-cart and dragged back several hundredweight of coal from a yard near Lot's Road, to Paulton's Square. Food was every day more scarce, and our ration that winter was again one pound of onions per person. Not that any of these things worried us: they were part of the life that we were living and intended to go on with for as long as we could. It must have been much harder for middle-aged or elderly people who had prewar standards to judge by, but for us it was life as life came. Paulton's Square, whatever else it might have been, was never dull. At breakfast time the Wrens from Crosby Hall at the bottom of the street drilled in front of us. Mouche hated these squadrons of women stomping about outside her house, and although not an aggressive dog her one ambition was to get out and chase them. This only happened once or twice but it pleased the girls very much, though not the officers, as a welcome break from routine.

Feeding a large standard poodle was sometimes a problem, but she more than earned her keep. She insisted on carrying the small torch we used during the blackout, and the light shone just where one needed it, on the pavement. At the kerb she would wait until we had reached it. Where the oncoming people thought the light was coming from must have posed quite a problem, until they passed by, sometimes loud in their praise, but the strong-minded Mouche was immune to their blandishments when doing her job. She also loved taxis and was adept at getting them. At that time only the driver's compartment was enclosed in the front, the remainder being free to put luggage in. Some taxi drivers had the habit of putting their glove over the meter while still on a rank. This meant they weren't working. Mouche was oblivious to the glove, and would jump up on to the luggage part and sit there, putting an appealing face through the driver's window. It almost always worked; in fact there was one taxi driver from Battersea who was so flattered that he used to take her for a ride when he had another fare and then bring her back to me. There were also the puppies, which sold quite lucratively. Con once said he had heard of men living on women, but he'd never heard of one living on a dog!

I bought horsemeat when available, but sometimes after queueing for an hour there would be only bones left, so I made a stew of them with flour dumplings. I did get whale meat twice which was much appreciated: when I tasted it once, I found it extremely rich. Ends of bread were baked in the oven and sometimes when there would be nothing else, she ate those with made-up dried milk powder and a few drops of cod liver oil. Then there were the pig bins: these were large drums situated in most streets where you put your edible waste. First thing in the morning Mouche would make a tour of these, but I don't think she got much, as they contained mostly vegetable peelings. She found many friends of her own, one being a dear old man from the workhouse who always had a few crusts for her in his pocket. She would go to Dovehouse Street where the workhouse was to wait for him. I think she was probably his only friend. In pubs there was sometimes an arrowroot biscuit; large ones were kept in jars on the bar, and these she liked with a drop of Guinness in the ashtray.

One day when Dylan was staying the subject of hypnotizing chickens with a white line came up. I went out with a piece of string and laid it out straight, then put the birds' beaks on it. It worked: both Dylan and Constantine, who were hiding behind trees in the garden, thought me very brave to pick up pecking birds like that. In a way, it was country life in the town. I thought a lot about Ireland and my father's family there, but it became more and more difficult to get back even for a short while.

On an evening in December I heard a taxi flag down outside the house; I peered out and the man getting out appeared familiar, yet strange. Perhaps he was going next door where Ford Madox Ford's wife lived, as did Herma Briffault, wife of the French writer. Nevertheless my doorbell rang and I answered the door. It was my father.

Chapter Nine

My father was the *pater nonfamilias* for we hardly ever saw him. His adult life was spent mostly in India and he would appear from time to time, years apart, without warning, for an indefinite stay. Nevertheless I was always delighted to see him for his arrival meant complete disorganization of whatever you were doing and tremendous excitement.

As a small child I had seen him perhaps half a dozen times and on every occasion something unusual happened. When he came to visit me at my convent school the nuns were charmed by him, and whereas other parents left in the afternoon, my father was still there being royally entertained in the evening. He had the ability of making everyone with him seem special. If that is called charm, he was endowed with it in a very natural way. He had a quick and ready wit, a remarkably hasty temper and a most infectious laugh.

His passions, in the true sense of the word, were beautiful horses and beautiful women, followed by good food and drink, the theatre and books. He had several children, only one being born in his own wedlock. He was definitely not the marrying sort. Nevertheless I never met anyone who didn't like him.

When I was very young he was like a myth to me and if someone had told me he was really Jupiter disguised in human form I wouldn't have been at all surprised. He would, it seemed, swoop down and carry me off to faraway places where everything looked and was quite different from anything I could have imagined. Very occasionally my mother came too, but usually it was just me. To an only child brought up in convents, when at the age of about eleven they expressed the wish that I should leave, and I went to live with my seventy-year-old maternal grandmother, it was an enchanted world he opened up for me. I believe he genuinely liked being with some children, for surprisingly late one night in the Gargoyle Club in Soho, the granite-faced Maurice Richardson told me he often had been taken out by him when he was about sixteen years old.

As I grew a little older the trips got longer. I was never treated as a child but as an equal, and expected to behave accordingly. It was he who, when I was sixteen years old, gave me my first cigar as he said he didn't like smoking alone. He was also full of worldly advice, which even today I reflect on and sometimes follow. He gave me a leather-covered flask filled with whisky on my seventeenth birthday.

'Never,' he said, 'ever go on a journey, or to stay with friends, without it. There will always be the time when you will want a drink and they don't.'

I have profited many times by that advice, never more than during the war when trains stopped, sometimes all night, during an air raid. Today that same flask still goes with me.

When, as a girl, my grandmother thought I had made an undesirable friend and hoped to win my father to her way of thinking, he replied that she couldn't expect *us* to have the morals of a haberdasher!

However, he did draw the line at what he called 'curly-headed counter-jumpers' and I was warned never to get involved with one.

We travelled together over most of Europe, the Middle East and parts of India. We stayed in castles and cottages and everywhere we went he seemed to know people, albeit mostly pretty women. Once in France we rose at dawn and drove for miles to visit one such charmer who lived in a magnificent hilltop château where we stayed for two days. She had a chubby, angelic-looking baby boy of whom she was very proud. When we were driving away, my father turned to me and said:

'Do you think that baby looks like me?'

I replied that it had a certain similarity.

'Nonsense,' he snapped, 'all blond blue-eyed babies look like me. Did you look at his ears or eyebrows?'

I said it hadn't occurred to me, and the subject was never mentioned again.

His clothes were always of the finest materials and he expected his female companions to be so attired. Unlike most men he loved shopping with pretty women and if you found it hard to choose between two dresses, then he bought you both. I once went home with six new pairs of shoes. He was highly critical of what you wore, and one time when I thought I looked just right, he said:

'Where do you think you're going? To a dog show?'

But if you had nothing else suitable to wear, he would take you out to buy something really beautiful immediately.

It was largely due to him I discovered my immense interest in different foods, for not only did we travel to many countries to taste it, but his interest stimulated mine. He insisted that we ate the food of the country, even a sheep's eye in Arabia, a fearsome, huge object which I don't recommend. He disliked people who tried to stick to roast beef, and was a firm believer that 'travel reinforces prejudice' in many. All dishes he ate had to be what they purported to be. If it said Potage Dubarry on the menu, I pitied the waiter who didn't bring a good cauliflower soup. When a Sole Veronique was presented with a white sauce over it, and not the glazed juices, it would be thrown on the floor with the words:

'That's what I think of your Sole Veronique.'

However, simple well-cooked food was also enjoyed, particularly calf's head with vinaigrette sauce, a dish seldom seen today. It is no doubt due to this training that I so dislike dishes called Hawaiian or Polynesian simply because they have a slice of pineapple on them.

Having eaten a good dish he would assume I would either know, or find out, how to cook it, and after a while I learned to do just that. One time we were having friends to dinner and I complained about the smell of garlic on my fingers.

'The hand that cuts the garlic is the one that gets kissed the most often,' he said tersely.

He had a marvellous way of describing people in a sentence.

'The sort of person who would be *seen* cutting up a lettuce.'

His method of summing up a man was in these words:

'You can usually tell what a man is really like by the expression on his wife's face!'

How often have I seen the truth of that remark.

Once when someone's legitimacy was being questioned, he took a large swig of whisky before saying:

'It's a wise cork that knows its own pop!'

He gave me the taste very early on for perfection. To a child used to the severity of a convent (breaking the ice on the jug to wash in wintertime was normal) the luxury of first-class hotels was impressive, although I was also taught not to despise the humble.

However, sitting in the sumptuous Gritti Palace in Venice, he once remarked:

'Thank God, at least we *look* rich.'

He went through a lot of money during his lifetime, but as my half-sister said:

'It was worth it: we learnt a lot.'

On my eighteenth birthday he gave me a thousand pounds, which was a vast sum in those days, and told me not to expect anything more. From time to time I think lump sums were handed out to his ladies as well as to his children, but never when you expected it. I will never know how spontaneous those trips were, but I do know that after a certain time, perhaps sitting in an hotel somewhere, he would give that wonderful laugh and say: 'Time we went back to the ancestral home,' and off we would go back to Ireland the next day. The enchantment was over until the next time he swooped down.

During all those years I was only once given any indication of what to do in strange surroundings. That was when he told me not to talk so freely to the footman. A few words would do.

Like most Irishmen, eventually he went back to Ireland, and once on a visit I found he had ten pretty servant girls all called Brigit.

'But why do you want ten, all with the same name?' I asked.

'Simple,' he replied, 'If I shout Brigit down the stairs at least one of them answers.'

This night in Chelsea in 1945 there was no possibility of being carried off anywhere. He was, although I didn't know it, a dying man. Flashes of the old wit were displayed, but they were like sparklers instead of rockets. He asked for whisky, but alas we had none, only beer, which he shouldn't have drunk. He was delighted to meet Constantine and unexpectedly my mother also called. It was a domesticity we had never known together.

The difficulty of finding him a taxi in blacked-out London was solved by the arrival of Diana Graves and Michael Gough, for he was able to take theirs. Foolishly, in my joy at seeing him I forgot to ask where he was staying. Two days later he telephoned me, and in the middle of the conversation we were cut off. It was the last time I was ever to hear from him. Adam, for that was his name, had left my life as abruptly as he had entered it.

Some years later, when I had returned home from the other side of the world, I heard this story. As his funeral cortege was slowly going its winding way to Ballymackey cemetery, the mourners were startled to hear the clatter of horses' hooves in the narrow country lane.

Ahead of the hearse, a young chestnut thoroughbred horse had leapt a five-barred gate and was rearing up in front of the coffin. He was led back into the field and the gate shut. Twice more he raced along the fields, jumping hedges and gates, and the performance was repeated along the road. The mourners murmured among themselves:

'It's a sign. He would have like that,' they said. 'God rest his soul.'

Chapter Ten

Spring came early and with it our spirits revived, for not only were the days warmer and longer, but the course of the war seemed to take a turn in our favour. Warm days meant one needed less food and fewer clothes, for those too were on a 'coupon' system. Even the watery-thin sunlight meant we could dispense with wool or silk stockings (nylons were almost only obtainable through a member of the US forces) and heavy top-coats. The coupon allowance, like all the rations, was only the barest minimum. Elderly people who didn't buy much would sell these coupons for small sums of money. Maybe one of the reasons the GIs were so popular was that they were given vast quantities of coupons. Shops dealing in second-hand clothes opened up, and when the clothes were well cut they often sold for high prices, but were worth it for special occasions.

Warm days also meant going out more, and further afield. Harold Scott, the actor whom Bernard Shaw had in mind to play the Dauphin in *St Joan,* and the originator of the famous Riverside Nights with Elsa Lanchester, would call from time to time. Then we would sometimes take the tube to Tower Hill, by the Tower of London, have some drinks, then walk down the almost deserted, bombed dockland of St Katherine's Way, calling at some of the little pubs, until we reached the Prospect of Whitby. At this time it was almost entirely patronized by dock workers and their families. There was an ancient piano and there Harold would play and in his light sweet voice sing old music-hall songs such as 'My Old Man Says Follow the Van' or 'The Boy I Love Is Up in the Gallery'. He was immensely popular and we were always assured of a warm welcome when he was there, sometimes even some hot wartime sausages would be handed round. It is curious that the only war song was 'Lili Marlene', a German one.

Harold was a remarkable person, a true bohemian in many ways. He always looked scruffy and penniless, yet to my knowledge he was seldom out of work over a span of at least fifty years. He was extremely well read, but his knowledge sat lightly on him. He was the most quietly entertaining person, and perhaps because of this he was usually with very pretty women.

Dylan was often in London writing his film scripts, and about this time he was collaborating with Philip Lindsay, the prolific historical novelist, brother of Jack and a member of the talented Australian family. Phil was a curious little man who resembled a small nocturnal animal with a large carbuncle on his forehead. He was in the Crossed Keys every evening, sitting by the fireplace drinking beer. Occasionally his correct-looking wife (who in fact wasn't correct at all) would be there for a little while, usually later in the evening to accompany him home. How he got all the writing done is still a mystery to me, but the long well-researched books would appear regularly despite the paper shortage.

Dylan and Phil were collaborating on a script about the life of Dickens. Dylan was anxious to use as far as possible Dickens' own words, but the collaborators did not always have the same ideas. One night or early morning Dylan and Phil were arguing about it in our house. Phil turned to me and said: 'Dylan's too f— intellectual, he ruins the bloody film.' In any case the film was never made. Another time Dylan turned up with a Welsh policeman called Walter Flower, and the art critic Tommy Earp. D. H. Lawrence once wrote these lines about Tommy after he had given Lawrence an unfavourable review of his exhibition of paintings.

He can't write
But he can chirp,
His name is Tommy
Tommy Earp.

I think Lawrence was wrong, for not only was Tommy a fine critic, far better than Lawrence was a painter, but also a much underestimated writer as the following last verse of his poem *Five Christs* shows:

Now, in the Rue de la Paix,
In a shop-window,
A small glass Christ,
Fragile and expensive,
'A Dainty Christ for the Dressing-table'.

Tommy was an extremely tall, thin man with a long narrow head. He waved his arms about a lot and seemed to me like an enormous upright dragonfly. The reference to his 'chirping' was a comment on his voice – not a chirp, but high and fluting – with which he enunciated the most exact English with an exaggerated Oxford accent. I don't know what the quiet blond policeman made of it all, for although we drank a certain amount in the pubs, we also did the most elaborate dances (at which Tommy was very good) and improvised plays about Goethe, Dylan being the young Goethe, Tommy the old, me Lotte, and Constantine an unlikely Schiller.

Then a new figure came to live in Paulton's Square, and figure is an appropriate word for John Davenport. He was not a very tall man, but immensely wide with a Beethovenesque head. One had no difficulty in believing he had been a boxing blue at Cambridge, both for his build and his strength. He was however a man with a deep love and knowledge of literature, painting and music. He had a large circle of friends both in the intellectual and social milieu, a ready and precise wit. For such an enormous man he had a very soft voice and the trick of dropping it when telling a story, so that you were literally sitting on the edge of your seat to hear it. John had spent some time in Hollywood in order to write a script for a Robert Donat film about the Young Pretender, which however came to nothing as Donat broke his contract and left. He stayed on for a little, and used the money to collect such modern painters as Roualt, Picasso and Tanguy which sold for very little then. Just before the war and at the beginning of it he entertained lavishly at his house in Gloucestershire.

Dylan and Caitlin had been his guests for over three months in 1940, and it was during this time that John and Dylan started writing a thriller together, subsequently published as *The Death of the King's Canary*, which was a *roman à clef*. John had written a book of poems at Cambridge, but subsequently he found himself with that condition most dreaded by writers, an increasing writing block. He did however write excellent, succinct literary criticism.

This then was the man who, having spent most of his fortune, came to live in a small flat in Dolly Donn Byrne and Kathleen Raine's house in Paulton's Square. He was often in the Black Lion or the Crossed Keys and we became great friends. Dolly adored him and had many amusing anecdotes about him. It appears that at this time he met Margery Morrison, who had been one of my *locataires* at Rossetti House. She was brought to the Paulton's Square flat to live. Dolly, eyes shining with delight, told of knocking on his door one day to ask a simple question, to which he replied: 'Come in.'

On entering she saw them both lying on the sofa *au naturel*; John raised himself up on his elbow and in his soft voice murmured:

'Dolly, I'm glad you called. I wanted you to meet Margery. She's a charming girl, her father was a captain in the Scots Greys.'

For some time past we had seen an elderly white-haired man in the Crossed Keys, usually in conversation with Desmond Ryan, flamboyant in his black Inverness cape. One evening I was sitting next to the white-haired man when he turned to me and almost querulously asked:

'What's your name then?'

'Theo FitzGibbon.'

'Nonsense,' he replied, 'that was my wife's name.'

And it was, although her name had been Theobaldina, but as it happened she was the daughter of Augustus FitzGibbon, Constantine's great-uncle and also a distant cousin of her husband.

This was the writer Norman Douglas, or 'Uncle Norman' as he became, author of *South Wind* and many even finer books, such as *Siren Land, Fountains in the Sand, Old Calabria* and some twenty others. He was at that time seventy-seven years old and was to be a constant friend until his death in 1952.

He had arrived in wartime London in 1941 after a circuitous journey across Europe from Italy, first to France and, when that was occupied by the Germans, to Portugal. He had thought never to return to England again, certainly he couldn't have picked a worse time. Life was not easy even for regular inhabitants, but for an elderly hedonist it must have seemed even more dismal and restrictive. However, self-pity was not one of Norman's faults and whatever his private feelings may have been, he stimulated and fascinated all who met him by his scholarship and wit. Most of all he loved to shock and it was this mixture of immense and diverse knowledge, classicism, lucidity and bluntness to the point of bawdyness which made him perhaps the most interesting person I have ever met. He belonged more to the eighteenth or early nineteenth century than the twentieth and this carried through to his appearance.

When I first met him he looked remarkably robust for a man of his years: tall and broad with a strong physique, a large noble head covered with thick but silky white hair, which went well with his ruddy complexion, clear-cut features and shrewd but twinkling eyes. His friend in Florence, Reggie Turner, has described him as 'a mixture of Roman emperor and Roman cab-driver', which combined his distinction and shrewdness to perfection, as well as his heritage, a Scottish father and an Austrian mother. All his life he had been very active, climbing and walking miles, and this habit of walking, even in the blackout, continued well into his eighties. Almost nightly he would walk from his room in South Kensington to Chelsea to dine or drink with us or other friends. He would sometimes take my arm, but one knew better than to take his. One evening when we had been drinking in the Crossed Keys for many hours with Desmond Ryan and

Brian Howard, we wandered towards our house at closing time. In the blackout there were sounds of a conversational scuffle between Norman and Brian.

'Do stop holding my arm, please.'

'But the steps are very difficult to see, Norman.'

'I had to live on nothing but carrots in Estoril for three weeks and my eyesight is much better than yours, duckums, I'm sure.'

While Constantine was working at his army duties during the day Norman would often call on me, his arrival heralded by a loud tapping on the window with his walking stick. Sometimes we would simply go for a drink and a pub lunch, and he would walk round Chelsea or Kensington first to see which provided the better value. As meals were still restricted to five shillings wherever you went, it was simply a question of sometimes finding a change of menu.

'Fish pie, shepherd's pie or sausage and mash, what are you having?' he would say. 'Whatever you have I shall have something different, for that way you get better helpings.'

And when we had finished he would invariably conclude by saying: 'Robbed, starved and poisoned, duckums,' and then make that extraordinary 'hah' sound which sounded like a minor explosion. Sometimes we would wander to the Queen's Restaurant in Sloane Square, or Caletta's, a homely little Italian restaurant where the canneloni weren't bad, in the King's Road. It was Desmond Ryan who introduced us all to the Ladder Club in a mews off Bruton Street with its genial Irish owner, Mossie. She served quite good snacks, it was warm, comfortable and there was always a fair supply of spirits to drink. Most important, she was open during the long bleak hours of the pub-less afternoon, closing early in the evening.

Norman had a great capacity for almost everything except humbug. He ate heartily, drank everything available, yet I never saw him even remotely drunk and no matter how long the evening he would insist on walking home. He could get very merry, however, and one evening, Norman, John Davenport, Constantine and I did a pub crawl of Chelsea and each place we left Norman had acquired a new hat in exchange for one he had left, which he would slap on his head saying:

'This one's rather cinquecento, isn't it? Does it suit my style of beauty?'

He was never without his hat, stick, snuff box and pipe and walking home he would stop to strike a match to refuel his pipe.

'I must light up my nose,' he would chuckle.

The constant pipe smoke turned the forelock of his white hair yellowish.

'How can I get rid of this yellow part?'

I gave him a blue-bag to dip into the rinsing water, but alas the first time he used too much.

'Rather smart, duckums, don't you think?' But after that he didn't bother so much about the yellow streak.

Nevertheless he could be most persistent about small things, forever asking where he could get a child's cash-box. I had no idea in wartime London, but he kept on until finally I found one in Hamleys, but I don't think it was quite right. When he wasn't smoking he was taking snuff and many times I made the journey to the Haymarket to the gracious eighteenth-century tobacconists Fribourg and Treyer to get the right kind for him.

He was an intensely curious man which is no doubt why he got on with so many different kinds of people. For although his knowledge on many subjects scientific and intellectual was vast, he enjoyed the company of friends with quite simple minds. It was through Norman that we came to know Viva and Willie King. Viva was a large friendly woman and Willie small, eccentric and erudite. Viva held a *salon* every Sunday afternoon where one was likely to meet some of the liveliest minds in England.

Viva and Willie adored Norman, Viva saying:

'He was so gay and amusing and Rabelaisian, I used to think of him as old Silenus – sometimes I used to look under the table for his goat's feet.'

Willie, who worked at the British Museum, became his literary executor. Viva once greeted Norman with:

'You're the best advertisement for the evil life.'

To which he replied:

'Humph, it's uphill work now, still I try to do my best.'

We went to Hampstead Heath together one Bank Holiday for he wanted to see the English enjoying themselves. We wandered over that vast heath, eating jellied eels (pronounced excellent), winkles (too much trouble for too little) and crab sandwiches.

'They should be good, my dear, so many dead bodies for them to feed on.'

Every so often he would stop and remark on a pretty girl, decrying those that had what he called 'the industrial eye'. Having heard a little about his unusual sex life I remarked on this interest, to get the sharp answer:

'Pretty girls are my business!'

We went to all the freak shows: the bearded lady; the 'mermaid'; the six-legged pony and the largest rat in the world, at which Norman said in a loud voice that it wasn't a rat at all but a European beaver. We walked and walked until I pleaded exhaustion, so we sat on the rather damp grass near to a large woman with two or three wild children. They all seemed quite out of hand and it was most unrestful. Then one tough, dirty little boy of about four years old charged up and said:

'I'm thirsty, Mum, give us a swig of the titty!'

'Well, he's enjoying himself at least,' said Norman. 'Come on, duckums, we've seen enough for one day.'

Norman was immensely interested in food and had been at one time a good cook. During his travels he had missed nothing, nor forgotten anything. He would sit in my kitchen while I was preparing meals and give me little tips, such as cutting tough meat up small, and putting a spoonful of grated chocolate into inferior coffee to improve the flavour. Mostly his tips were almost impossible to carry out as the ingredients weren't available, but he approved of a shashlik I made out of two meat rations one day for a luncheon of eight people. Sam Langford was helping me to cut up the meat, and went out into the garden to pick small twigs which he pared down to make skewers: 'Pick an aromatic wood,' said Norman, but alas we didn't have any.

I did however have bay leaves and a rosemary bush, which he would pinch every time he went past and say they reminded him of Italy. Also I still had my home-grown garlic, which impressed him.

'Put plenty in, it's good for the stomach, and other things, my dear.'

We had no rice to accompany the shashlik so we broke up Soho-bought spaghetti quite small, and Norman told me to put a spoon of oil into the boiling water to stop it clumping together, something I have done ever since.

At the end of the lunch, with stuffed eggs from the hens first, Brian Howard said:

'Delicious, why don't we have meals like this at home, Sam?'

To which Sam replied: 'Because we don't have a home, Brian.' For once he had no answer.

Norman told me how to cook a leg of lamb or mutton so that it tasted like wild boar, but I had neither leg of lamb nor the ingredients, which consisted of a litre of dry white wine, pinoli, candied peel and powdered dark chocolate. Later on I read it in his book *Birds and Beasts of the Greek Anthology* and then I did try it. His comments afterwards were:

'Not a dish for every day, someone may remark. Assuredly not. The longer one lives the more one realizes that nothing is a dish for every day.'

He would talk of his collection of aphrodisiac recipes and ask if I had any. Oysters and truffles were all I had heard of: he would look thoughtful and say a few would be nice now, duckums. His last book was this collection which he called *Venus in the Kitchen* and it was published posthumously in 1952 although he had been collecting for it for over twelve years. Some of it was maybe tongue-in-cheek, but I met at least one person who swore it had done him a lot of good.

During all this time Norman had very little money, and what he had was supplemented by giving Italian lessons, for he was an excellent linguist, speaking French, Italian and German fluently as well as having a good knowledge of others such as Russian, for in his early days he had been a diplomatist in St Petersburg.

It was particularly galling to see a pirated edition of his famous privately printed *Some Limericks*, with the succinct footnotes, being sold in thousands to the American forces, for which he got not one penny. Likewise the reprinting of *South Wind* earlier by Bennett Cerf in America, for which he received no money owing to copyright problems.

He had however written *An Almanac* in 1941, dedicated to the Honourable Neil Hogg of the British Embassy, Lisbon, as a token of thanks for his kindness in putting a room at his disposal in Lisbon after leaving Italy in 1940. It was a charming book published by Chatto and Windus with an aphorism for every day of the year. The one for my birthday, 21 October, was: 'I always know when a man is drunk, even when I'm drunk myself.' In 1944 he was compiling *Late Harvest,* which was published by Lindsay Drummond after Nancy Cunard had introduced them. Owing to the paper shortage and other things it was not brought out until 1946.

The book contained, amongst other writings, the whole of *Summer Islands,* those two beautiful essays written earlier about the idyllic, magical islands and islets off the coast of Naples. Then he had said:

'I have shut up my little writing shop for good.'

Although then I had no thought of ever writing anything, there are many times when I think of his advice:

'Never stop writing at a sticky spot; always leave it in the middle of a good, flowing part, for then you will be able to continue easily.'

It does work.

For Norman, at seventy-seven years old, uprooted from all he knew and loved, living in one room in Kensington with his few treasured belongings in a small bag and a child's cash-box, during the bleak and dangerous years of wartime London, it must have seemed the most impossible dream that he would ever again see his beloved Italy.

Chapter Eleven

We had learned never to plan anything ahead of time; too many places disappeared, friends never returned and our attempts at two brief holidays had resulted in either the trains not going, or the place we wished to go to being in a restricted area. The fact that you woke up in one piece was something to be thankful for, and we were. We continued to take advantage of the chance meeting, to enjoy life as we found it.

Nevertheless, as the spring came the four-page newspaper, still lamentably short of news, was eagerly read. In March, General Montgomery crossed the Rhine and, in early April, General Alexander's armies broke into the Po Valley. Paris was liberated on 25 August and Constantine with his great foresight and determination had managed to get himself transferred there, briefly, together with a letter of introduction to Nancy Cunard, who had gone back after the liberation, and one from Francis Rose, the painter, to Gertrude Stein. Norman worried about his flat in Florence and the fate of Emilio, who had been left in charge of it. The dream of getting back to Italy was not so distant. Yet he was inexpressibly sad, as he wrote to Nancy Cunard in France in 1945.

'I spend half my days now in climbing stairs and asking people whether they have a room to let. A dog's life . . . instead of my becoming used to this country, I get more homesick every day. Went for a solitary walk down the Serpentine this afternoon. Yesterday for a solitary walk in Battersea Park . . .'

There was however an excitement in the air for many, which became more so when the Allies landed in the south of France. However, there was still fighting in the Far East. It was not until the two dictators were dead that it appeared the fighting in Europe would stop. This all happened at the end of April when Mussolini and his mistress were shot by partisans and, on 30 April, Hitler killed his mistress, then committed suicide. On 8 May the long-awaited ending of the European war was announced.

It was an emotional time for almost everybody. Church bells rang out once more (during the war they were only to be rung to announce a gas attack), flood-lighting and drawn curtains took the place of the blackout, strangers hugged and kissed in the streets and there was dancing and singing around the boarded-up Eros in Piccadilly Circus and in Trafalgar Square. The pubs were full, work seemed to stop for the day, but the few shops that opened gave good measure on the ration books. Desmond Ryan turned up with a battered car and said we should go to Piccadilly. Norman Douglas threw out anecdotes of peace day in 1918 with vivid descriptions of lovemaking in the streets. Yes, we would go: I said I would stand on the bonnet of the car the length of Piccadilly. Not quite though, for after about twenty yards I tripped forward and all I did was chip my front tooth, so I retired to a safer place inside.

What did we see? A thin crowd of people straggling towards the Circus and Augustus John, hands behind his back, looking furious, going in the opposite direction. Not enough licentiousness, I would imagine. We went on and at the Circus found thicker crowds, very good natured, singing and dancing. We decided to go to the Café Royal and enjoy the marble and plush. The lights were all blazing, it was very crowded, but at a table we saw Brian Howard and Sam Langford, whom we joined. The drink flowed as it had not done for nearly five years, and it was then that Sam and I decided to go out and climb lamp-posts. Like white Irish monkeys we shinned up the tall Regent Street stands and had a marvellous view of everything. Then back home, pubs all open after hours on the way, and a night-cap at the Black Lion. People there were discussing when Jack or Bill would be home, when rationing would be over, and when would the Japanese pack it in? Everyone had theories, none of which proved right as it turned out. It was after all only half the war which had ended but it was something to be going on with.

Nevertheless, some of the forces did come home but it was not always the homecoming they had dreamed about. Wives found that husbands who had left as young, almost innocent men returned as disillusioned, weary and war-shocked individuals unable to settle down to family life or to find a job. Wives too had changed after years of living alone bringing up a family or, if they hadn't lived alone, that only complicated matters further and added to the frustration and feeling of uselessness. These were violent times and very few were untouched by them.

One such man who had been a commando officer behind the German lines in Greece returned home to his wife, a childhood friend of Dylan's, to a bungalow near the Thomases in New Quay, Cardiganshire. During an evening in the local pub, Dylan, a secretary Donald Taylor had sent down to help Dylan to finish an overdue film script, the officer and his wife were drinking together. Dylan's account was that a verbal skirmish took place between the secretary and the commando, who then taunted her with being Jewish, an unfortunate happening at any time but especially when the savagery of the concentration camps was being revealed. The secretary attacked him, and he hit back, to be forcibly removed from the pub by Dylan and the other male drinkers. He went on his own to another pub, drank heavily and thought of revenge.

Dylan and the wife went back to Caitlin at the flimsy bungalow they lived in, had a few more beers, no doubt trying to dismiss the incident from their minds. Of a sudden they were startled by sten-gun bullets coming through the walls. Caitlin with foresight pushed the babies up the wide chimney minutes before the door was kicked in. Dylan, with a bravery one wouldn't have connected with him, got the gun away, only to find that the man had a hand-grenade in his pocket. He threatened to pull the pin unless the gun was returned. Naturally Dylan complied with his wishes and, after trying to reason with him, left with his wife and children. The man was subsequently prosecuted for attempted murder, but released on the grounds of temporary insanity brought on by provocation.

Although a terrifying and upsetting experience, it was somehow not so surprising, for the climate of Britain at the end of the war was one of exhausted brutality, and it was maybe one amongst many other incidents.

Meanwhile, the euphoria gradually passing, we all went about the daily tasks, looking for food to eat, for rationing had in no way decreased, working, and relaxing at whichever pub had their beer ration. In July a general election brought the Labour Party to power, which caused great hopes amongst many of the returned forces. The atmosphere was once more excited and electric. The hungry thirties were still very real for many people and the Labour programme with promise of work and social security seemed attractive. Francis Rose told of a large luncheon he was at in one of London's big hotels: 'where, my dears, all the waiters were *quite* tipsy. The courses were all out of order, ice-cream served after the fish! Lady Colefax exclaimed, "Oh, delicious, a sorbet!" ' But alas it was simply vanilla ice-cream. The working classes thought the time had come for them to inherit the earth.

There were murmurs that Constantine would soon be sent back to America and from July onwards it was merely a question of when. Norman Douglas had applied for a renewal of his passport to Italy, which he got, mainly perhaps due to the answer he gave to the interviewing official:

'So you want to go back to live in Italy?'

'No, I want to go back to die.'

We realized that we too would shortly be packing up, probably to go to some unknown part of America. We started to sell furniture and some books. Norman came round when we were sorting the books and said:

'Oh, I'll sign them for you; it'll make them much more valuable.'

He did, not only sign his own books, but some of Hardy, Conrad and so on. 'Best wishes' from Thomas Hardy, 'A memorable meeting', Joseph Conrad. Alas when we did come to sell some of them, the buyer said he couldn't give us full price as they had been defaced!

It was to be another year before Norman was to see Italy

and Capri again. However, while we were all still together we would often meet during the summer months, in the garden of the Pier Hotel at the bottom of Oakley Street. One day Constantine and I had joined John Davenport and a rather tall, ill-looking American soldier to whom we were introduced. It was pleasant under the trees and even a hard pear falling on Con's head didn't disturb the tranquillity. We were joined by Norman well wrapped up in overcoat, scarf and hat despite the heat. He seemed in sombre mood and not very talkative. Then he looked up and in a loud voice said:

'I thought I was coming here to meet W. H. Auden.'

He hadn't heard John's soft-voiced introduction, but thought it amusing when he realized he had been talking to Auden for nearly an hour. Once more he was in an ebullient mood.

When the final victory did come it was at the terrible cost of the atomic bomb being dropped on innocent victims of American war-strategy. There were outcries about it, but to be fair I will say that the ordinary person did not realize, for we were never told then, the monstrous and lasting effect it was to have on so many people. A little under a month after the first bomb on Hiroshima being dropped, VJ–Day as it was called was officially celebrated on 2 September 1945.

This time the celebrations seemed more ordered and more restrained. The crowds, at least in Chelsea, were not so evident as after the European peace, but there were many private and street parties. The Black Lion announced they were giving us all a party in the pub and outside in Paulton's Street, and many pubs did likewise for their customers. How many of the pubs had been safe harbours for us during those long years – places of congeniality and friendliness, the hum of conversation, the warmth in winter, the kindness and cheerfulness shown by many publicans – will never be forgotten by those who experienced it.

The weather was still very summer-like. Mouche the poodle, heavily pregnant, puffed about the house trying to find a cool spot; we opened a few hoarded tins for lunch and looked forward to the party the next day. At about five o'clock, almost as if he knew there would be a party, Dylan turned up with a rather dreary, adoring fan who hung on his every word and flattered him so outrageously that even he told her to stop. We told them of the party and through the window we could see benches being put in the street, huge barrels of beer rolled out and put on to wooden trestles, then finally a piano. We had none of us ever been to a street party before and no children were ever more excited. Then, what were they doing now? Hanging up rather faded bunting left over from George VI's coronation.

At opening time precisely, Francis Butterfield arrived, to be followed by Norman, and over they all went, I saying I would follow when I had fed the dog and the poultry. Mouche puffed even more and refused her dinner. I thought she had caught our excitement, but within minutes the first little brown poodle puppy was born. I led her to her prepared bed and waited, but nothing more happened, so I comforted her and decided she would be better on her own for a bit. I went over to join the fun, and fun it was too. Free beer, the piano thumping out with whatever repertoire the pianist had. Dolly, Janie and most of our chums were there. Two enormous women were dancing and the young girls were doing their best to persuade fathers, uncles, anyone who would volunteer, to dance. First we sat on the benches then, as the evening progressed, the kerbstone. I would keep going back to see to Mouche, until finally the eighth puppy was born. I gave her glucose and water and straightened up the nuzzling, wandering bunch. As dusk lengthened into evening we wandered inside the pub. It was there, at the bar, that I found myself standing next to Bill Gee, the guest of our wedding night. It took me a moment to recognize him, then he smiled and said:

'Hullo, my child, how's hubby?'

It became evident that the adoring fan was not going to be easily shaken off, so Dylan, supreme actor that he was, simulated such extreme drunkenness that I took him home where, although not sober, he perked up considerably.

'Has she gone?' he said conspiratorily.

'I've left her with Francis, he'll take care of her.'

'Good, let's have another drink.'

Norman had wandered off into the darkness muttering that it wasn't a patch on Armistice Night, but we had all enjoyed it. Constantine came home, with Francis, then we all had some supper and went to bed.

Much later, when we were all asleep, I woke up to find a cowering Dylan by the side of the bed.

'I think there's been a mistake', he said. 'There's an awful noise of aeroplanes flying very low. I think it's a raid.'

I got up and went down to see what it was. Nothing, but after a while a faint buzzing sound.

'Dylan, it's the puppies nuzzling on the verandah just next to you.'

We went out to see them, and the noise did sound quite loud in the still night. Then, fascinated and reassured, he went back to bed with a bar of chocolate I had tucked away for just such a special occasion.

Chapter Twelve

About two weeks later Constantine was sent to a port, prior to embarking for America, destination unknown, but he would write when he could. Meanwhile I was to see about finding homes for the puppies, hens and ducks, go to the American Express and Cook's, every shipping line and every airline I could find to 'put my name down'. That is just about what I did, for to this day I have never heard a word from any of them. Also I was to pack up the house and find somewhere to stay when I'd done it. When there seemed no urgency I tried to carry on as usual. I saw quite a lot of Norman Douglas who, like myself, just waited for news, any news of leaving England. Nothing. We wandered about having our fish pie or shepherd's pie at various pubs, and sometimes he would come to dinner with me, but now I had only one ration book and no eggs, as the poultry had gone.

Dolly Donn Byrne's two sons returned from the Far East and sometimes you would see a friend you had thought never to hear from again, in the street or on a bus, thus giving the illusion that life had returned to a prewar level. But this was never to happen, Britain had changed greatly, and had taken an important leap forward in many ways into the twentieth century. After years of what had seemed like stagnation, people were anxious to progress. Many young men of my acquaintance had joined mounted regiments only to find them rapidly mechanized. The trend was from agriculture to industry.

Constantine had been sent to Camp Ritchie in Maryland, where he was interrogating captured German generals, such material being edited into a book for the United States Army. His letters made it sound a pleasant place and the work not arduous. When was I coming over? he wanted to know, to which of course I had no answer. He suggested I went to the United States Embassy to see what they had to say. This I did; they were attentive, but nothing had been decided, they said. They would let me know.

After the long hot summer, the winter of 1945 to 1946 was extremely hard and there was no relaxation in coal supplies or food. The house seemed comfortless and cheerless. For the first time I felt lonely. Dylan and Caitlin came up to stay a couple of times, separately, and once with the baby Aeronwy, now a sturdy two-year-old with the determination of a dictator and the strength of Hercules. She was not an easy child, but Caitlin seemed to go on placidly making her huge cauldron of soup. After a while I went to stay with my mother, taking the dogs with me. Maurice Richardson then complained about my leaving the Thomases in charge, so finally they went to stay in a flat found for them by Nicolette Devas, Caitlin's sister, in a basement in Markham Square, Chelsea, where they were for some time.

After a bleak Christmas I was ill again, and had to go to a very out-of-the-way hospital for an operation which left me very weak and dispirited. So in February, Constantine got compassionate leave to join me. He was at that time working with General Laegeler, ex-Chief of Staff of the Home Army in Germany, who replaced the gallant Count Stauffenberg who was hanged after his attempt on Hitler's life. General Laegeler remarked:

'I expect your General will lend you his private plane. I would to one of my officers.'

It was, however, the old army transport which flew him over for the few weeks he was here. Before he left I heard from the Embassy that they were in fact going to transport the 'fireside companions' as we seemed to be called.

The remaining things were either sold or stored with my family, including Mouche who was looked after by my grandmother until such time as I could send for her. All the puppies were in good homes, and really my clothes were so few and so old that they hardly seemed worth packing. I did take the most precious of my books with me.

From the moment the Embassy sent me four labels, three

for my luggage and one to tie on the lapel of my coat, with a covering letter enclosing my 'orders', everything promised to be unusual. I had become that unlikely person for me, a 'GI bride'. Just before I left I had a cable from Constantine giving me an address in Park Avenue, also sending me love and kisses from the Stork Club. Later I heard my grandmother telling her friends, her grandson-in-law was staying at the Stork *Hotel*.

I arrived at Waterloo Station, labelled and with my luggage, on 14 March 1946. My grandmother had pressed five pounds into my hand and a bottle of whisky for the journey. A porter said to me: 'You a bride, miss?' which rather amused me as I had at that time been married for two years. He led me to a special train which was to take us all, not to the boat, but to an army camp at Tidworth on Salisbury Plain. I settled in the first compartment I came to, and watched the leave-takings of the other 'brides'. One fond mother produced a hot-water bottle which was disdainfully handed back with the message that 'where I'm going to everything's properly heated'. I wondered if it was.

The unheated train rattled slowly through the London suburbs. In Middlesex the first sign of fields appeared and I noticed a rather pretty farmhouse in the middle of a field, the small town about a mile away to the left. My reverie was disturbed by a dark girl, well wrapped in a travelling rug, sitting opposite me.

'My, I wouldn't like to live in that isolated spot,' she said in a very false American accent. I asked her where she was going to in America.

'Montana,' she replied calmly. I hadn't the heart to disillusion her.

It was dark when we arrived at Tidworth Camp. We were helped out of the bus by shadowy male figures. I heard the girl in front of me say, 'Thank you,' but as she came into the lamplight she wheeled round to me and cried:

'My mother would be furious with me if she knew I'd said thank you to a German.'

I saw then that our assistants were German prisoners. From then on the German prisoners looked after us entirely.

In the bare room I shared with sixteen other 'brides', Fritz or Hans stood by while we made our beds and commiserated with us for the dust on the bare wooden boards. They cooked for us and served the food into our tin trays. We were frequently told over loudspeakers that we mustn't fraternize with them. My limited knowledge of German was a great nuisance as I found myself let in for many things. In this barrack room was a central old-fashioned coke stove around which we huddled in the evenings. I shared Grandmother's whisky with a chosen few.

It was all nightmarish. The beds were as hard as boards, the food uneatable, there were two baths only in an out-house between two hundred of us. Also the American Army's passion for youth was a bit overwhelming: only one other girl apart from myself was in her middle twenties, all the others were teenagers, with the exception of one rather jolly old lady of about fifty, whom I took to be a relic of 1918.

We were not allowed out of the perimeter at all, and the Red Cross 'rest' room was built to hold about a quarter of us. The two public telephones it housed were beseiged at all hours by long queues of girls shouting inanities like 'and we had tinned peaches for dinner' down the mouthpiece. Most of the time you couldn't get through, and if you did you couldn't hear what was said at the other end because of the noise in the 'rest' room.

On the third day of our stay we were herded into various rooms for vaccinations, medical inspections and interviews. It was refreshing to have something to do rather than just sitting in the cold barracks. However, some who had never been vaccinated before got very ill, and very homesick. By this time I had made the acquaintance of Joan Ogle, or 'Oggles' as she preferred to be called, who occupied the bed next to mine. I think I might have lost my sense of humour but for her.

She was a pretty girl of about nineteen, dark-haired and eyed, with clear-cut features which bespoke her Italian blood. She had been bred in one of the toughest London city districts. Oggles swore incessantly, yet with such charm that it seemed like anyone else's normal conversation. She told me her grandmother said she remembered 'women with cleavers fighting bare to the waist on the street corners'. 'Bloody old liar' was Oggles' only comment. It was she who stood by me at the baggage inspection when it was made known that I was married to a captain and my address was Park Avenue. This information was stencilled in large white paint on the cases by the prisoners. Nobody it appeared had married an officer. That night Oggles said to me:

'My husband's only a private, first class. Do you think it matters?' I thought of saying that none of it would matter in a little while when everyone had been demobilized, but instead I said that my husband was only a captain in the Intelligence, not in the fighting line, and anyway we had been lent the flat, and it was way downtown and not up to much. Yes, it was despicable, but I valued Oggles' friendship.

Two days later, early in the morning we went by train to Southampton, labelled and numbered, to be shepherded on to what I thought was a very small ship to be crossing the Atlantic at that time of year. It was the SS *James Parker* and it was my wedding anniversary. After Tidworth Camp the ship although small was quite luxurious, although the cabins weren't really equipped to hold four of us and two babies. The saloon was well proportioned and would have been comfortable for half the number. Nevertheless it was considerably better than I had expected. Larger luggage was stowed in the hold. We were allowed, indeed there was only room for, one small case each, and one for each baby. After being allocated our cabins we were summoned by bells to go down to lunch.

The dining saloon was attractive and for the first time we had tables laid with cloths and proper cutlery. Remarkably there were also well-trained stewards. The food was plentiful and good considering the numbers they had to cater for, with mostly American dishes. All in all it was a pleasant surprise. It was interesting to wander over the ship, but that soon palled, especially as it got much, much colder. Reading, my main occupation, was out; there were too many people about all the time, and a scarcity of chairs. So it was that Oggles and I volunteered to do some work in the office.

The work was routine, making duplicate forms of the names and addresses we were to be dispatched to. A cheery little sergeant called Charlie was in charge of us, a small man with twinkling eyes behind spectacles, always smiling and ready with a quip. We were his favourites and one day he offered us a coke.

'Wouldn't drink the bloody stuff,' said Oggles determinedly. 'Haven't you got anything decent?'

'I think you'll like this one,' he replied. 'Try it and see.'

I took a deep swig and coughed violently. It had been half emptied and filled up with rum: delicious, especially on a dry ship. From then on, one or two was our daily ration, very much looked forward to.

Class-consciousness is something I have never been in contact with, but it soon became apparent when my luggage and labels were exhibited that it was rife on the ship. I suppose I got what was coming to me when I asked what the abbreviation for Staff Sergeant was, during our work-time.

'I expect you'd know how to abbreviate General,' was the only reply I got. Whereupon Oggles chipped in on my behalf with a mild obscenity.

After we passed the coast of Ireland at night we struck a northern route. The ship was fairly stable, but at that time of year I felt we could be in for bad weather later on.

During that ten-day voyage I became an information bureau. Because I had been to America before I was expected to know in detail about all the cities and towns of every state. They seldom got my name right. Usually I was called Bedelia after the heroine of a current film; they knew it was long and ended with an 'a', that was all. I used to wonder and worry a little as to how some of them would make out, they had such odd ideas of what they were going to. One very pretty Welsh girl would spend long hours on her bunk gazing at her husband's photograph, which I thought omened well, until she confided that she had always hated tall men and her husband was six feet five inches. She wondered whether *it* was worth it; *it* being that she loved her busy home port of Cardiff and she was going to a box number in Iowa. There were large notices over the ship saying: *Orientation Meetings*, with an arrow afterwards. The lieutenant in charge of the meetings told me of the poor attendances. I inquired among the girls and found that most of them thought that if they went to the meetings they would come out resembling Geisha girls.

I always regretted that Oggles wasn't in my cabin. There were three others and two babies but no Oggles. She did make an appearance one evening when I went to bed early because I had a slight cold. She opened the door and stood there with two lemons in her hand and a pot of hot water.

'Well, don't bloody say I never bloody well do a bloody thing for you.'

Dropping the lemons on my bunk, she left. The mothers inquired if my friend always talked like that. I murmured something and squeezed the lemons into the remaining whisky. Dear Oggles.

When we were being de-loused she left the powder in her hair and looked liked Marie Antoinette on her way to the scaffold. 'Too much bloody brushing,' she commented when I asked why her hair still had a grey powdery look. Then there were the physical jerks. I refused to do them for several days until I saw the fifty-year-old bending at the knees and felt ashamed. Oggles got herself made a section leader under the impression she would be exempt from the 'bloody things' but found she wasn't and in the bargain had to round up the other girls. Her comments were choice.

The selection of films shown to us during the voyage was most unfortunate. The one that caused the most distress was called *Grapes Have Tender Vines*, which depicted a prosperous farm in Wisconsin, but not so prosperous, as it got flooded regularly every year. Groans went up from that part of the audience that was destined for the farming states, especially when Edward G. Robinson, who played the prosperous farmer, had to lie on the floor because his wife was sitting in the only chair. The other film was apparently made in Australia and called *The Man From Down Under*, starring Charles Laughton. It started in 1914 when Sergeant Laughton adopted two children in France, became an idle drunk in Australia with Binnie Barnes and ended up by killing with his bare fists six Japanese soldiers who, believe it or not, came down the chimney while he was in a semi-alcoholic stupor. If anything was guaranteed to set off our pent-up hysteria, that film was. These films were shown at least four times. The other nights we had rough and competitive 'states' competitions, in which you had to sing a song connected with the state you were going to. This was a non-starter except for those going to Texas. We had an amateur dramatic show, given to us by the American Red Cross girls, and a horse-race with cardboard horses. It was eerie, like being at an old-fashioned Kindergarten school. For me it was a far cry from Paris or Chelsea, and very funny sometimes.

I was right about the weather, when the little Arctic owl landed on deck, that it presaged a storm. We were fairly far out, past mid Atlantic, when it came and it blew for two or three days. The small ship rolled and heaved, faces turned green and eventually, apart from the crew and Red Cross staff, only Oggles and I were still on our feet. Except for the banging of the storm, the ship was quiet for the first time; we had it almost to ourselves and Oggles was determined not to miss a meal. Unfortunately the dining saloon was on the deck below and to get to it we had to pass on the way huge bins full of vomit. This almost turned me up, but the next time we went Oggles was ready for them.

'Put a peg on your nose,' she said, and painfully snapped one over mine. Where she got them I will never know, but she was very resourceful.

The stewards, delighted with our strong stomachs, plied us with food and we would sit there for hours having second helpings of course after course. The games were suspended as there were not enough people, and Charlie's rum and coke in the afternoons was most welcome. It was almost like a regular crossing until we got back to our cabins with their heavy, sickly smell.

At last 30 March arrived and we started up the Hudson at

about eight o'clock in the morning. A tug drew alongside with a coloured band on it playing 'Sentimental Journey'. Everyone was in tears including the Red Cross girls and we had to use all our powers of persuasion to get the brides to decide to leave the ship when it docked. Not that it was as easy as that to leave the ship. Unless your husband was there to claim you, you weren't allowed off. I was quite worried because I had been unable to send word of the exact sailing date and the Park Avenue address was unknown to me. I had very little hope of Constantine being there at nine o'clock to meet me. If you were met you had to pay your own fare to wherever your destination was, but if nobody turned up you had to stay on board for two days, then you got a free ticket. With no address they kept you on board until further inquiries were made.

At nine o'clock precisely, the immigration people came on board and questioned us. All those who had husbands meeting them were called out. My name wasn't on the list. I was beginning to feel I would never get off the ship, when Charlie appeared, cheerful as ever, and I told him what had happened. Oggles passed me in the queue, still looking a bit powdery, and said her bloody husband hadn't turned up, but Indiana was a bloody long way. Well, I thought, it won't be so bad if Oggles is here too. Then Charlie eased me out of my queue and took me to look through a porthole to see if Con was on the dock. No sign. I gave him Con's name, number, rank, address and in a panic even suggested him ringing up the Stork Club. Eventually, by what means I don't know, he reappeared with a man in a smart uniform who checked a list then took me to a lower deck. Pointing through a porthole he said:

'Is that your husband?'

There were a lot of men in a sort of giant playpen, but following his direction, surprisingly, I saw him.

On getting off the boat there was the usual business about finding my luggage despite the indelible white stencilling. However, once again Charlie sorted it out for me and down the gangplank we went.

Constantine stepped forward from the other husbands and said:

'Darling, it's lovely to see you. Look, I've been promoted to Major, so we've got two things to celebrate.'

I hurried him away quickly lest one of the other GI brides should overhear. I had no Oggles with me and it had been bad enough being a captain's wife.

'How did you find me?'

'I rang up of course, but the fools first sent me to the wrong pier. I've only just arrived.'

'Where are we going to celebrate? At the apartment on Park Avenue?'

'For heaven's sake, no, that's Teddy Rose's place. I had to give some address otherwise they wouldn't have let you off.'

'But where . . .?'

'Oh, don't fuss, we'll find somewhere.'

It was the end of the month so the paycheque was a bit low. We took a taxi and Constantine went to an office which found accommodation for 'veterans'. He came out, eyes shining.

'It's marvellous, darling. I've taken us a suite at the Plaza Hotel overlooking the Park. Damn fine hotel, we're lucky to get in.'

'What are we using for money?' I inquired.

'It costs practically nothing. Apparently if any hotel has spare rooms they have to rent them at a nominal sum to service personnel. They only had this suite left.'

So it was that we arrived at what seemed like the bridal suite at the Plaza with our battered old luggage. It was very luxurious with huge bowls of flowers, such as I had never seen, and fruit of all different kinds. At dinner that night the menu confused me, it was so vast and varied, I thought I would never decide: swordfish, kidneys in Madeira and fresh pineapple and bananas . . . m.m.mm, all things I hadn't had or even thought of for years. For the first time for many months there was warmth, plenty of food and drink, an atmosphere of gaiety and peace, and a soft, inviting-looking bed.

Tomorrow, we said, we would have to make plans: there was the New World to be explored, money to be found and a new way of life to be discovered.